ISBN 978-1-330-66212-0
PIBN 10089008

1 MONTH OF
FREE
READING

at
www.ForgottenBooks.com

By purchasing this book you are eligible for one month membership to ForgottenBooks.com, giving you unlimited access to our entire collection of over 700,000 titles via our web site and mobile apps.

To claim your free month visit:

www.forgottenbooks.com/free89008

English
Français
Deutsche
Italiano
Español
Português

www.forgottenbooks.com

Mythology Photography **Fiction**
Fishing Christianity **Art** Cooking
Essays Buddhism Freemasonry
Medicine **Biology** Music **Ancient
Egypt** Evolution Carpentry Physics
Dance Geology **Mathematics** Fitness
Shakespeare **Folklore** Yoga Marketing
Confidence Immortality Biographies
Poetry **Psychology** Witchcraft
Electronics Chemistry History **Law**
Accounting **Philosophy** Anthropology
Alchemy Drama Quantum Mechanics
Atheism Sexual Health **Ancient History**
Entrepreneurship Languages Sport
Paleontology Needlework Islam
Metaphysics Investment Archaeology
Parenting Statistics Criminology
Motivational

MATRICULATION CAESAR

BELL. GALL., B. IV, CHAPTERS 20-38
AND
BELL. GALL., B. V, CHAPTERS 1-23

BY

JOHN HENDERSON, M.A.

AND

R. A. LITTLE, B.A.

TORONTO
THE COPP, CLARK COMPANY, LIMITED

CONTENTS

I.—PRESCRIBED CAESAR

ILLUSTRATIONS

TO

.REV. WILLIAM ROBERTSON, A.M.

"justissimus unus
qui fuit et servantissimus aequi."

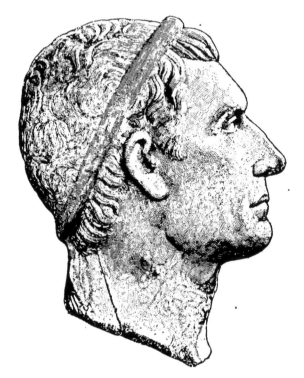

Caius Julius Caesar.

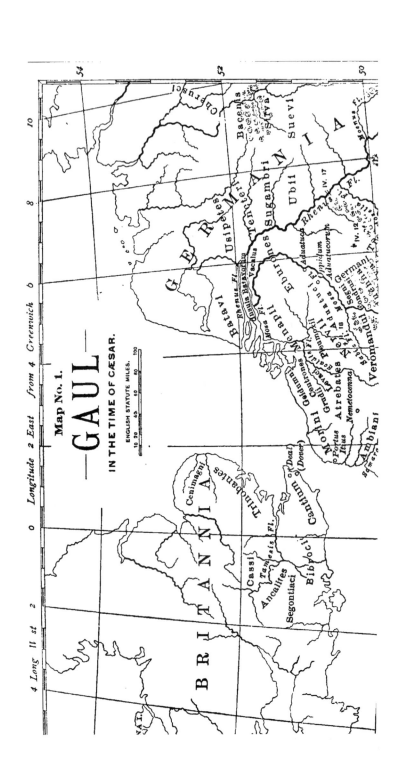

Map No. 1.

GAUL

IN THE TIME OF CÆSAR.

ENGLISH STATUTE MILES.

10 20   40   60   80   100

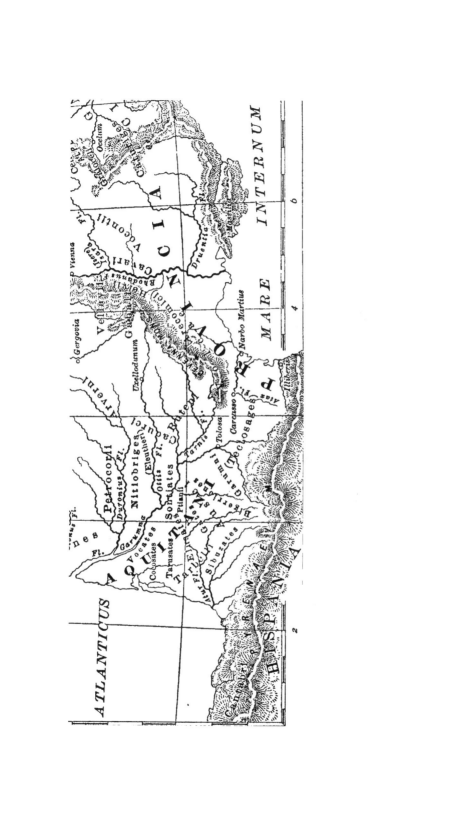

INTRODUCTION

I

The Life of Caius Julius Caesar

"The noblest man that ever lived in the tide of times." —SHAKESPEARE

Caius Julius Caesar[1] was born July 12th, 100 B.C.[2]   He *Birth* was thus six years younger than Cicero, the orator, and than Pompey, his rival in politics and war.   His family was not *His family* only one of the oldest but also one of the most respected of the patrician families of Rome.   On his father's side, it traced its origin to Iulus, son of Aeneas, the founder of the Roman line, and on his mother's side, it claimed, as an ancestor, Ancus Martius, one of the early kings.

Little is known of Caesar's father except that he held at *Caesar* one time the office of *praetor*, and that he died suddenly at *father* Pisa, 84 B.C.   To Aurelia, his mother, a woman of primitive *Caesar's* frugality in the management of her household, but charac- *mother* terized by a lofty ambition and a firm belief in the noble destiny of her son, was entrusted the direction of his edu- cation.   What the Gracchi owed to their mother Cornelia, Caesar owed to Aurelia.   Mother and son showed mutual reverence, and undoubtedly Caesar's future life was largely affected by his mother's influence.

---

[1] A Roman citizen had regularly *three* names: the *praenomen* .(*Caius*) answering to our Christian name, marking the individual: the *nomen* (*Julius*), designating the clan or *gens : cognomen* (*Caesar*) telling the family.   Sometimes another *cognomen* was added for honorary distinction · as *Africanus* to Publius Cornelius Scipio.

[2] Mommsen argues that Caesar was born 102 B.C.   His main reason for assigning this date is that the *lex annalis* which prescribed the minimum age at which a citizen could hold certain offices was observed in Caesar's case.   By this law no one could hold the office of *quaestor* before he was 31, of *aedile* before 37, of *praetor* before 40, of *consul* before 43.   By referring to the chronology of Caesar's life the plausibility of the argument appears.   But (1) the law was often broken as it had been in the case of Pompey ; (2) Suetonius says that Caesar was 16 when his father died ; (3) Plutarch, Suetonius, and Appian say that Caesar was 54 when he was assassinated.

Related to Marius

His aunt Julia was married to Caius Marius, who saved Italy in the war against the Cimbri and Teutones, and was the sturdy supporter of the popular party against the narrow senatorial faction led by Cornelius Sulla. Though aristocratic by birth, Caesar was no doubt led through the influence of Marius to side with the popular party.

Flamen Dialis

At the age of 14,.Caesar was appointed priest of Jupiter (*flamen Dialis*), and by virtue of this office he became a member of the sacred college and received a handsome income. In 83 B.C., at the age of 17, he married Cornelia,

Marries Cornelia

daughter of L. Cornelius Cinna, the leader of the popular party and the avowed opponent of Sulla. Soon afterwards Sulla returned from Asia and proscribed Marius and all his adherents. As the nephew of Marius and the husband of Cornelia, Caesar was especially an object of displeasure. He was ordered to divorce Cornelia, but refused to obey. Accordingly a price was set upon his life, and it was only through the earnest intercession of his friends that he was pardoned.

Serves his first campaign 80-78 B.C.

In consequence of having thwarted the will of the imperious Sulla, Caesar found it unsafe to remain at Rome. He went to Asia, where he served with distinction at the siege of Mitylene and in the war against the Cilician pirates. On the report of Sulla's death, 78 B.C., he returned to Rome to resume his studies.

Goes to Rhodes 76-75 B.C.

Oratory and military skill were in Rome the two great avenues to success. To improve his skill in oratory, Caesar went to Rhodes, 76 B.C., to study rhetoric and oratory under Apollónius Molon, the most celebrated teacher of that time. On the way thither Caesar's vessel was captured by pirates and Caesar was detained till a heavy ransom was paid. During his detention he is said to have joined these marauders in their sports and to have told them half-jestingly that he would, when liberated, have them hanged. This threat he made good. Landing at Miletus, he collected a small fleet. captured them and brought them to Pergamus, where they were executed. He stayed at the school of Molon for two years.

Quaestor 68 B.C.

Caesar began his political career in 68 B.C., by gaining the *quaestorship*, and by virtue of this office he was connected with the public treasury and entitled to a seat in the senate.

In 65 B C., he was elected to the office of *curule aedile*, which *Curule aedile 65 B.C.* had charge of public buildings and the oversight of public festivals and games. While holding this office he increased his popularity and also his debts by the costly gladiatorial shows which he gave. He also more than ever identified himself with the popular party by his devotion to the memory of Marius. He caused the trophies of that great commander, which had been destroyed by Sulla, to be replaced.

In 63 B.C., a year memorable for the conspiracy of Catiline, *Pontifex maximus 63 B.C.* Caesar was elected *pontifex maximus* against the strong opposition of the *optimates*. This office, though not a civil office, conferred great power and dignity on Caesar. In 62 B.C., he was elected *praetor*, an office chiefly of a judicial *Praetor* nature. On resigning this office, he went to Spain, as *pro-praetor*, when he managed to gain money enough to pay off his enormous debts.

On his return from Spain, he united with Pompey and *First Trium-virate 60 B.C.* Crassus to form the *First Triumvirate*. Pompey may be said to have been the representative of the aristocratic class; Caesar, of the democratic; while Crassus represented the monied interests.

In 59 B.C., Caesar became consul. To further cement the *Consul* union, Pompey married Julia, Caesar's daughter. During this year, Caesar passed an Agrarian law for the division of lands among the poor of Italy. The object of the bill was to restore to the peasant freeholders lands of which they had been dispossessed by the rich. He also caused to be passed a *Laws passed* body of laws called *Leges Juliae*, the object of which was to guard the rights of individuals, to secure justice in the courts, to improve public and private morality, and to obtain generally good government for the state. Before laying down his consulship, he procured the passage of a bill by *Goes to Gaul* which he was invested for five years with pro-consular powers over the two Gauls and over Illyricum.

II

The Conquest of Gaul

The Gauls The Gauls were a Celtic race, of the same stock as the Welsh, the Erse or Celts of Ireland, and the Highlanders of Scotland. When the Romans became acquainted with them, they were in a primitive state of civilization. They are described as a tall, blue-eyed, fair-haired race, nomadic in their habits, pasturing their flocks and herds, and paying little heed to agriculture. They dwelt in open villages or collections of primitive huts without fortifications. The clan system prevailed amongst them ; at the head of each clan was the chief, and they never got beyond this form of government. According to Mommsen, they had shaken all states but founded none. Though individually a match for the Romans in physical strength and personal courage, they had not the qualities to endure a campaign or to make any permanent use of their conquests. According to Cato, the Elder, they cared for little else than for wit and war. The influence of the chief depended on his fame as a warrior or his skill as an orator. They lived by plundering each other or their common enemies. They excelled, however, in horsemanship, and were active warriors, but were better fitted for aggressive than for defensive war.

Danger from the Gauls The Romans had been defeated at the Alia in 390 B.C., and the city had been plundered and burned by this race. Again, in the days of Marius, it was saved only by the skill of that general at Vercellae, 101 B.C.

Rome had succeeded in gaining dominion over all the surrounding nations with one exception. She had successively got into her power Sicily, Sardinia, Spain, Africa, Greece, Asia Minor, Syria, Egypt. The only nation around the Mediterranean not under her power was Gaul.

Caesar's Province Gallia Cisalpina, Gallia Transalpina and Illyricum were the three provinces given to Caesar by the Senate. Gallia Cisalpina comprised that part of *Italy north of the Rubicon and the Macra;* Illyricum included a part of *Croatia,* the whole of *Dalmatia, Bosnia,* and part of *Albania ;* Gallia
Roman Provincia Transalpina included the whole of *France, Belgium,* and

parts of *Holland, Switzerland* and *Germany*. In the southern part was the *Provincia* around the southern part of the Rhone. This was acquired by the Romans in 121 B.C., and Narbo Martius (now *Narbonne*) was made the capital of the *Provincia*, a word which still survives in the word *Provence*. The rest of Gallia Transalpina was divided *Divisions of Gaul* into three parts. Aquitania included the country *between the Pyrenees and the Garonne;* Gallia Celtica the land *between the Garonne and the Seine ;* all *between the Seine and Marne* on the south *and the Rhine* on the north was called Gallia Belgica. The Aquitani were akin to the *Basques;* the rest of Gaul outside the *Provincia* was inhabited by people of Celtic origin, comprising about sixty tribes, which were always at war with each other or their common enemies.

Just before the days of Caesar two factions existed in the *Parties in* country, one headed by the Haedui, who were in league with *Gaul* the Romans, and the other headed by the Arverni and the Sequani. The Haedui, proud of the alliance with Rome, had been lording it over the others, and as a counterbalance for the support of the Romans the Arverni and the Sequani had invited the aid of the neighboring Germans.

The immediate cause of Caesar's departure was the news *Cause of* that reached Rome that the *Helvetii* were setting out from *Caesar's departure* Switzerland on an expedition into Gaul, just as the Cimbri had done about fifty years before. They had left their homes, burned their towns and villages, passed through the *First* territories of the Sequani and were plundering those of the *Campaign* Haedui. Their presence was a standing menace to the Roman *58 B.C.* *B 1.* *Provincia.* Caesar left Rome with five legions and by rapid marches soon overtook the enemy and defeated them at *Defeat of the* Bibracte (now *Autun*). *Helvetii*

Not content with protecting the Province against its invaders, Caesar now accepted the invitation of the Haedui to drive out of Gaul the Germans under Ariovistus. This leader had *Ariovistus* made overtures to Caesar to divide Gaul between them, but the proposal was rejected by Caesar. Ariovistus was *Defeat of* defeated near the modern town of *Bâsle*, and the Romans by *Ariovistus* their victory extended their territory as far as the Treviri.

Second Campaign 57 B.C. B. II.

The second year in Gaul was occupied with a war against the Belgae. Alarmed at the encroachments of the Romans, the tribes between the Seine and the Rhine had formed a league against Caesar. Only the Remi were favorable to him. After reducing the weaker tribes, Caesar marched against the Nervii, one of the most warlike of the Gallic tribes, and

Defeat of the Nervii

fought a desperate battle, which was won only by his skill and personal daring. So signal was this victory that a public thanksgiving of fifteen days, an unprecedented honor, was granted to Caesar. By this victory all Eastern Gaul, from the Mediterranean to the English Channel, was now in the hands of the Romans.

Third Campaign 56 B.C. B. III.

During the spring of the third year in Gaul, Caesar saw clearly that his work there could not be completed at the expiration of the five years, which would end in December, 54 B-C. He did not wish to run the risk of having his policy reversed by the Senate as Pompey's had been in the war against Mithridates, nor did he desire to leave his veterans unprovided for, or to have the laws passed in his consulship ignored or repealed. There were now signs of the coming struggle. Cicero had already assailed the acts of the triumvirs and dissensions were arising between Pompey and Crassus. The influence of Pompey and the optimates was gradually being eclipsed by the brilliant successes of Caesar in Gaul. At

Conference at Luca

Luca, Caesar held a conference with Pompey and Crassus, at which it was agreed that Pompey and Crassus should be consuls for the year 55 B.C., that Pompey should receive the command of the two Spains (*Hispania citerior et ulterior*) for five years at the end of 53 B.C., and Crassus the government of Syria for the same period, and that Caesar should remain in Gaul till December 31, 49 B.C., and that he should stand for the consulship of the following year 48 B.C. Caesar would thus lay down his consulship a year before Crassus or Pompey.

Conquest of the Veneti

In the third campaign Caesar completed the conquest of Gaul. He defeated the Veneti, a daring, sea-faring people of north-western Gaul. He then turned his army against the Morini and Menapii, two tribes in the neighborhood of *Calais*. Though the Gauls had been defeated, still the spirit of the nation was not broken, and only lacked an opportunity to rise against the conquerors.

The news on the German frontier called out Caesar earlier *Fourth* than usual during the spring of this year. The Usipetes and *Campaign 55 B.C.* Tencteri, two German tribes, had been driven out of their *B. IV.* territories by the Suevi, and had crossed the Rhine with the intention of settling in Eastern Gaul. Caesar defeated them with great slaughter after detaining the ambassadors who had come to sue for peace. After this victory, Caesar decided to cross the Rhine to strike terror into the hearts *Crosses the* of the inhabitants. In ten days he built a bridge in the *Rhine* neighborhood of *Cologne*, and, crossing the river, remained about eighteen days on the eastern side. He then crossed back, broke down the bridge, and returned to Gaul. He then resolved to cross the channel and invade Britain. With *First* two legions (the *seventh* and the *tenth*), and eighty ships he *Invasion of* *Britain* set out from Port Itius (probably *Boulogne*), and landed, *55 B.C.* probably, at *Deal*. Beyond securing the submission of a few British tribes in the southern part of the Island, the invasion effected nothing, for the season was too far advanced to permit a regular campaign. A public thanksgiving of twenty days was decreed, not without opposition, for Cato proposed that Caesar should be given up to the Germans in consequence of his treacherous acts towards the ambassadors of the Usipetes and the Tencteri.

The expedition against Britain had flattered the vanity of *Fifth* the Romans. The island was said to abound with rich mines, *Campaign.* *Second* and the sea with pearls. Here, therefore, was a rich field for *Invasion of* *Britain* Roman enterprise. Accordingly he wished to complete the *54 B.C.* conquest he had begun in the previous summer. Again he *B. V.* started from *Port Itius* with five legions and landed at the same place as in the previous year. The Britons had put in supreme command Cassivellaunus, chief of the Trinobantes, whose state lay north of the *Thames*. Caesar advanced north, crossed the *Thames*, probably above *London*, defeated the *Britons,* and advanced as far as *St. Albans*. After taking hostages and determining the amount of tribute Britain should pay yearly, Caesar returned to the Continent. Caesar's absence from Gaul had been attended with danger to the Roman cause, for a rebellion was maturing in Gaul. This

Caesar helped to foster by arranging his legions at considerable distances from each other—a policy he was compelled to
pursue in consequence of the scarcity of corn in Gaul.
Accordingly the Eburones, a Gallic tribe, attacked the camp
Uprising in
Gaul
of Sabinus and Cotta and cut to pieces their command. They
next besieged Quintus Cicero, the brother of the orator, who
was stationed among the Nervii.   Cicero was relieved by the
timely aid of Caesar.

Sixt.
Campaign
53 B.C.
B. VI.
The defeat of Sabinus and Cotta had inspired the nation of
Gaul to make an effort to regain its independence.   Caesar
strengthened his army by levying two new legions in Cisalpine Gaul and receiving another from Pompey, who was
now at Rome.   He defeated in turn several tribes in North-
Eastern Gaul.   As the chief of these tribes, the Treviri, had
A second
time across
the Rhine
been aided by the Germans, Caesar determined to cross the
Rhine again.   After receiving the submission of the Ubii,
he devastated the lands of the Suevi, and, on his return to
Gaul, he laid waste the lands of the Eburones.

Seventh
Campaign
52 B.C.
B. VII.
This year was marked by a general uprising of Gaul.   Even
the Haedui, the former friends of the Romans, joined in the
general revolt.   At the head of the insurgents was Vercingetorix, the chief of the Arverni, and by far the best general
Caesar had ever met in his Gallic campaign.   Caesar's success
in this, as in all his campaigns, was due to the unexampled
rapidity of his movements.   With incredible celerity he
concentrated his forces and attacked the enemy before they
were aware of his presence.   After capturing several towns,
he attacked Vercingetorix, who had strongly fortified himself
at Gergovia (near *Clermont*).   Caesar was unsuccessful in
his attempt to take this town.   Vercingetorix then took
up his position at Alesia, but Caesar finally compelled
its surrender, and soon after the Arverni and Haedui
surrendered.

Eighth
Campaign
57 B.C.
B. VIII.
The last campaign was spent by Caesar in reducing several
of the minor states, and in employing himself with the details
of the pacification of Gaul.   His policy towards the Gauls
was conciliatory, and after so many years of fighting, Caesar
left the province of Gaul loyal to the Roman cause, and
patiently submissive to the Roman yoke.

III

Life of Caesar after the Conquest of Gaul

While these stirring events were occurring in Gaul, equally stirring events were taking place at Rome. The conference at Luca was a hollow truce, and it was evident that a rupture was imminent. The first break in the link that bound the triumvirate together was the death of Julia, the *Death of Julia* daughter of Caesar and wife of Pompey. Another link was *54 B.C.* broken by the death of Crassus who was slain at Carrhae in *Death of* an expedition against the Parthians. By his removal the *Crassus* *53 B.C.* state was now at the mercy of Caesar and Pompey. While Caesar, however, was actively reducing the province of Gaul and gaining fresh laurels with every conquest, Pompey, instead of setting out to his province of Spain, remained inactive in the city resting on the honors he had gained in the Mithridatic war.

The state of affairs at Rome showed clearly the need of an *Need of a* absolute ruler to put down the lawlessness that prevailed. *strong ruler* During the years 54 B.C. and 53 B.C., bloody brawls had been of frequent occurrence between the two old foes Clodius and Milo and their hired gladiators. Finally Clodius was slain. During the funeral of Clodius, the senate-house was burned, and in consequence of the constant riots of the two factions the Senate met and appointed Pompey sole consul. Milo was tried and sent to Massilia.

Pompey now became the sturdy supporter of the aristocratic party. After the death of Julia he married Cornelia, daughter of Metellus Scipio, whom he had as his colleague *Breaks with* in the consulship in the following August. Pompey now *Pompey* brought forward an old law that no one could become consul while absent from Rome. This would have compelled Caesar to resign his command at the end of 49 B.C. At the same time Pompey would, by virtue of the agreement made at the conference of Luca, still be at the head of the army, since his term of office would not expire till a year after the expiration of the time of Caesar's command. Marcellus, the consul, also proposed that Caesar should give up his military power since all Gaul had been subdued. Cato,

the uncompromising foe of Caesar, also declared that in case
Caesar should appear in Rome, he would bring him up for
trial for his acts in Gaul. The quarrel was evidently begun
by the Senate and not by Caesar. It would have been in
vain for Caesar to give up his command and retire into
private life while Pompey was invested with the imperium
and at the head of his legions at Rome. The tribune
Curio laid before the Senate the proposal of Caesar, that
the latter would disband his legions if Pompey would
do the same. The proposal was made on January 1st, 49
B.C., when the new consuls, L. Cornelius Lentulus, and C.
Claudius Marcellus, took office. With difficulty Marc
Antony (afterwards the triumvir), and L. Cassius Longinus,
at that time tribunes of the *plebs*, obtained a hearing for
the proposal of Caesar. At length, after a stormy debate,
Final order
of the
Senate
the motion was passed "that Caesar should disband his
soldiers by a certain day, and if he did not, he should be
declared a public enemy." This meant a declaration of war.
Five days after the consuls were invested with dictatorial
power, and Pompey was appointed to carry on the war in
case Caesar did not obey.

Caesar was at Ravenna when the news of the action of the
Senate reached him. He was not long in maturing his plans.
Caesar
crosses the
Rubicon
At midnight he left Ravenna with one legion and crossed the
Rubicon, a small stream that divided his province from
Italy proper. To do so without the permission of the Senate
was equivalent to a declaration of war. Town after town
succumbed to him, and by the beginning of February he
had Umbria and Picenum at his feet. To all opponents he
granted amnesty. In this respect the conduct of Caesar in
carrying on the war against his fellow-citizens was in striking
contrast with his policy in his Gallic campaign. By the
middle of February he was reinforced by two other legions
from Gaul.

Pompey
flees to
Greece
Pompey and the chiefs of the aristocracy, on hearing the
action of Caesar, were thrown into consternation, and abruptly
left Rome. Pompey hastened to Brundusium and afterwards crossed over to Epirus. Caesar with his troops, which
now numbered six legions, followed Pompey to Brundusium,
but lack of ships prevented his further advance at that time.

He had now Gaul and Italy on his side, and he decided to go over to Spain, which soon fell under his power. Most of the soldiers of Pompey's army in Spain enlisted under Caesar's banners.

Having acquired possession of Spain, Gaul, and Italy, Caesar embarked in the beginning of 48 B.C. at Brundusium, and finally the two armies met at Pharsalia when Caesar, in spite *Defeat of* of disparity in numbers, gained a signal victory. Pompey *Pompey at Pharsalia* fled to Lesbos, to Cyprus, and finally to Egypt, where he was *48 B.C.* treacherously murdered as he was being conveyed to the shore. *Death of* Caesar pursued Pompey to Alexandria. A dispute at that *Pompey* time for the throne of Egypt arose between Ptolemy and his sister Cleopatra. Caesar sided with Cleopatra and established her on the throne.

After settling the affairs of Egypt, he marched northward against Pharnaces, son of Mithridates, whom he defeated at *Victory at* Zela. His laconic despatch to the Roman Senate—*veni, vidi,* *Zela* *vici* - is well known. By the battle of Thapsus in Africa, 46 B.C., he crushed the only opposition left of Pompey's party in that country.

On his return to Rome he was made dictator for ten years. *Returns to* He then celebrated his four triumphs—over Gaul, Egypt, *Rome* Pontus and Numidia—purposely avoiding all reference to the civil wars. His dictatorship was marked by many reforms.

In Spain an insurrection broke out, which, however, he crushed by the decisive battle at Munda, 45 B.C. On his return he was granted a triumph. The Senate at once began *Honors* *granted to* to shower honors on him. He was styled Father of his *Caesar* Country (*pater patriae*), statues of him were erected in the temples, his effigy was placed on coins, the month *Quinctilis* was changed to *Julius*. By his office of Imperator for life he was the supreme ruler of the Roman world. He was *consul* for ten years, *dictator* and *praefectus morum* for life and practically all the offices of the state were centred in him.

It may be said that he used his power mercifully. No *Plans of* proscriptions followed his assumption of absolute power. *Caesar* His mind was bent on schemes for the benefit of the Roman world. He proposed to codify the Roman laws, to establish public libraries, to enlarge the harbor of Ostia, drain the Pomptine marshes, and cut a canal through the Isthmus of Corinth.

No doubt Caesar wished to perpetuate his power in his own family. Having no legitimate children, he made his sister's grandson, Octavius, his successor. He wished also to have the title as well as the power of king, and accordingly it was agreed that at the *Lupercalia*, Marc Antony should offer Caesar a diadem in public ; but Caesar, seeing that the people were opposed to this, refused to accept the offer.

Conspiracy formed

Meanwhile a conspiracy was afoot. It was probably started by C. Cassius, a personal foe, and included upwards of sixty persons, many of whom had taken active part in the war against Caesar. Among the most prominent of the conspirators was M. Junius Brutus, who had fought against him at Pharsalia, but was pardoned and had since been raised to the praetorship. It was arranged to assassinate Caesar 15th March—the Ides of March. This plan was carried out, and Caesar fell at the base of Pompey's statue pierced with twenty-three wounds.

Death of Caesar 44 B.C.

IV

Character of Caesar

Caesar's death was a loss, not merely to Rome, but to the civilized world. Had his master genius executed the plans he had in mind, the whole of future history would have been changed. With his death were renewed those civil wars that brought carnage and disorder to the Roman world. Equally gifted as a jurist, statesman, historian and general, his versatility of genius was remarkable. His successes as a general were all achieved after his fortieth year. According to Cicero he might have been a great orator ; his Commentaries prove that he was a great historian. His true greatness is shown by the entire absence of vanity. Power he loved above all things, and in employing the means to attain this, he probably was no worse or no better than the other Roman political leaders of his day.

V

Works of Caesar

(1) *Extant;* (a) *Commentarii de Bello Gàllico,* in *seven* books. This work contains an account of the Conquest of Gaul, from 58 B.C. to 52 B.C. In the beginning of the first book we have the Conquest of the Helvetii mentioned, while the opening of the seventh refers to the death of Clodius as lately taking place. An eighth book was added by Aulus Hirtius, one of Caesar's officers, to complete the narrative.

(b) *Commentarii de Bello Civili,* in *three* books. This gives an account of the civil wars down to the time of the Alexandrine war. The history of the Alexandrine, African and Spanish campaigns was afterwards added in three books. *Hirtius* probably wrote the account of the *Alexandrine* campaign; *Oppius,* that of the *African;* the account of the *Spanish* war was written probably by a *Centurion* of Caesar's army, according to Niebuhr, who discovers a change in style and expression from that of the other two accounts.

(2) *Lost Works,*

(a) *Anticato.* A reply to Cicero's panegyric on Cato Uticensis, who fell at Thapsus, 46 B.C.

(b) *De Analogia,* or as Cicero calls it, *De Ratione Latine Loquendi,* dedicated to Cicero, and written while Caesar was crossing the Alps.

(c) *Libri Auspiciorum* or *Auguralia,* written 63 B.C. when Caesar was *Pontifex maximus.*

(d) *De Astris,* written also 63 B.C.

(e) *Apothegmata* or *Dicta Collectanea,* a collection of witticisms made at different times.

(f) *Poemata,* nearly all written in his youth. To these belong *Œdipus, Laudes Herculis,* and *Iter* (describing his going to Spain in 46 B.C.).

VI

The Roman Army

Infantry

Cavalry

The legion (*legio*) numbered in Caesar's time from 3,000 to 5,000 infantry and 30.) cavalry. The infantry (*peditatus*) was divided into 10 cohorts (*cohortes*); each cohort into 3 maniples (*manipuli*), and each maniple into 2 centuries (*centuriae*). The cavalry (*alae, equitatus*) was divided into 10 *turmae*, each *turma* into 3 *decuriae* or squads. Generally, the effective strength of a legion was 3,600 infantry; so that a cohort would number 3.0 men; a maniple, 120; a century, 60; a *turma*, 30; a squad of cavalry, 10. The variation in number of the legion would arise from furloughs, sickness, losses in battle, for usually such losses were not filled by new recruits, since such recruits were usually formed into new legions. Legions were numbered according to their enrolment.

Acies triplex

The usual formation in battle was the *acies triplex*. Four cohorts formed the first line, three the second, and three the third, thus ·—

4   3   2   __

7   6   5

10   9   8

The men usually stood 10 deep, so that each cohort would have a front of from 30 to 40 men. We have no means of knowing the space between the different cohorts, or even between the maniples. The cavalry was usually posted on the wings (*alae*); so were the light-armed troops (*velites*),

Light armed

such as the slingers (*funditores*) and bowmen (*sagittarii*).

Artisans

Attached to the army were the engineers and artisans (*fabri*), often formed into a separate company under a chief engineer (*praefectus fabrum*). These were employed in building bridges, building vessels, constructing winter quarters, repairing weapons. When Caesar was in Britain, the *fabri* were scattered among the legions, and not formed as a separate corps. (*B.* V, 11.)

The artillery of the Romans (*tormenta*) consisted of large *Artillery* engines formed on the principle of the cross-bow. These were *catapultae*, *ballistae*, and *scorpiones.* The *catapultae* hurled large arrows and darts ; the *ballistae* threw large stones, while the *scorpiones* were smaller than the *catapultae* and had a less range. In sieges the battering-ram (*aries*) was often used.

VII

The Officers of the Army

The officers of the army were :—

The *Commander* (*imperator*, *dux belli*) appointed by the *Imperator* Senate. He possessed the *imperium*, and his power was practically unlimited in the field. He usually received the title *imperator* after his first successful battle with the enemy.

Under him were the *legati* or staff officers appointed by the *Legati* Senate. They were of senatorial rank, *i.e.*, they had held before their appointment a curule office, as consul, praetor, chief aedile, or censor. The Senate appointed them and also determined the number. Caesar at first had six and afterwards ten.

The *quaestores* were elected annually by the people. They *Quaestores* were attached to the general or the governor of a province. They managed all financial affairs connected with the army, had charge of the money chest, paid the soldiers, provided the food and clothing. They corresponded to the modern quartermaster or paymaster.

The *tribuni militum* were six in number to each legion, *Tribuni* appointed by the Senate. They were not all exercising this *Militum* power at once. Probably one held the command for two months. They kept the roll-call, attended to the levying, discipline, equipment of the troops, presided at court-martials, and took part in the council of war

The *centuriones* were sixty in number in each legion, and *Centuriones* were appointed by the general. The six centurions of the first cohort were admitted to the council of war. These were called *primipili.* The centurions carried a wand (*vitis*) as a badge of office.

VIII

Arms

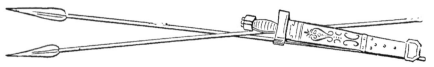

Offensive armor

The arms of a Roman soldier were of two kinds, offensive and defensive.

(a) *Offensive weapons.* The regular soldier (*miles legionarius*) was armed with (1) a short sword (*gladius*), about two feet long and double-edged. It was kept in a light scabbard hung from a belt (*balteus*) passing over the left shoulder to the right side. The other offensive weapon was (2) the javelin (*pilum*), a strong heavy pike, consisting of a square shaft of wood four feet long, into which was fitted a long slender iron shank ending in a barbed head.

Defensive armor

(b) *Defensive weapons* consisted of (1) helmet (*cassis* of bronze or *galea* of leather) surmounted with a white crest;

SCUTUM.

CLIPEUS.

(2) cuirass (*lorica*), or coat of mail made of leather or strips of metal fastened on the leather; (3) shield (*scutum*) rectangular in shape, about four feet long and two wide ; made of wood, slightly curved, and covered with leather. In early days the *clipeus* also was used, but was discarded when the Roman soldiers received pay. The soldier had beneath his armor his tunic (*tunica*), a thick, sleeveless, woolen garment reaching to the knees. In severe weather he wore his cloak (*sagum*) of heavy, woolen stuff, fastened with a broach (*fibula*) on the right shoulder. Around his waist was a strong leather belt (*cingulum*). On his feet were heavy half-boots (*caligae*).

IX

Standards

Any standard was called by the general term *signum*. The standard of the legion was the eagle (*aquila*). This was of gold, silver, or bronze on a wooden staff. It was generally carried by the first centurion (*primipilus*). To lose the eagle was regarded as the greatest disgrace. The standards of the cohorts or maniples were called *signa*. These were of various designs, sometimes a dog, horse, wolf, serpent, figure of victory, etc. The standard of the cavalry was called *vexillum*, a square or oblong banner.

Standards
(1) *Aquila*

(2) *Signa*

(3) *Vexillum*

X

The Musical Instruments

Musical instruments The musical instruments of the army were (I) *tuba*, trumpet ; straight and deep-toned, and used to give the order for the advance or retreat ; (2) *bucina* and *cornu* crooked, having a shrill tone, and generally used to indicate a change in the watch ; (3) *lituus*, formed like an augur's staff, and used for cavalry.

XI

The Army on the March

The army on the march may be divided into :—

Divisions of army on the march (1) *agmen primum*, or van ; (2) *exercitus, agmen legionum*, or main body ; (3) *agmen novissimum*, or rear. The van was generally composed of light-armed troops of infantry or cavalry. Their chief duty was to find out the force of the enemy, or to hold the enemy at bay till the main body arrived. The main body, with the baggage train (*impedimenta*), followed. The rear consisted of cavalry, or light-armed skirmishers. The average march (*iter justum*) was from six to seven hours, or from fifteen to twenty miles a day. On a forced march (*iter magnum*) fifty miles were often covered. On the march the legionary carried his pack (*sarcina*), in which he had to carry his corn (*frumentum*), cooking utensils *vasa*), his arms, blanket, and two stakes (*valli*).

XII

The Army in Camp

Metatores When an army was on the march, men (*metatores*) were sent forward to select a place suitable for a camp. If possible, high ground (*locus superior*) was selected. The camp was square or oblong. An embankment (*vallum*), formed from the ground thrown up from the ditch (*fossa*), surrounded the *Gates of the Camp* camp. The camp had four gates : (1) *porta praetoria*, near the *praetorium*, or the general's tent, facing the enemy ; (2) *porta decumana*, opposite to this ; (3) *porta principalis sinistra*, on the left ; (4) *porta principalis dextra*, on the right. Connecting the two latter was the *via principalis*, and parallel to the street was the *via quintana*. Connecting the *porta praetoria* and *porta decumana* was the *via praetoria*.

The subjoined cut will explain this.

PLAN OF A CONSULAR CAMP

This is the camp described by Polybius :—

The lines across the cavalry, etc., denote the divisions of troops or maniples.
A Praetorian gate.
B Decuman gate.
C Porta principalis sinistra.
D Porta principalis dextra.
E Praetorium.

H Roman cavalry.
I Triarii.
K Principes and Velites.
L Hastati and Velites.
M Cavalry of allies.
N Infantry of allies.
O Consul's and Quaestor's horse guards.
P do. foot guards.
Q Extraordinary cavalry of the allies.

R do. foot of the allies.
S Strangers and occasional allies.
1 2 3 4 5 6 7 8 9 10 11 12
The twelve tribunes.
a b c d e f g h i j k l,
The prefects of allies.
¸*¸ The figures on the right, and bottom, are the measures of length in feet.

The average pay of the legionary in Caesar's time was 12½ cents; that of the centurion was 25 cents. Often their pay was increased from the sale of booty.

C. JULII CAESARIS

COMMENTARIORUM

DE BELLO GALLICO

LIBER QUARTUS

Caesar determined to invade Britain; his reasons for crossing.

20. Exigua parte aestatis reliqua, Caesar, etsi in his locis,
quod omnis Gallia ad septentriones vergit, maturae sunt
hiemes, tamen in Britanniam proficisci contendit, quod
omnibus fere Gallicis bellis hostibus nostris inde subministrata
auxilia intellegebat ; et, si tempus anni ad bellum gerendum
deficeret, tamen magno sibi usui fore arbitrabatur, si modo
insulam adisset et genus hominum perspexisset, loca, portus,
aditus cognovisset; quae omnia fere Gallis erant incognita.
Neque enim temere praeter mercatores illo adit quisquam,
neque iis ipsis quicquam praeter oram maritimam atque eas
regiones, quae sunt contra Gallias, notum est. Itaque vocatis
ad se undique mercatoribus, neque quanta esset insulae
magnitudo, neque quae aut quantae nationes incolerent, neque

NOTE.—The numeral after a verb shows the conjugation. If a verb is regular, the
conjugation is simply indicated.

exiguus, -a, -um, adj., small.

reliquus, -a, -um, adj., remaining.

septentriones, -um, M., the seven
stars forming the constellation of the Great Bear, hence
the North.

vergō, 3, no pf., no sup., incline,
slope.

mātūrus, -a, -um, adj., early.

contendō, 3, -dī, -tum, v. intr.,
proceed.

subministrō, 1, furnish secretly.

dēficiō, 3, -fēcī, -fectum, v. intr.,
be insufficient.

modo, adv., only.

perspiciō, 3, -spexī, -spectum,
v. tr., observe, become
thoroughly acquainted with.

aditus, ūs, M., approach, landing
place.

incognitus, -a, -um, adj., unknown.

temere, adv., without reason.

illō, adv., thither.

incolō, 3, coluī, no sup., v. tr.,
live in, inhabit

20

quem usum belli haberent aut quibus institutis uterentur, neque qui essent ad majorum navium multitudinem idonei portus, reperire poterat?

Sends Volusenus, who returns and reports to him.

21. Ad haec cognoscenda, priusquam periculum faceret, idoneum esse arbitratus, Caium Volusenum cum navi longa praemittit. Huic mandat, ut exploratis omnibus rebus ad se quam primum revertatur. Ipse cum omnibus copiis in Morinos proficiscitur, quod inde erat brevissimus in Britanniam trajectus. Huc naves undique ex finitimis regionibus, et quam superiore aestate ad Veneticum bellum effecerat, classem, jubet convenire. Interim, consilio ejus cognito, et per mercatores perlato ad Britannos, a compluribus ejus insulae civitatibus ad eum legati veniunt, qui polliceantur obsides dare atque imperio populi Romani obtemperare. Quibus auditis, liberaliter pollicitus, hortatusque, ut in ea sententia permanerent, eos domum remittit; et cum iis una Commium, quem ipse Atrebatibus superatis regem ibi constituerat, cujus et virtutem et consilium probabat, et quem sibi fidelem

---

usus, ūs, M., experience.

institūtum, -ī, N., custom, usage.

reperiō, 4, repperī, repertum, v. tr., find out, learn.

---

cognoscō, 3, cognōvī, cognitum, v. tr., learn, ascertain.

mandō, 1, v. intr. (governs dat), command, instruct.

explōrō, 1, v. tr., investigate.

inde, adv., thence, from that point.

trājectus, ūs, M., passage.

perferō, -ferre, -tulī, -lātum, v. tr., carry through, report.

complūrēs, -plūria, adj., pl., several.

polliceor, 2, pollicitus, v. dep., promise.

obtemperō, 1 (governs dat.), obey.

līberāliter, adv., kindly.

sententia, -ae, F., feeling, sentiment.

ūnā, adv. ; una cum, along with.

Atrebātēs, -ium, M., pl., the Atrebates.

constituō, 3, -stituī, -stitūtum, v. tr., establish.

probō, 1, v. tr., approve of.

fidēlis, -e, adj., faithful.

arbitrabatur, cujusque auctoritas in iis regïonibus magni habebatur, mittit. Huic imperat, quas possit adeat civitates horteturque, ut populi Romani fidem sequantur, seque celeriter eo venturum nuntiet. Volusenus, perspectis regïonibus omnibus, quantum ei facultatis dari potuit, qui navi egredi ac se barbaris committere non auderet, quinto die ad Caesarem revertitur quaeque ibi perspexisset renuntiat.

Caesar levies hostages from the Morini.

22. Dum in his locis Caesar navium parandarum causa moratur, ex magna parte Morinorum ad eum legati venerunt, qui se de superioris temporis consilio excusarent, quod homines barbari et nostrae consuetudinis imperiti bellum populo Romano fecissent, seque ea, quae imperasset, facturos pollicerentur. Hoc sibi satis opportune Caesar accidisse arbitratus, quod neque post tergum hostem relinquere volebat, neque belli gerendi propter anni tempus facultatem habebat neque has tantularum rerum occupationes sibi Britanniae anteponendas judicabat, magnum iis obsidum numerum imperat. Quibus adductis, eos in fidem recepit. Navibus

---

magnī (gen. of value), of great value.

habeō, 2, v. tr., hold, consider.

facultās, -ātis, F., opportunity.

egredior, -dī, egressus, v. dep., go out; disembark.

committō, 3, -mīsī, -missum, v. tr., intrust.

audeō, 2, ausus sum, v. semi-dep., dare.

excūsō, 1, v. tr., excuse, justify.

consuētūdō, -inis, F., custom.

imperītus, -a, -um (governs gen.), adj., unacquainted with.

satis, adv., enough, sufficiently.

opportūnē, adv., opportunely.

accidō, 3, accidī, v. intr., happen.

accidit, accidēre, accidit, v. impers., it happens.

tergum, -ī, N., back.

relinquō, 3, -līquī, -lictum, v. tr., leave, leave behind.

tantulus, -a, -um, adj., trifling.

occupātiō, -ōnis, F., business, engagement.

antepōnō, 3, -posuī, -positum, v. tr., place before, prefer.

jūdicō, 1, v. tr., judge, decide.

circiter octoginta onerariis coactis contractisque, quot satis
esse ad duas transportandas legiones existimabat, quicquid
praeterea navium longarum habebat, quaestori, legatis, prae-
fectisque distribuit.   Huc accedebant octodecim onerariae
naves, quae ex eo loco ab millibus passuum octo vento tene-
bantur, quominus in euntdum portum pervenire possent ; has
equitibus distribuit.   Reliquum exercitum Quinto Titurio
Sabino et Lucio Aurunculeio Cottae legatis in Menapios
atque in eos pagos Morinorum, ab quibus ad eum legati non
venerant, deducendum dedit.   Publium Sulpicium Rufum
legatum cum eo praesidio, quod satis esse arbitrabatur, portum tenere jussit.)

Caesar reaches Britain.

23. His constitutis rebus, nactus idoneam ad navigandum
tempestatem, tertia fere vigilia solvit equitesque in ulteriorem
portum progredi et naves conscendere et se sequi jussit.
A quibus cum id paulo tardius esset administratum, ipse
hora diei circiter quarta cum primis navibus Britanniam
attigit atque ibi in omnibus collibus expositas hostium

---

cōgō, 3, coēgī, coactum, v. tr.,
  force, collect.

contrahō, 3, -traxī, -tractum, v.
  tr , bring together.

existimō, I, v. intr., think, consider.

praetereā, adv., besides.

quaestor,-ōris, M.,quarter-master.

praefectus, -ī, M., captain.

distribuō, 3, -uī, -ūtum, v. tr.,
  divide.

accēdō, 3,-cessī,-cessum, v. intr.,
  am added.

nanciscor, 3, nactus, v. dep.,
  obtain.

tempestās, -ātis, F., storm,
  weather.

solvō, 3, solvī, solūtum, v. tr.,
  loosen, set sail.

conscendō, 3, -dī, -sum, v. tr., go
  on board.

paulō, adv , a little.

tardē, adv., slowly.

administrō, 1, v. tr., carry out.

attingō, 3, attigī, no sup., v. tr.,
  reach.

expono, 3, -posuī, -positum, v.
  tr., draw up.

copias armatas conspexit. Cujus loci haec erat natura ·
adeo montibus augustis mare continebatur, uti ex locis
superioribus in litus telum adjici posset. Hunc ad egrediendum
nequaquam idoneum arbitratus locum, dum reliquae naves
eo convenirent, ad horam nonam in ancoris exspectavit.
Interim, legatis tribunisque militum convocatis, et quae ex
Voluseno cognovisset, et quae fieri vellet, ostendit, monuitque, ut rei militaris ratio, maxime ut maritimae res postularent, ut quae celerem. atque instabilem motum haberent,
ad nutum et ad tempus omnes res ab iis administrarentur.
His dimissis, et ventum et aestum uno tempore nactus
secundum, dato signo, et sublatis ancoris, circiter millia
passuum septem ab eo loco progressus, aperto ac plano
litore naves constituit.

The natives attack the Romans.

24. At barbari, consilio Romanorum cognito, praemisso
equitatu et essedariis, quo plerumque genere in proeliis uti
consuerunt, reliquis copiis subsecuti, nostros navibus egredi,

---

armātus, -a, -um, p. p. p. used as
    an adj., armed.
conspicio, 3, -spexī, -spectum,
    v. tr., observe, espy.
nātūra, -ae, F., character.
adeō, adv., so, to such an extent.
angustus, -a, -um, adj., narrow,
    precipitous.
contineō, 2, -tinuī, -tentum, v. tr.,
    hem in.
adjiciō, 3, -jecī, -jectum, v. tr.,
    throw upon.
nequaquam, adv., by no means.
ancora, -ae, F., anchor.
fīō, fierī, factus sum, v. irreg., be
    done.
ostendō, 3, -dī, -tum, v. tr., show,
    point out.

ratiō, -ōnis, F., method.
maxime, adv., especially
instābilis, -e, adj.. unsteady.
mōtus, -ūs, M., motion.
nūtus, -us, M., nod.
ventus, -ī, M., wind.
aestus, -us, M., tide.
tollō, 3, sustulī, sublātum, v. tr.,
    raise up, weigh.
apertus, -a, -um, adj., open.
plānus, -a, -um, adj., level.

---

at, conj., but.
essedāriī, -ōrum, M., pl., chari-
    oteers.
plērumque, adv., generally.
consuescō, 3, -suevi, -suetum, v.
    intr., become accustomed.

prohibebant.) Erat ob has causas summa difficultas, quod naves propter magnitudinem nisi in alto constitui non poterant; militibus autem, ignotis- locis, impeditis manibus, magno et gravi armorum onere oppressis, simul et de navibus desiliendum et in fluctibus consistendum et cum hostibus erat pugnandum; cum illi aut ex arido aut paululum in aquam progressi, omnibus membris expeditis, notissimis locis, audacter tela conjicerent, et equos insuefactos incitarent. Quibus rebus nostri perterriti, atque hujus omnino generis pugnae imperiti, non eadem alacritate ac studio, quo in pedestribus uti proeliis consueverant, utebantur.)

Caesar's device; bravery of the standard-bearer of the 10th legion; Roman advance.

25. Quod ubi Caesar animadvertit, naves longas, quarum et species erat barbaris inusitatior et motus ad usum expeditior, paulum removeri ab onerariis navibus, et remis

---

prohibeō, 2, v. tr., prevent.
ignōtus, -a, -um, adj., unknown.
impedītus, -a, -um, p. p. p. used as adj., hampered.
opprimo, 3, -pressī, -pressum, crush, weigh down.
simul, adv., at one and the same time.
dēsiliō, 4, -siluī, -sultum, v. intr., leap down.
fluctus, -us, M., wave.
consistō, 3, -stitī, no sup., come to a stand.
aridus, -a, -um, dry.
paululum, adv., a short distance.
prōgredior, -dī, -gressus, advance.
membrum, -ī, N., limb.
expedītus, -a, -um, adj., free.
conjiciō, 3, -jēcī, -jectum, v. tr., throw, hurl.

insuēfactus, -a, -um, adj., trained.
incitō, 1., spur on.
omnīnō, adv., wholly.
imperītus, -a, -um (governs gen.), adj., unskilled in.
alacritās, -ātis, F., eagerness.
studium, -ī, N., zeal.
pedestĕr, -tris, -tre, adj., on foot, on land.

---

animadvertō, 3, -vertī, -versum, v. tr., notice.
speciēs, -ēī, F., appearance.
inūsitātus, -a, -um, adj., strange, unfamiliar.
paulum, adv., a little, a short distance.
removeo, 2, -mōvī, -mōtum, v. tr., remove.
remus, -ı, M., oar.

incitari, et ad latus apertum hostium constitui, atque inde
fundis, sagittis, tormentis hostes propelli ac summoveri jussit;
quae res magno usui nostris fuit. Nam, et navium figura
et remorum motu et inusitato genere tormentorum permoti,
barbari constiterunt ac paulum modo pedem retulerunt.
Atque, nostris militibus cunctantibus, maxime propter alt-
itudinem maris, qui decimae legionis aquilam ferebat, contestatus deos, ut ea res legioni feliciter eveniret: "Desilite,"
inquit, "commilitones, nisi vultis aquilam hostibus prodere;
ego certe meum reipublicae atque imperatori officium praestitero." Hoc cum magna voce dixisset, ex navi se projecit,
atque in hostes aquilam ferre coepit. Tum nostri, cohortati
inter se, ne tantum dedecus admitteretur, universi ex navi
desiluerunt. Hos item ex proximis navibus cum conspex
issent, subsecuti hostibus appropinquarunt.

Rout of the enemy.

26. Pugnatum est ab utrisque acriter. Nostri tamen,
quod neque ordines servare neque firmiter insistere neque

funda, -ae, F., sling

tormentum, -ī, N., engine.

propellō, 3, -pulī, -pulsum, v. tr.,
drive forward.

summoveō, 2, -mōvī, -mōtum,
v. tr., dislodge.

figura -ae, F., shape.

cunctor, 1, v. dep., waver, hesitate.

altitūdo, -inis, F., height

contestor, 1, v. dep., invoke.

eveniō, 4, -venī, -ventum, v. intr.,
turn out, happen.

commīlitō, -onis, M., comrade.

prōdō, 3, prōdidī, prōditum, v.
tr., betray.

certē, adv., at least.

officium, -i, N., duty.

praestō, 1, -stitī, -stitum, v. tr.,
show, perform.

prōjiciō, 3, -jēcī, -jectum, v. tr.,
throw forward.

dedecus, -oris, N., disgrace.

admittō, 3, -mīsī, -missum, v. tr.,
incur.

universī, -ae, -a, adj. pl., all together, in a body.

item, adv., likewise.

appropinquo, 1 (governs dat.),
approach.

uterque, utraque, utrumque, pro.
adj., either, both.

ordō, -inis, M., rank.

firmiter, adv., steadily.

insistō, 3, -stitī, no sup., stand.

signa subsequi poterant, atque alius alia ex navi, quibuscum-
que signis occurrerat, se aggregabat, magno opere perturbabantur. Hostes vero, notis omnibus vadis, ubi ex litore
aliquos singulares ex navi egredientes conspexerant, incitatis
equis impeditos adoriebantur, plures paucos circumsiste-
bant, alii ab latere aperto in universos tela conjiciebant.)
Quod cum animadvertisset Caesar, scaphas longarum navium,
item speculatoria navigia militibus compleri jussit et, quos
laborantes conspexerat, iis subsidia submittebat. Nostri,
simul in arido constiterunt, suis omnibus consecutis, in
hostes impetum fecerunt, atque eos in fugam dederunt;
neque longius prosequi potuerunt, quod equites cursum
tenere atque insulam capere non potuerant. Hoc unum
ad pristinam fortunam Caesari defuit.

Several states submit to Caesar.

27. Hostes proelio superati, simul atque se ex fuga
receperunt, statim ad Caesarem legatos de pace miserunt,
obsides daturos quaeque imperasset sese facturos polliciti
sunt. Una cum his legatis Commius Atrebas venit, quem

---

quicumque, quaecumque, quodcumque, rel. pron., whoever,
whatever.
signum, -ī, N., standard.
occurro, 3, -currī, -cursum (governs dat.), meet.
aggrego, 1, v. tr., join, unite.
perturbō, 1, v. tr., disorder, throw
into confusion.
vēro, conj., but, on the other
hand.
vadum, -ī, N., ford.
aliquis, aliquae, aliquid, adj.
pron., any.
singulāris, -e, adj., singly.

adorior, -orīrī, -ortus, v. dep.,
attack.
scapha, -ae, F., light boat.
speculātorius, -a, -um, adj., spy,
scouting.
navigium, -ī, M., boat.
compleō, 2, -plēvī, -plētum, v. tr.,
fill, man.
labōrō, 1, v. intr., be in trouble.
subsidium, -ī, N., support, reinforcement.
pristinus, -a, -um, adj., former.
desum, -esse, -fuī, v. intr., (governs dat.), am lacking.

supra demonstraveram a Caesare in Britanniam praemissum}
Hunc illi e navi egressum, cum ad eos oratoris modo
imperatoris mandata deferret, comprehenderant atque in
vincula conjecerant: tum, proelio facto, remisèrunt et in
petenda pace ejus rei culpam in multitudinem contulerunt et
propter imprudentiam ut ignosceretur, petiverunt. Caesar
questus, quod, cum ultro in continentem legatis missis pacem
ab se petissent, bellum sine causa intulissent, ignoscere impru-
dentiae dixit obsidesque imperavit; quorum illi partem statim
dederunt, partem ex longinquioribus locis arcessitam paucis
diebus sese daturos dixerunt. Interea suos remigrare in agros
jusserunt, principesque undique convenire et se civitatesque
suas Caesari commendare coeperunt.}

Fate of the eighteen cavalry troop ships.

28. His rebus pace confirmata, post diem quartum, quam
est in Britanniam ventum, naves octodecim, de quibus supra
demonstratum est, quae equites sustulerant, ex superiore portu
leni vento solverunt. Quae cum appropinquarent Britanniae
et ex castris viderentur, tanta tempestas subito coörta est, ut

---

suprā, adv., above.

dēmonstrō, 1, v. tr., show, point
out.

modō, in the manner of.

mandātum, -i, N., order.

dēferō, -ferre, -tulī, -lātum, v. tr.,
deliver.

comprehendō, 3, -dī, -sum, v. tr.,
seize.

vinculum, -ī, N., chain.

culpa, -ae, F., blame, fault.

ignoscō, 3, ignovı, ıgnotum, v.
intr., (governs dat.) pardon.

queror, querī, questus, v. dep.,
complain.

ultrō, adv., of one's own accord.

continens, -ntis, (sc. *terra*) continent.

arcessō, 3, arcessīvī, arcessītum,
v. tr., send for, summon.

remigrō, 1, v. intr., go back,
return.

commendō, 1, v. tr., intrust.

---

confirmō, 1, v. tr., establish.

lēnis, -e, adj., gentle.

coorior, -orīrī, -ortus, v. dep.,
arise.

nulla earum cursum tenere posset, sed aliae eodem, unde erant
profectae, referrentur; aliae ad inferiorem partem insulae,
quae est propius solis occasum, magno sui cum periculo
dejicerentur: quae tamen, ancoris jactis, cum fluctibus
complerentur, necessario adversa nocte in altum provectae
continentem petierunt.

A storm and high tides wreck Caesar's transports.

29. Eadem nocte accidit, ut esset luna plena, qui dies
maritimos aestus maximos in Oceano efficere consuevit, nos-
trisque id erat incognitum. Ita uno tempore et longas naves,
quibus Caesar exercitum transportandum curaverat, quasque
in aridum subduxerat, aestus compleverat; et onerarias, quae
ad ancoras erant deligatae, tempestas afflictabat, neque ulla
nostris facultas aut administrandi aut auxiliandi dabatur.
Compluribus navibus fractis, reliquae cum essent—funibus,
ancoris reliquisque armamentis amissis — ad navigandum
inutiles, magna, id quod necesse erat accidere, totius exercitus
perturbatio facta est. Neque enim naves erant aliae, quibus
reportari possent, et omnia deerant, quae ad reficiendas eas
usui sunt, et, quod omnibus constabat hiemari in Gallia
oportere, frumentum his in locis in hiemem provisum non erat.

eōdem, adv., to the same place
necessāriō, adv., of necessity.
prōvehō, 3, -vexī, -vectum, v. tr.,
    carry forward, carry out.

efficiō, 3, -fēcī, -fectum, v. tr.,
    make, render.
subdūcō, 3, -dūxī, -ductum, v. tr.,
    draw up on shore, beach.
dēligō, 1, v. tr., bind.
afflictō, 1, v. tr., shatter.
administrō, 1, v. tr., manage.
auxilior, 1, v. dep., aid.

frangō, 3, frēgī, fractum, v. tr.,
    wreck, shatter.
fūnis, -is, M., rope, cable.
armāmentum, -ī, N., tackle.
inūtilis, -e, adj., useless.
perturbātiō, -onis, F., panic.
reficiō, 3, -fēcī, -fectum, v. tr.,
    repair.
constat, constāre, constitit, v.
    impers., it is agreed.
oportet, -ēre, oportuit, v. impers.,
    it behoves, ought.
prōvideō, 2, -vīdī, -vīsum, v. tr.,
    foresee, provide.

Conspiracy of British Chiefs.

30. Quibus rebus cognitis, principes Britanniae, qui post proelium factum ad ea, quae jusserat Caesar, facienda convenerant, inter se collocuti, cum equites et naves et frumentum Romanis deesse intellegerent, et paucitatem militum ex castrorum exiguitate cognoscerent, quae hoc erant etiam angustiora, quod sine impedimentis Caesar legiones transportaverat, optimum factu esse duxerunt, rebellione facta, frumento commeatuque nostros prohibere, et rem in hiemem producere, quod, iis superatis, aut reditu interclusis, neminem postea belli inferendi causa in Britanniam transiturum confidebant. Itaque, rursus conjuratione facta, paulatim ex castris discedere ac suos clam ex agris deducere coeperunt.

Caesar suspects their intentions; forms plans accordingly.

31. At Caesar, etsi nondum eorum consilia cognoverat, tamen et ex eventu navium suarum et ex eo, quod obsides dare intermiserant, fore id, quod accidit, suspicabatur. Itaque ad omnes casus subsidia comparabat. Nam et frumentum ex

---

colloquor, -loqui, -locūtus, v. dep., converse.

intellegō, 3, -lexī, -lectum, v. tr., perceive.

paucitās, -ātis, F., fewness.

exiguitās, -ātis, F., smallness.

hōc, for this reason.

factū, supine in -u, to be done.

rebelliō, -ōnis, F., renewal of war.

commeātus, -us, M., supplies.

reditus, -ūs, M., return.

interclūdō, 3, -clūsī, -clusum, v. tr., cut off.

nemo, acc. neminem, no one.

posteā, adv., afterwards.

transeo, -īre, -iī, -itum, v. tr., go across, cross over.

confīdō, 3, confīsus sum, v. semidep., trust.

rursus, adv., again.

conjurātiō, -onis, F., league.

paulātim, adv., gradually.

discēdō, 3, -cessī, -cessum, v. intr., go away, depart.

clam, adv., secretly.

---

nōndum, adv., not yet.

ēventus, -ūs, M., accident.

intermittō, 3, -mīsī, -missum, v, tr., cease, stop.

suspicor, 1, v. dep., suspect.

casus, -us, M., emergency.

subsidium, -ī, N., resource.

agris cotidie in castra conferebat, et quae gravissime afflictae
erant naves, earum materia atque aere ad reliquas reficiendas
utebatur; et quae ad eas res erant usui ex continenti com-
portari jubebat. Itaque, cum id summo studio a militibus
administraretur, duodecim navibus amissis, reliquis ut navigari
commode posset, effecit.

Sudden attack of the British.

32. Dum ea geruntur, legione ex consuetudine una frumentatum missa, quae appellabatur septima, neque ulla ad id
tempus belli suspicione interposita, cum pars hominum in
agris remaneret, pars etiam in castra ventitaret, ii, qui pro
portis castrorum in statione erant, Caesari renuntiarunt,
pulverem majorem, quam consuetudo ferret, in ea parte videri,
quam in partem legio iter fecisset. Caesar id, quod erat,
suspicatus, aliquid novi a barbaris initum consilii, cohortes,
quae in stationibus erant, secum in eam partem proficisci.
duas ex reliquis in stationem succedere, reliquas armari et
confestim sese subsequi jussit. Cum paulo longius a castris
processisset, suos ab hostibus premi, atque aegre sustinere, et
conferta legione ex omnibus partibus tela conjici animadvertit.

cotidie, adv., daily.
affligo, 3, --flixi, -flictum, v. tr., shatter.
materia, -ae, F., timber.
aes, -aeris, N., metal.
amitto, 3, -misi, -missum, v. tr., lose.
commode, adv., conveniently.

frumentor, 1, v. dep., forage.
suspicio, -onis, F., suspicion.
ventito, 1, v. intr., come often, come and go.
statio, -onis, F., outpost, guard.
pulvis, -eris, M., dust.

ineo, -ire, -ii, -itum, v. tr., go into, enter upon, form.
succedo, 3, -cessi, -cessum, v. intr., take the place of.
armo, 1, v. tr., arm.
confestim, adv., immediately.
procedo, 3, -cessi, -cessum, v. intr., advance.
premo, 3, pressi, pressum, v. tr., press, press hard.
aegre, adv., with difficulty.
sustineo, 2, -tinui, -tentum, v. tr., hold out, withstand.
confertus, -a, -um, adj., in close array, crowded together.

Nam quod, omni ex reliquis partibus demesso frumento, pars una erat reliqua, suspicati hostes huc nostros esse venturos noctu in silvis delituerant; tum dispersos, depositis armis, in metendo occupatos, subito adorti, paucis interfectis, reliquos incertis ordinibus perturbaverant, simul equitatu atque essedis circumdederant.

The British mode of fighting.

33. Genus hoc est ex essedis pugnae. Primo per omnes partes perequitant, et tela conjiciunt, atque ipso terrore equorum et strepitu rotarum, ordines plerumque perturbant; et cum se inter equitum turmas insinuaverunt, ex essedis desiliunt et pedibus proeliantur. Aurigae interim paulatim ex proelio excedunt, atque ita currus collocant, ut, si illi a multitudine hostium premantur, expeditum ad suos receptum habeant. Ita mobilitatem equitum, stabilitatem peditum in proeliis praestant, ac tantum usu cotidiano et exercitatione

---

dēmetō, 3, -messui, -messum, v. tr., reap.

noctū, adv., in the night time.

dēlitescō, 3, -lituī, no sup., lie hid, hide one's self.

dispersus, -a, -um, p. p. p. used as an adj., scattered.

metō, 3, messui, messum, v. tr., reap.

occupātus, -a, -um, p. p. p. used as an adj., engaged.

incertus, -a, -um, adj., uncertain, confused.

esseda, -ae, F., chariot.

circumdō, -dăre, -dedī, -datum, v. tr., surround.

---

prīmō, adv., at first.

perequitō, 1, v. intr., ride through, drive through.

terror, -ōris, M., fright, terror.

strepitus, -ūs, M., noise, din.

rota, -ae, F., wheel.

turma, -ae, F., squadron [of cavalry].

insinuo, 1, v. tr., cause to go into; insinuant sē, they work their way into.

dēsiliō, 4, -siluī, -sultum, v. intr., leap down.

proelior, 1, v. dep., fight.

aurīga, -ae, M., charioteer.

interim, adv., meanwhile.

paulātim, adv., gradually.

receptus, -us, M., retreat.

mōbilitās, -ātis, F., mobility.

stabilitās, -ātis, F., steadiness.

cotīdiānus, -a, -um, adj., daily.

exercitātiō, -ōnis, training, practice, exercise.

efficiunt, uti in declivi ac praecipiti loco incitatos equos sustinere, et brevi moderari ac flectere, et per temonem percurrere, et in jugo insistere, et inde se in currus citissime recipere consuerint.

Caesar acts on the defensive: severe storms keep the Romans within their camp.

34. Quibus rebus, perturbatis nostris novitate pugnae, tempore opportunissimo Caesar auxilium tulit; namque ejus adventu hostes constiterunt, nostri se ex timore receperunt. Quo facto, ad lacessendum et ad committendum proelium alienum esse tempus arbitratus, suo se loco continuit, et brevi tempore intermisso, in castra legiones reduxit. Dum haec geruntur, nostris omnibus occupatis, qui erant in agris reliqui discesserunt. Secutae sunt continuos complures dies tempestatés, quae et nostros in castris continerent, et hostem a pugna prohiberent. Interim barbari nuntios in omnes partes dimiserunt, paucitatemque nostrorum militum suis praedi

---

dēclīvis, -e, adj., sloping.

praeceps, -cipitis, adj., headlong, steep.

incitātus, -a,-um, p. p. p. used as an adj., at full speed.

brevī (sc. *tempore*), in a short time.

moderor, 1, v. tr., control.

flectō, 3, flexuī, flexum, v. tr.,turn.

tēmō, -ōnis, M., pole, tongue.

citō, adv. (citius, citissimē) quickly, swiftly.

---

novitās, -ātis, F., strangeness, novelty.

opportūnus, -a, -um, adj., fit, suitable, opportune.

namque, conj., for.

timor, -ōris, M., fear.

lacessō, 3, -sīvī, sītum, v. tr., harass, provoke, attack.

alienus, -a, -um, adj., belonging to another, unfavorable.

contineō, 2, -uī, -tentum, v. tr., hem in, keep.

discēdō, 3, cessī, -cessum, v. intr., go away, depart, scatter.

continuus, -a, -um, adj., successive.

prohibeō, 2, v. tr., prevent, keep from.

praedicō, 1, v. tr., announce, boast.

caverunt et, quanta praedae faciendae atque in perpetuum sui liberandi facultas daretur, si Romanos castris expulissent, demonstraverunt. His rebus celeriter magna multitudine peditatus equitatusque coacta, ad castra venerunt.

Defeat and pursuit of the enemy.

35. Caesar, etsi idem, quod superioribus diebus acciderat, fore videbat, ut, si essent hostes pulsi, celeritate periculum effugerent, tamen nactus equites circiter triginta, quos Commius Atrebas, de quo ante dictum est, secum transportaverat, legiones in acie pro castris constituit. Commisso proelio, diutius nostrorum militum impetum hostes ferre non potuerunt, ac terga verterunt. Quos tanto spatio secuti, quantum cursu et viribus efficere potuerunt complures ex iis occiderunt, deinde, omnibus longe lateque aedificiis incensis, se in castra receperunt.

Caesar makes peace; sets sail for Gaul.

36. Eodem die legati ab hostibus missi ad Caesarem de pace venerunt. His Caesar numerum obsidum, quem antea imperaverat, duplicavit eosque in continentem adduci jussit, quod, propinqua die aequinoctii, infirmis navibus, hiemi

---

praeda, -ae, F., booty, plunder.
perpetuus, -a, -um, adj., constant, unbroken; in perpetuum, forever.
expellō, 3, -pulī, -pulsum, v. tr., drive out.
cogō, 3, coegī, coactum, v. tr., collect.

celeritās, -ātis, F., speed.
effugiō, 3, -fūgī, -fugitum, v. tr., escape.
constituō, 3, -uī, -utum, v. tr., draw up, post.
committō, 3, -mīsī, -missum, v. tr., engage, engage in.

spatium, -ī, N., distance.
tantus—quantus, as great as.
cursus, -ūs, M., running.
occīdō, 3, -cīdī, -cīsum, v. tr., cut down, kill, slay.
deinde, adv., then, next, afterwards.
incendō, 3, -dī, -sum, v. tr., set on fire, burn.

anteā, adv., before, previously.
duplicō, 1, v. tr., double, demand . . . double.
propinquus, -a, -um, adj., near.
aequinoctium, -ī, N., equinox.
infirmus, -a, -um, adj., weak.

navigationem subjiciendam non existimabat. Ipse, idoneam tempestatem nactus, paulo post mediam noctem naves solvit; quae omnes incolumes ad continentem pervenerunt; sed ex his onerariae duae eosdem, quos reliquae, portus capere non potuerunt et paulo infra delatae sunt.

Sudden attack of the Morini.

37. Quibus ex navibus cum essent expositi milites circiter trecenti, atque in castra contenderent, Morini, quos Caesar in Britanniam proficiscens pacatos reliquerat, spe praedae adducti, primo non ita magno suorum numero circumsteterunt, ac, si sese interfici nollent, arma ponere jusserunt Cum illi, orbe facto, sese defenderent, celeriter ad clamorem hominum circiter millia sex convenerunt. Qua re nuntiata, Caesar omnem ex castris equitatum suis auxilio misit. Interim nostri milites impetum hostium sustinuerunt, atque amplius horis quatuor fortissime pugnaverunt, et paucis vulneribus acceptis complures ex iis occiderunt. Postea vero quam equitatus noster in conspectum venit, hostes, abjectis armis, terga verterunt, magnusque eorum numerus est occisus.

---

subjicio, 3, -jeci, -jectum, v. tr., place near, expose.

incolumis, -e, adj., safe.

onerarius, -a, -um, adj., of burden; navis oneraria, a transport.

infra, adv., below.

defero, -ferre, -tuli, -latum, v. tr., carry down.

---

expono, 3, -posui, -positum, v. tr., land, disembark.

trecenti, -ae, -a, num. adj., 300.

contendo, 3, -di, -tum, v. intr., proceed, hasten.

pacatus, -a, -um, p. p. p. used as adj., at peace.

circumsto, 1, -steti, -statum, v. tr., surround.

nolo, nolle, nolui, v. irreg., not.. wish, am unwilling.

orbis, -is, M., circle.

defendo, 3, -di, -sum, v. tr., defend, protect.

vulnus, -eris, N., wound.

accipio, 3, -cepi, -ceptum, v. tr., receive.

posteaquam, conj., after.

vero, adv. conj., in truth, but, however.

conspectus, -us, M., sight.

abjicio, 3, -jeci, -jectum, v. tr., throw away.

Conquest of the Morini and Menapii.

38. Caesar postero die Titum Labienum legatum, cum iis legionibus, quas ex Britannia reduxerat, in Morinos, qui rebellionem fecerant, misit. Qui cum propter siccitates paludum, quo se reciperent, non haberent, quo perfugio superiore anno fuerant usi, omnes fere in potestatem Labieni venerunt. At Quintus Titurius et Lucius Cotta legati, qui in Menapiorum fines legiones duxerant, omnibus eorum agris vastatis, frumentis succisis, aedificiis incensis, quod Menapii se omnes in densissimas silvas abdiderant, se ad Caesarem receperunt. Caesar in Belgis omnium legionum hiberna constituit. Eo duae omnino civitates ex Britannia obsides miserunt, reliquae neglexerunt. His rebus gestis, ex litteris Caesaris dierum viginti supplicatio a senatu decreta est.

rebellio, -ōnis, F., renewal of war.
siccitās, -ātis, F., dryness.
palūs, -ūdis, F., marsh.
perfugium, -ī, N., refuge.
ferē, adv., almost, about.
potestās, -ātis, F., power.
frūmentum, -ī, N., corn; pl., crops.
succīdō, 3, -cīdī, -cīsum, v. tr., cut down.
abdō, 3, abdidī, abditum, v. tr., hide, conceal.

hībernus, -a, -um, adj., winter, wintry; hīberna, -orum, N., pl. (sc. castra), winter camp, winter quarters.
eo, adv., thither.
omnīnō, adv., in all.
neglegō, 3, -lexī, -lectum, v. tr., neglect.
supplicātio, -onis, F., thanksgiving.
decerno, 3, -crēvī, -crētum, v. tr., decree.

LIBER QUINTUS

Caesar orders a fleet to be built.   The Pirustae give hostages.

1. L. Domitio Ap. Claudio consulibus, discedens ab hibernis Caesar in Italiam, ut quotannis facere consuerat, legatis imperat, quos legionibus praefecerat, uti quam plurimas possent bieme naves aedificandas veteresque reficiendas curarent. Earum modum formamque demonstrat. Ad celeritatem onerandi subductionesque paulo facit humiliores, quam quibus in nostro mari uti consuevimus, atque id eo magis, quod propter crebras commutationes aestuum minus magnos ibi fluctus fieri cognoverat ; ad onera ac multitudinem jumentorum transportandam, paulo latiores, quam quibus in reliquis utimur maribus. Has omnes actuarias imperat fieri, quam ad rem humilitas multum adjuvat. Ea, quae sunt usui ad armandas naves, ex Hispania apportari jubet. Ipse, conventibus Galliae citerioris peractis, in Illyricum proficiscitur, quod a Pirustis finitimam partem provinciae incursionibus vastari audiebat. Eo cum venisset, civitatibus milites imperat

---

ut, conj., as.

quotannīs, adv., yearly.

consuesco, 3, -suēvi, -suētum, v. intr., become accustomed ; consuēvī, I am accustomed.

praeficiō, 3, -fēcī, -fectum, v. tr., (governs acc. and dat.), place over, place in command of

curō, 1, v. tr., care for (see general vocab.)

modus, -ī, M., measure, size.

forma, -ae, F., shape, plan.

onerō, 1, v. tr., load.

subductiō, -onis, F., drawing up on shore, beaching.

humilis, -e, adj., low.

eō, adv., for this reason.

crēber, -bra, -brum, adj., frequent.

commūtātiō, -ōnis, F., change.

jūmentum, -i, N., baggage animal, beast of burden.

actuārius, -a, -um, adj., driven by oars (as well as sails), rowing fast sailing.

humilitās, -ātis, F., lowness.

multum, adv., much.

adjūvō, 1, -jūvī, -jūtum, v. tr., aid, help.

apportō, 1, v. tr., bring.

conventus, -ūs, M., assize.

perago, 3, -egi, -actum, v. tr., conduct, hold.

incursiō, -ōnis, F., raid, inroad.

certumque in locum convenire jubet. Qua re nuntiata,
Pirustae legatos ad eum mittunt, qui doceant nihil earum
rerum publico factum consilio, seseque paratos esse demon-
strant omnibus rationibus de injuriis satisfacere. Percepta
oratione eorum, Caesar obsides imperat eosque ad certum
diem adduci jubet; nisi ita fecerint, sese bello civitatem
persecuturum demonstrat. Iis ad diem adductis, ut imper
averat, arbitros inter civitates dat, qui litem aestiment
poenamque constituant.

The soldiers praised for their zeal. Fleet ordered to rendezvous at Portus Itius.

2. His confectis rebus, conventibusque peractis, in citeriorem Galliam revertitur, atque inde ad exercitum proficiscitur.
Eo cum venisset, circuitis omnibus hibernis, singulari militum
studio, in summa omnium rerum inopia, circiter sexcentas ejus
generis, cujus supra demonstravimus, naves et longas viginti

---

certus, -a, -um, adj., stated, definite, certain.
doceō, 2, -uī, doctum, v. tr., teach,
inform, tell.
publicus, -a, -um, public, common.
parātus, -a, -um, p. p. p. used as
adj., ready.
ratiō, -ōnis, F., account, claim.
injuria, -ae, F., wrong, injustice.
satisfaciō, 3, -fēcī, -factum, v. tr.,
satisfy, meet.
percipio, 3, -cēpī, -ceptum, v. tr.,
take in, hear.
nisi, conj., unless, if . . . not.
ita, adv., so.
persequor, 3, -secutus, v. tr.,
follow up, pursue.
arbiter, -trī, M., arbitrator, as-
sessor.

līs, lītis, F., law suit, damages.
aestimō, 1, v. tr., value, estimate,
assess.
poena, -ae, F., punishment,
penalty.

revertor, revertī, revertī, reversum, v. semi-dep., turn back,
return.
circueo, -īre, -iī, -itum, v. tr., go
around, visit.
singulāris, -e, adj., remarkable,
extraordinary.
studium, -ī, N., zeal, enthusiasm.
inopia, -ae, F., want, lack, scarcity.
sexcentī, -ae, -a, num. adj., 600.
suprā, adv., above.

octo invenit instructas, neque multum abesse ab eo, quin
paucis diebus deduci possint. Collaudatis militibus, atque iis,
qui negotio praefuerant, quid fieri velit, ostendit, atque omnes
ad portum Itium convenire jubet, quo ex portu commodissimum in Britanniam trajectum esse cognoverat, circiter
millium passuum triginta a continenti : huic rei quod satis
esse visum est militum reliquit. Ipse cum legionibus expeditis quattuor et equitibus octingentis in fines Treverorum
proficiscitur, quod hi neque ad concilia veniebant, neque
imperio parebant, Germanosque Transrhenanos sollicitare
dicebantur.

The Treveri and their rival chieftains.

3. Haec civitas longe plurimum totius Galliae equitatu
valet, magnasque habet copias peditum, Rhenumque, ut supra
demonstravimus, tangit. In ea civitate duo de principatu
inter se contendebant, Indutiomarus et Cingetorix ; e quibus
alter, simul atque de Caesaris legionumque adventu cognitum

---

invenio, 4, vēnī, -ventum, v. tr.,
  find
instruo, 3, -struxī, -structum, v.
  tr., draw up, build, equip.
dēdūco, 3, -dūxi, -ductum, v.
  tr., draw down (into water),
  launch.
collaudō, 1, v.tr., commend, praise.
negōtium, -ī, N., business, work.
praesum, -esse, -fuī, v. intr.
  (governs dat.), be in charge of.
fīō, fierī, factus sum, v. irreg.,
  am done, become.
ostendō, 3, -dī, -tum, v. tr., show.
commodus, -a, -um, adj., fit,
  handy, suitable, convenient.
trājectus, -ūs, M., passage.
circiter, adv., about.

videor, 2, vīsus, v. dep., seem,
  appear.
expedītus, -a, -um. adj., free,
  ready for action.
octingenti, -ae, -a, num. adj, 800.
concilium, -ī, N., council.
sollicitō, 1, tamper with, stir up.

---

longe, adv., by far.
plūrimum, adv., very, most.
valeō, 2, v. intr., am strong, have
  power.
tangō, 3, tetigī, tactum, v. tr.,
  touch, border on.
principātus, -ūs, M., leadership.
simul atque, conj., as soon as.
adventus, ūs, M., arrival.

est, ad eum venit; se suosque omnes in officio futuros, neque
ab amicitia populi Romani defecturos confirmavit; quaeque in
Treveris gererentur ostendit. At Indutiomarus equitatum
peditatumque cogere, iisque, qui per aetatem in armis esse
non poterant, in silvam Arduennam abditis, quae ingenti
magnitudine per medios fines Treverorum a flumine Rheno
ad initium Remorum pertinet, bellum parare instituit. Sed
posteaquam nonnulli principes ex ea civitate, et familiaritate
Cingetorigis adducti, et adventu nostri exercitus perterriti, ad
Caesarem venerunt, et de suis privatim rebus ab eo petere
coeperunt, quoniam civitati consulere non possent, veritus, ne
ab omnibus desereretur, Indutiomarus legatos ad Caesarem
mittit: Sese idcirco ab suis discedere atque ad eum venire
noluisse, quo facilius civitatem in officio contineret, ne omnis
nobilitatis discessu plebs propter imprudentiam laberetur:
itaque esse civitatem in sua potestate, seseque, si Caesar
permitteret, ad eum in castra venturum, suas civitatisque
fortunas ejus fidei permissurum.

---

officium, -i, N., duty, allegiance.
deficio, 3, -feci, -fectum, v. intr.,
fail, revolt.
confirmo, 1, v. tr., assure.
aetas, -atis, F., age.
abdo, 3, -didi, -ditum, v. tr., hide,
conceal.
ingens (gen. ingentis), adj., large,
huge, immense.
initium, -i, N., beginning.
instituo, 3, -ui, -utum, v. tr., draw
up, decide, begin.
familiaritas, -atis, F., intimacy,
friendship.
privatim, adv., privately, individually.
quoniam, conj., since.

consulo, 3, -sului, -sultum, v. tr.,
with acc. consult; intr. with
dat. consult for, consult the
interests of.
desero, 3, -serui, -sertum, v. tr.
desert.
idcirco, adv., for this reason.
quo, conj., in order that.
nobilitas, -atis, F., nobility.
discessus, -us, M., departure.
imprudentia, -ae, F., thoughtlessness.
labor, 3, lapsus, v. intr., slip,
glide away, revolt.
fortunae, -arum, F. pl., fortunes,
interests.

Cingetorix honored and Indutiomarus offended.

4. Caesar, etsi intellegebat, qua de causa ea dicerentur, quaeque eum res ab instituto consilio deterreret, tamen, ne aestatem in Treveris consumere cogeretur, omnibus ad Britannicum bellum rebus comparatis, Indutiomarum ad se cum ducentis obsidibus venire jussit. His adductis, in iis filio propinquisque ejus omnibus, quos nominatim evocaverat, consolatus Indutiomarum, hortatusque. est, uti in officio maneret; nihilo tamen secius, principibus Treverorum ad se convocatis, hos singillatim Cingetorigi conciliavit, quod cum merito ejus a se fieri intellegebat, tum magni interesse arbitrabatur ejus auctoritatem inter suos quam plurimum valere, cujus tam egregiam in se voluntatem perspexisset. Id tulit factum graviter Indutiomarus, suam gratiam inter suos minui, et, qui jam ante inimico in nos animo fuisset, multo gravius hoc dolore exarsit.

intellegō, 3, -lexī, -lectum, v. tr., perceive, am aware.

qua dē causā, for what reason.

institūtus, -a, -um, p. p. p. used as an adj., appointed, predetermined.

dēterreo, 2, v. tr.; keep from, deter.

consumo, 3, -sumpsī, -sumptum, v. tr., spend.

propinquus, -ī, M., relative.

nōminātim, adv., by name, specially, individually.

evôcō, 1, v. tr., summon.

consōlor, 1, v. dep., console, comfort, cheer.

nihilō secius, none the less.

singillātim, adv., one by one, individually.

conciliō, 1, v. tr., win over, reconcile.

cum . . . tum, both . . . and.

meritum, -ī, N., service, deserts.

interest, -esse, -fuit, v. impers., it is of interest, importance.

magnī interesse, to be of great importance.

egregius, -a, -um, adj., remarkable, signal.

voluntās, -ātis, F., goodwill.

factum, -ī, N., act, deed.

graviter fero, am offended at, am annoyed at.

grātia, -ae, F., favor, influence.

minuo, 3, -uī, -ūtum, v. tr., lessen.

inimīcus, -a, -um, adj., unfriendly, hostile.

multō, adv., much.

dolor, -ōris, M., grief, resentment.

exardescō, 3, -arsī, -arsum, v. intr., be kindled, burst forth.

Caesar prepares to sail.

5. His rebus constitutis, Caesar ad portum Itium cum legionibus pervenit. Ibi cognoscit quadraginta naves, quae in Meldis factae erant, tempestate rejectas cursum tenere non potuisse atque eodem, unde erant profectae, revertisse; reliquas paratas ad navigandum atque omnibus rebus instructas invenit. Eodem equitatus totius Galliae convenit numero millium quattuor; principesque ex omnibus civitatibus, ex quibus perpaucos, quorum in se fidem perspexerat, relinquere in Gallia, reliquos obsidum loco secum ducere decreverat, quod, cum ipse abesset, motum Galliae verebatur.

Dumnorix gives trouble.

6. Erat una cum ceteris Dumnorix Haeduus, de quo ante ab nobis dictum est. Hunc secum habere in primis constituerat, quod eum cupidum rerum novarum, cupidum imperii, magni animi, magnae inter Gallos auctoritatis cognoverat. Accedebat huc, quod in concilio Haeduorum Dumnorix dixerat, sibi a Caesare regnum civitatis deferri; quod dictum Haedui graviter ferebant, neque recusandi aut deprecandi causa legatos ad Caesarem mittere audebant. Id factum ex suis hospitibus Caesar cognoverat. Ille omnibus primo precibus

rejicio, 3, -jēcī, -jectum, v. tr., throw back.
perpaucī, -ae, -a, pl. adj., very few.
locō, in the place of, as.
dēcernō, 3, -crēvī, -crētum, v. tr., decree, determine, decide.
absum, -esse, -fuī, v. irreg., am absent.
mōtus, -us, M., rising.

unā cum, along with.
in prīmīs, among the first, especially.

rēs novae, F. pl., new things, change, revolution.
accēdēbat huc quod, to this was added the fact that.
dēferō, -ferre, -tulī, -latum, v. tr., report, offer.
dictum, -ī, N., saying, statement.
recuso, 1, v. tr., refuse, object.
deprecor, 1, v. dep., protest.
audeō, 2, ausus sum, v. semi-dep. dare.
hospes, -itis, M., guest, friend.
preces, precum, pl. F., (see Vocab.) prayer, request.

petere contendit, ut in Gallia relinqueretur, partim quod
insuetus navigandi mare timeret, partim quod religionibus
impediri sese diceret. Posteaquam id obstinate sibi negari
vidit, omni spe impetrandi adempta, principes Galliae
sollicitare, sevocare singulos, hortarique coepit, uti in
continenti remanerent; metu territare, non sine causa fieri,
ut Gallia omni nobilitate spoliaretur; id esse consilium
Caesaris, ut, quos in conspectu Galliae interficere vereretur,
hos omnes in Britanniam traductos necaret; fidem reliquis
interponere, jusjurandum poscere, ut, quod esse ex usu
Galliae intellexissent, communi consilio administrarent.
Haec a compluribus ad Caesarem deferebantur.

Death of Dumnorix.

7. Qua re cognita, Caesar, quod tantum civitati Haeduae
dignitatis tribuebat, coercendum atque deterrendum, quibus-
cumque rebus posset, Dumnorigem statuebat; quod longius
ejus amentiam progredi videbat, prospiciendum ne quid sibi
ac reipublicae nocere posset. Itaque dies circiter viginti

---

partim, adv., partly.
insuĕtus, -a, -um, adj. (governs
  gen.), unaccustomed, unused.
timeō, 2, uī, no sup., fear, am afraid.
rēligiō, -ōnis, F., religious feeling,
  religious scruple.
impediō, 4, v. tr., prevent.
obstinātē, adv., resolutely.
impetrō, 1, v. tr., obtain a request.
adimō, 3, -emi, -emptum, v. tr.,
  take away, remove.
sevoco, 1, v. tr., call aside.
singulī, -ae, -a, distrib. num. adj.,
  one by one
territō, 1, v. tr., terrify, alarm.
spoliō, 1, v. tr., despoil, rob.
necō, 1, v. tr., kill, murder.

fidem interponō, pledge one's
  word.
jūsjūrandum, jurisjūrandi, N.,
  oath.
ex usu, in the interests of.
communis, -e, adj., common.
administrō, 1, v. tr., carry out.

---

tribuō, 3, -uī, -ūtum, v. tr., assign,
  give.
coerceō, 2, restrain, check.
amentia, -ae, F., madness, folly.
prōspiciō, 3, -spexī, -spectum,
  v. tr., foresee, take care, take
  precautions.
noceō, 2, v. intr. (governs dat.),
  injure, harm.

quinque in eo loco commoratus, quod Corus ventus navigationem impediebat, qui magnam partem omnis temporis in his
locis flare consuevit, dabat operam ut in officio Dumnorigem
contineret, nihilo tamen secius omnia ejus consilia cognosceret;
tandem idoneam nactus tempestatem, milites equitesque con
scendere in naves jubet: At, omnium impeditis animis, Dum
norix cum equitibus Haeduorum a castris, insciente Caesare,
domum discedere coepit.   Qua re nuntiata, Caesar, intermissa
profectione, atque omnibus rebus postpositis, magnam partem
equitatus ad eum insequendum mittit, retrahique imperat;
si vim faciat neque pareat, interfici jubet, nihil hunc se
absente pro sano facturum arbitratus, qui praesentis imperium
neglexisset.   Ille enim, revocatus, resistere ac se manu
defendere, suorumque fidem implorare coepit, saepe clamitans,
liberum se liberaeque esse civitatis.   Illi, ut erat imperatum,
circumsistunt hominem atque interficiunt; at equites Haedui
ad Caesarem omnes revertuntur.

Caesar's second landing in Britain, 54 B.C.

8.   His rebus gestis, Labieno in continente cum tribus
legionibus et equitum millibus duobus relicto, ut portus

---

commoror, 1, v. dep., delay
Cōrus, -ī, M., north-west wind.
nāvigātiō, -ōnis, F., sailing, navi-
    gation.
flō, I, v. intr., blow.
operam dō ut, take pains to.
nihilō secius, none the less.
conscendō, 3, -dī, -sum, v. tr. and
    intr., go on board.
insciens (gen. inscientis), adj.,
    not knowing, ignorant.
intermittō, 3, -mīsī, -missum,
    v. tr., stop, delay.
profectiō, -ōnis, F., departure.

insequor, 3, -secūtus, v. dep.,
    pursue, overtake.
retrahō, 3, -traxī, -tractum, v. tr.,
    bring back.
sanus, -a, -um, adj., sane.
prō sānō, like a sane man.
praesens (gen. praesentis), adj.,
    present.
neglegō, 3, -lexī, -lectum, v. tr.,
    neglect, disregard.
clāmitō, 1, v. intr., shout often.
circumsistō, 3, -stetī, no sup.,
    v. tr., surround.

tueretur, et rem frumentariam provideret, quaeque in Gallia.
gererentur cognosceret, consiliumque pro tempore et pro re
caperet, ipse cum quinque legionibus et pari numero equitum,
quem in continenti reliquerat, ad solis occasum naves solvit ;
et leni Africo provectus, media circiter nocte vento intermisso,
cursum non tenuit ; et longius delatus aestu, orta luce, sub
sinistra Britanniam relictam conspexit. Tum rursus aestus
commutationem secutus, remis contendit, ut eam partem
insulae caperet, qua optimum esse egressum superiore aestate
cognoverat. Qua in re admodum fuit militum virtus laudanda,
qui vectoriis gravibusque navigiis, non intermisso remigandi
labore, longarum navium cursum adaequarunt. Accessum est
ad Britanniam omnibus navibus meridiano fere tempore,
neque in eo loco hostis est visus : sed, ut postea Caesar ex
captivis cognovit, cum magnae manus eo convenissent, multitudine navium perterritae, quae cum annotinis privatisque,
quas sui quisque commodi fecerat, amplius octingentae uno
erant visae tempore, a litore discesserant ac se in superiora
loca abdiderant. ·

tueor, 2, tuitus, v. dep., protect, defend.
res frūmentāria, F., corn supply.
par (gen. paris), adj., equal.
lēnis, -e, adj., gentle, mild.
Africus, -ī, M., south-west wind.
prōvehō, 3, -vexī, -vectum, v. tr., carry forward.
sinistra, -ae (sc. manus), F., left hand, left.
orior, orīrī ortus, v.dep.,rise, arise.
rēmus, -ī, M., oar.
quā (sc. parte), where.
egressus, -ūs, M.. landing, landing place.
admodum, adv., very.

vectōrius, -a, -um, adj., adapted for carrying.
vectōrium navigium, transport ship.
remigō, 1, v. intr., row.
adaequō, 1, v. tr., equal.
merīdiānus, -a, -um, adj., mid-day.
manus, -us, F., hand, band.
annōtinus, -a, -um, adj., of last year.
prīvātus, -a, -um, adj., private.
commodum, -ī, N., convenience, advantage.
amplius, adv., more (than).
octingentī, -ae, -a, num. adj., 800.

The Britons oppose his march inland.

9. Caesar, exposito exercitu, et loco castris idoneo capto, ubi ex captivis cognovit, quo in loco hostium copiae consedissent, cohortibus decem ad mare relictis et equitibus trecentis, qui praesidio navibus essent, de tertia vigilia ad hostes contendit eo minus veritus navibus, quod in litore molli atque aperto deligatas ad ancoram relinquebat, et praesidio navibusque Quintum Atrium praefecit. Ipse, noctu progressus millia passuum circiter duodecim, hostium copias conspicatus est. Illi, equitatu atque essedis ad flumen progressi, ex loco superiore nostros prohibere et proelium committere coeperunt. Repulsi ab equitatu, se in silvas abdiderunt, locum nacti egregie et natura et opere munitum, quem domestici belli, ut videbantur, causa jam ante praeparaverant: nam, crebris arboribus succisis, omnes introitus erant praeclusi. Ipsi ex silvis rari propugnabant, nostrosque intra munitiones ingredi prohibebant. At milites legionis septimae, testudine facta, et aggere ad munitiones adjecto, locum ceperunt eosque ex silvis expulerunt, paucis vulneribus acceptis. Sed eos fugientes

---

expōnō, 3, -posuī, -positum, v. tr., land, disembark.

consīdō, 3, -sēdī, -sessum, settle, encamp.

vigilia, -ae, F., watch.

eo, adv., for this reason.

mollis, -e, adj, soft.

dēligō, 1, v. tr., bind.

conspicor, 1, v. dep., see, behold.

repellō, 3, -pūlī, -pulsum, v. tr., drive back, repulse.

egregie, adv., admirably, excellently.

domesticus, -a, -um, adj., domestic, civil.

praeparō, 1, v. tr., prepare beforehand.

crēber, -bra, -brum, adj., frequent, numerous.

succīdō, 3, -cīdī, -cīsum, v. tr., cut down.

introitus, -ūs, M., entrance.

praeclūdō, 3, -clūsī, -clūsum, v. tr., close, shut.

rarus, -a, -um, adj., thin, few, in small bodies.

propugnō, 1, v. intr., fight

mūnītiō, -ōnis, F., fortification.

ingredior, -gredī, -gressus, v. dep., go into, enter.

testūdō, -inis, F., testudo (see Vocab.)

adjiciō, 3, -jēcī, -jectum, v. tr., throw up, throw against.

longius Caesar prosequi vetuit, et quod loci naturam ignorabat, et quod, magna parte diei consumpta, munitioni castrorum tempus relinqui volebat.

Bad news of the fleet.

10. Postridie ejus diei, mane, tripartito milites equitesque in expeditionem misit, ut eos, qui fugerant, persequerentur. His aliquantum itineris progressis, cum jam extremi essent in prospectu, equites a Quinto Atrio ad Caesarem venerunt, qui nuntiarent superiore nocte, maxima coorta tempestate, prope omnes naves afflictas atque in litore ejectas esse, quod neque ancorae funesque subsisterent, neque nautae gubernatoresque vim pati tempestatis possent : itaque ex eo concursu navium magnum esse incommodum acceptum.

Labienus builds new ships.   Cassivellaunus.

11. His rebus cognitis, Caesar legiones equitatumque revocari atque in itinere resistere jubet; ipse ad naves revertitur ; eadem fere, quae ex nuntiis litterisque cognoverat,

---

vetō, 1, vetuī, vetitum, v. tr., forbid.

ignōrō, 1, v. tr., not to know, am ignorant of.

—

manē, adv., in the morning.

tripęrtītō, adv., in three divisions.

expedītiō, -ōnis, F., foray.

aliquantus, -a, -um, adj., somewhat; aliquantum, neut. sing., some distance.

extremus, -a, -um, adj., last ; extrēmī, -ōrum, M. pl., the rear.

prōspectus, -us, M., sight, view.

coorior, -orīrī, -ortus, v. dep., arise.

afflīgō, 3, -flīxī, -flictum, v. tr., dash down, shatter.

ejiciō, 3, -jēcī, -jectum, v. tr., throw out, cast.

fūnis, -is, M., rope, cable.

subsistō, 3, -stitī, no sup., v. tr., make a stand, hold out.

gūbernātor, -oris, M., pilot, steersman.

patior, patī, passus, v. dep., endure, stand.

concursus, -ūs, M., collision.

incommodum, -ī, N., inconvenience, loss, damage.

—

resistō, 3, restitī, no sup., v. intr. (governs dat.), resist, withstand.

litterae, -arum, F. pl., letter, despatch.

coram perspicit, sic ut, amissis circiter quadraginta navibus, reliquae tamen refici posse magno negotio viderentur. Itaque ex legionibus fabros deligit, et ex continenti alios arcessi jubet; Labieno s. ribit, ut, quam plurimas posset, iis legionibus, quae sunt apud eum, naves instituat. Ipse, etsi res erat multae operae ac laboris, tamen commodissimum esse statuit, omnes naves subduci et cum castris una munitione conjungi. In his rebus circiter dies decem consumit, ne nocturnis quidem temporibus ad laborem militum intermissis. Subductis navibus, castrisque egregie munitis, easdem copias, quas ante, praesidio navibus reliquit, ipse eodem, unde iedierat, proficiscitur. Eo cum venisset, majores jam undique in eum locum copiae Britannorum convenerant, summa imperii bellique administrandi communi consilio permissa Cassivel launo; cujus fines a maritimis civitatibus flumen dividit, quod appellatur Tamesis, a mari. circiter millia passuum *l.* octoginta. Huic superiore tempore cum reliquis civitatibus continentia bella intercesserant; sed nostro adventu permoti Britanni hunc toti bello imperioque praefecerant.

coram, adv., face to face, before one's eyes.

perspicio, 3, -spexi, -spectum, v. tr., see, perceive.

reficio, 3, -feci, -fectum, v. tr., repair.

negotium, -i, M., trouble.

faber, -bri, M., workman.

deligo, 3, -legi, -lectum, v. tr., choose, select.

arcesso, 3, -cessivi, -cessitum, v. tr., summon.

opera, -ae, F., work, service.

subduco, 3, -duxi, -ductum, v. tr., draw up on shore, beach.

conjungo, 3, -junxi, -junctum, v. tr., join together.

nocturnus, -a, -um, adj., of the night.

ne . . . quidem, not even.

summa, -ae, F., whole; summa imperii, supreme command.

divido, 3, -visi, -visum, v. tr., divide, separate.

continens (gen. continentis), adj., continuous, incessant.

intercedo, 3, -cessi, -cessum, v. intr., intervene, occur.

The people.

12. Britanniae parѕ interior ab iis incolitur, quos natos in insula ipsi memoria proditum dicunt ; maritima pars ab ııs, qui praedae ac belli inferendi causa ex Belgis transierant (qui omnes fere ııs nominibus civitatum appellantur, quibus orti ex civitatibus eo pervenerunt) et bello illato ibi permanserunt, atque agros colere coeperunt. Hominum est infinita multitudo, creberrimaque aedificia fere Gallicis consimilia ; pecorum magnus numerus. Utuntur aut aere aut taleis ferreis ad certum pondus examinatis pro nummo. Nascitur ibi plumbum album in mediterraneis regionibus, in maritimis ferrum, sed ejus exigua est copia ; aere utuntur importato. Materia cujusque generis, ut in Gallia, est praeter fagum atque abietem. Leporem et gallinam et anserem gustare fas non putant; haec tamen alunt animi voluptatisque causa. Loca sunt temperatiora quam in Gallia, remissioribus frigoribus.

---

incolō, 3, -coluī, -cultum, v. tr , live in, inhabit.

nascor, nascī, natus, v. dep., am born.

memoria, -ae, F., memory, tradition.

prōdō, 3, -didī, -ditum, v. tr., hand down.

inferō, -ferre, -tulī, illātum, v. tr., bring against ; bellum infero, make war on.

transeō, -īre, -iī, -itum, v. tr., go across, cross.

infinītus, -a, -um, adj., boundless, countless.

consimilis, -e, adj., similar.

pecus, -oris, N., cattle (collectively).

aes, aeris, N., metal, bronze.

tālea, -ae, F., bar.

ferreus, -a, -um, adj., iron.

pondus, -eris, N., weight.

exāminō, 1, test, weigh.

nummus. -ī. M.. coin.

plumbum, -ī. N., lead ; plumbum album, tin.

mediterrāneus, -a, -um, adj., central.

importō, 1, v. tr., import.

māteria, -ae, F., timber.

quisque, quaeque, quidque or quodque, indef., pron., each.

praeter, prep. (governs acc.), except.

fāgus, -ī, F., beech.

abiēs, -ietis, F., fir.

lepus, -oris, M., hare.

gallīna, -ae, F., hen.

anser, -eris, M., goose

gustō, 1, taste.

fās, indecl. noun, right, divine law.

alō, 3, aluī, altum, v. tr., rear.

voluptās, -ātis, F., pleasure.

temperātus, -a, -um, adj., temperate.

remissus, -a, -um, adj., mild.

The island.

13. Insula natura triquetra,· cujus unum latus est contra Galliam. Hujus lateris alter angulus, qui est ad Cantium, quo fere omnes ex Gallia naves appelluntur, ad orientem solem, inferior ad meridiem spectat. Hoc pertinet circiter millia passuum quingenta. Alterum vergit ad Hispaniam atque occidentem solem ; qua ex parte est Hibernia, dimidio minor, ut existimatur, quam Britannia, sed pari spatio transmissus atque ex Gallia est in Britanniam. In hoc medio cursu est insula quae appellatur Mona; complures praeterea minores subjectae insulae existimantur ; de ·quibus insulis nonnulli scripserunt dies continuos triginta sub bruma esse noctem. Nos nihil de eo percontationibus reperiebamus, nisi certis ex aqua mensuris breviores esse quam in continenti noctes videbamus. Hujus est longitudo lateris, ut fert illorum opinio, septingentorum millium. Tertium est contra septentriones ; cui parti nulla est objecta terra, sed ejus angulus lateris maxime ad Germaniam spectat. Hoc millia passuum octingenta in longitudinem esse existimatur. Ita omnis insula est in circuitu vicies centum millium passuum.

---

triquetrus, -a, -um, adj., triangular.

angulus, -ī, M., angle.

appellō, 3, -pulī, -pulsum, v. tr., drive to, steer towards. ·

sol oriens, rising sun, east.

merīdiēs, -ēī, M., mid-day, south.

pertineō, 2, -uī, -tentum, v. intr., extend.

occidens sol, setting sun, west.

dīmidium, -ī, N., half.

transmissus, -ūs, M., passage.

praetereā, adv., besides.

subjectus, -a, -um, p. p. p., used as adj., lying near.

bruma, -ae, F. (=brevissima, sc. diēs), shortest day, winter solstice.

percontātiō, -ōnis, F., inquiry.

reperiō, 4, repperī, repertum, v. tr., find out.

mensura, -ae, F., measurement.

septingentī, -ae, -a, num. adj., 700.

circuitus, -ūs, M., circumference.

vicies, num. adv., twenty times.

Manners and customs.

14. Ex his omnibus longe sunt humanissimi, qui Cantium incolunt, quae regio est maritima omnis, neque multum a Gallica differunt consuetudine. Interiores plerique frumenta non serunt, sed lacte et carne vivunt pellibusque sunt vestiti. Omnes vero se Britanni vitro inficiunt, quod caeruleum efficit colorem, atque hoc horridiore sunt in pugna aspectu; capilloque sunt promisso atque omni parte corporis rasa praeter caput et labrum superius. Uxores habent deni duodenique inter se communes et maxime fratres cum fratribus parentesque cum liberis; sed si qui sunt ex his nati, corum habentur liberi, quo primum virgo quaeque deducta est.

More fighting, a surprise; death of a tribune.

15. Equites hostium essedariique acriter proelio cum equitatu nostro in itinere conflixerunt, tamen ut nostri omnibus partibus superiores fuerint atque eos in silvas collesque compulerint; sed compluribus interfectis, cupidius insecuti, nonnullos ex suis amiserunt. At illi, intermisso spatio, imprudentibus nostris atque occupatis in munitione

hūmānus, -a, -um, adj., civilized.
plērīque, plēraeque, plēraque, pl. adj.; most, the majority.
sero, 3, sēvī, satum, v. tr., sow, plant.
lac, lactis, N., milk.
caro, carnis, F., flesh.
pellis, -is, F., skin, hide.
vitrum, -ī, N., woad.
caeruleus, -a, -um, adj., sky-blue, blue.
horridus, -a, -um, adj., dreadful, frightful.
aspectus, -us, M., aspect.
capillus, -ī, M., hair.
promissus, -a, -um, adj., flowing, long.
rādō, 3, rāsī, rāsum, v. tr., shave,

lābrum, -ī, N., lip.
deni, -ae, -a, distrib. num. adj., ten by ten, ten apiece.
duodēnī, -ae, -a, distrib. num. adj., twelve by twelve, twelve apiece.
dēdūcō, 3, -dūxī, -ductum, v. tr., lead away; marry.

conflīgō, 3, -flixī, -flictum, v. tr., strike, engage.
compello, 3, -pulī, -pulsum, v. tr., drive.
cupidē, adv., eagerly.
nōnnūllī, -ae, -a, pl. adj., some.
imprūdens (gen. imprudentis), off one's guard.

castrorum, subito se ex silvis ejecerunt, impetuque in eos facto, qui erant in statione pro castris collocati, acriter pugnaverunt; duabusque missis subsidio cohortibus a Caesare, atque his primis legionum duarum, cum hae, perexiguo intermisso loci spatio inter se, constitissent, novo genere pugnae perterritis nostris, per medios audacissime perruperunt seque inde incolumes receperunt. Eo die Quintus Laberius Durus tribunus militum interficitur. Illi, pluribus submissis cohortibus, repelluntur.

British mode of fighting.

16. Toto hoc in genere pugnae, cum sub oculis omnium ac pro castris dimicaretur, intellectum est, nostros propter gravitatem armorum, quod neque insequi cedentes possent neque ab signis discedere auderent, minus aptos esse ad hujus generis hostem; equites autem magno cum periculo proelio dimicare, propterea quod illi etiam consulto plerumque cederent et, cum paulum ab legionibus nostros removissent ex essedis desilirent et pedibus dispari proelio contenderent. Equestris autem proelii ratio et cedentibus et insequentibus par atque idem periculum inferebat. Accedebat huc, ut nunquam conferti, sed rari magnisque intervallis proeliarentur stationesque dispositas haberent, atque alios alii deinceps exciperent, integrique et recentes defatigatis succederent.

---

subsidium, -ī, N., support, reinforcement.

perexiguus, -a, -um, adj., very small.

consistō, 3, -stitī, -stitum, v. intr., take one's stand.

audacter, adv., boldly (audacius, audācissimē).

perrumpō, 3, -rūpī, -ruptum, v. tr., break through.

---

dīmicō, 1, v. intr., fight, struggle.

gravitās, -ātis, F., weight.

cēdō, 3, cessī, cessum, v. intr., go, withdraw, retreat.

aptus, -a, -um, adj., fit, suited.

propterea, adv., for this reason; propterea quod, because.

consultō, adv., purposely.

dēsiliō, 4, -siluī, -sultum, v. intr., leap down.

dispār (gen. disparis), unequal.

ratiō, -ōnis, F., plan, method.

accēdēbat huc ut, to this was added the fact that.

deinceps, adv., in turn.

integer, -gra, -grum, adj., whole, fresh, vigorous.

dēfatigātus, -a, -um, adj., wearied.

The Britons repulsed.

17. Postero die procul a castris hostes in collibus constiterunt, rarique se ostendere, et lenius quam pridie nostros equites proelio lacessere coeperunt. Sed meridie, cum Caesar pabulandi causa tres legiones atque omnem equitatum cum Caio Trebonio legato misisset, repente ex omnibus partibus ad pabulatores advolaverunt, sic uti ab signis legionibusque non absisterent. Nostri, acriter in eos impetu facto, repulerunt, neque finem sequendi fecerunt, quoad subsidio confisi equites, cum post se legiones viderent, praecipites hostes egerunt; magnoque eorum numero interfecto, neque sui colligendi neque consistendi aut ex essedis desiliendi facultatem dederunt. Ex hac fuga protinus, quae undique convenerant auxilia discesserunt; neque post id tempus unquam summis nobiscum copiis hostes contenderunt.

Caesar crosses the Thames.

18. Caesar, cognito consilio eorum, ad flumen Tamesim in fines Cassivellauni exercitum duxit; quod flumen uno omnino loco pedibus, atque hoc aegre, transiri potest. Eo cum venisset, animadvertit ad alteram fluminis ripam magnas esse copias hostium instructas. Ripa autem erat acutis sudibus praefixis munita, ejusdemque generis sub aqua defixae

---

ostendō, 3, -dī, -sum (or -tum), v. tr., show, display.
lēniter, adv., gently.
pābulor, 1, v. dep., forage.
pābulātor, -ōris, M., forager.
advolō, 1, v. intr., fly at.
absistō, 3, -stitī, no sup., v. intr., keep away from.
quoad, conj., until.
confīdō, 3, confīsus sum, v. semi-dep., trust.

colligō, 3, -lēgī, -lectum, v. tr., collect, rally.
prōtinus, adv., forthwith.

---

aegrē, adv., with difficulty.
acūtus, -a, -um, adj., sharp.
sudes, -is, F., stake.
praefīgō, 3, -fīxī, -fīxum, v. tr., fix or place in front of.

sudes flumine tegebantur. His rebus cognitis a captivis
perfugisque, Caesar, praemisso equitatu, confestim legiones
subsequi jussit. Sed ea celeritate atque eo impetu milites
ierunt, cum capite solo ex aqua exstarent, ut hostes impetum
legionum atque equitum sustinere non possent, ripasque
dimitterent ac se fugae mandarent.

Tactics of Cassivellaunus.

19. Cassivellaunus, ut supra demonstravimus, ōmni de-
posita spe contentionis, dimissis amplioribus copiis, millibus
circiter quattuor essedariorum relictis, itinera nostra servabat; paulumque ex via excedebat, locisque impeditis ac
silvestribus sese occultabat, atque iis regionibus, quibus nos
iter facturos cognoverat, pecora atque homines ex agris in
silvas compellebat; et, cum equitatus noster liberius prae-
dandi vastandique causa se in agros ejecerat, omnibus viis
semitisque essedarios ex silvis emittebat, et magno cum
periculo -nostrorum equitum cum iis confligebat, atque hoc
metu latius vagari prohibebat. Relinquebatur, ut neque
longius ab agmine legionum discedi Caesar pateretur, et
tantum· in agris vastandis incendiisque faciendis hostibus
noceretur, quantum labore atque itinere legionarii milites
efficere poterant.

---

tegō, 3, texī, tectum, v. tr., cover,
   protect.
perfuga, -ae. M., deserter.
exstō, -stāre, no pf., no sup.,
   v. intr., stand out of.
mandō, 1, v. tr., consign.

---

contentiō, -ōnis, F., struggle.
servō, 1, v. tr., guard, watch.

silvester, -tris, -tre, adj.; woody.
occultō, 1, v. tr., hide.
līberē, adv., freely.
sēmita, -ae, F., path, by-path.
vagor, 1, v. dep., wander.
patior, patī, passus, v. dep., allow.
incendium, -ī, N., fire.
tantum ... quantum, as much ... as,
   as far ... as.

The Trinobantes submit to Caesar.

20. Interim Trinobantes, prope firmissima earum regionum civitas, ex qua Mandubracius adulescens, Caesaris fidem secutus, ad eum in continentem Galliam venerat, cujus pater Immanuentius in ea civitate regnum obtinuerat interfectusque erat a Cassivellauno, ipse fuga mortem vitaverat, legatos ad Caesarem mittunt, pollicenturque sese ei dedituros atque imperata facturos; petunt, ut Mandubracium ab injuria Cassivellauni defendat, atque in civitatem mittat, qui praesit imperiumque obtineat. His Caesar imperat obsides quadraginta frumentumque exercitui, Mandubraciumque ad eos mittit. Illi imperata celeriter fecerunt, obsides ad numerum frumentumque miserunt.

So do other tribes.   A British "town."

21. Trinobantibus defensis atque ab omni militum injuria prohibitis, Cenimagni, Segontiaci, Ancalites, Bibroci, Cassi, legationibus missis, sese Caesari dedunt. Ab his cognoscit non longe ex eo loco oppidum Cassivellauni abesse silvis paludibusque munitum, quo satis magnus hominum pecorisque numerus convenerit. Oppidum autem Britanni vocant, cum silvas impeditas vallo atque fossa munierunt, quo incursionis hostium vitandae causa convenire consuerunt. Eo proficiscitur cum legionibus; locum reperit egregie natura atque opere munitum; tamen hunc duabus ex partibus oppugnare contendit. Hostes paulisper morati militum nostrorum impetum non tulerunt seseque alia ex parte oppidi ejecerunt. Magnus ibi numerus pecoris repertus; multique in fuga sunt comprehensi atque interfecti.

---

firmus, -a, -um, adj., strong.

adulescens, -ntis, M., young man.

vito, 1, v. tr., avoid.

defendo, 3, -di, -sum, v. tr., defend, protect.

praesum, -esse, -fui, v. irreg., am at the head of, am in command of.

imperatum, -i, N., command.

legatio, -onis. F., embassy.

palus, -udis, F., marsh, swamp.

incursio, -onis, F. attack, raid.,

paulisper, adv., for a short time.

moror, 1, v. dep., delay.

comprehendo, 3, -di, -sum, v. tr., seize, arrest.

Four Kentish kings defeated. Cassivellaunus treats for peace.

22. Dum haec in his locis geruntur, Cassivellaunus ad
Cantium, quod esse ad mare supra demonstravimus, quibus
regionibus. quattuor reges praeerant, Cingetorix, Carvilius,
Taximagulus, Segovax, nuntios mittit atque his imperat, uti,
coactis omnibus copiis, castra navalia de improviso adoriantur
atque oppugnent. Ii cum ad castra venissent, nostri, eruptione
facta, multis eorum interfectis, capto etiam nobili duce
Lugotorige, suos incolumes reduxerunt. Cassivellaunus, hoc
proelio nuntiato, tot detrimentis acceptis, vastatis finibus,
maxime etiam permotus defectione civitatum, legatos per
Atrebatem Commium de deditione ad Caesarem mittit.
Caesar, cum constituisset hiemare in continenti propter
repentinos Galliae motus, neque multum aestatis superesset,
atque id facile extrahi posse intellegeret, obsides imperat, et,
quid in annos singulos vectigalis populo Romano Britannia
penderet, constituit; interdicit atque imperat Cassivellauno,
ne Mandubracio neu Trinobantibus noceat.

---

nāvālis, -e, adj., naval.
improvisus, -a, -um, adj., unfore-
    seen; dē improviso, unex-
    pectedly
adorior, -orīrī, -ortus, v. dep.,
    attack, assail.
nobilis, -e, adj., noble.
incolumis, -e, adj., safe.
dētrīmentum, -ī, N., loss, damage.
maximē, adv., especially.
etiam, adv., also.
dēfectiō, -ōnis, F., revolt.

repentīnus, -a, -um, adj., sudden,
    unexpected.
supersum, -esse, -fuī, v. irreg.,
    survive, remain.
extrahō, 3, -traxī, -tractum, v.
    v. tr., draw out, spend.
vectīgal, -ālis, N., tax, tribute.
pendō, 3, pependī, pensum, v. tr.,
    weigh out, pay.
interdīcō, 3, -dīxī, -dictum, v. tr.,
    forbid.

Caesar returns to GauL

23. Obsidibus acceptis, exercitum reducit ad mare, naves invenit refectas. His deductis, quod et captivorum magnum numerum habebat, et nonnullae tempestate deperierant naves, duobus commeatibus exercitum reportare instituit. Ac sic accidit, uti ex tanto navium numero tot navigationibus, neque hoc neque superiore anno, ulla omnino navis, quae milites portaret desideraretur ; at ex iis, quae inanes ex continenti ad eum remitterentur, et prioris commeatus expositis militibus, et quas postea Labienus faciendas curaverat numero sexaginta, perpaucae locum caperent ; reliquae fere omnes rejicerentur. Quas cum aliquamdiu Caesar frustra expectasset, ne anni tempore a navigatione excluderetur, quod aequinoctium suberat, necessario angustius milites collocavit ac, summa tranquillitate consecuta, secunda inita cum solvisset vigilia, prima luce terram attigit, omnesque incolumes naves perduxit.

---

dēpereō, -ire, -iī, -itum, v. irreg., perish, am lost.

nāvigātiō, -ōnis, F., voyage.

commeātus, ūs, M., trip, relay.

dēsīderō, 1, v. tr., want, miss ; pass., am lost.

inanis. -e, adj., empty.

aliquamdiū, adv., for some time.

exclūdō, 3, -clūsī, -clūsum, v. tr., shut out, prevent.

subsum, -esse, -fuī, v. irreg., am near.

necessariō, adv., of necessity.

angustē, adv., narrowly, closely

tranquillitās, -ātis, F., calm.

Sentence-Structure

If you compare a page of Caesar with a page of an English History, you will readily see that the sentences in Caesar are much longer and consequently fewer than in English. In English the narrative consists largely of independent statements, and the sentences contain one or more principal verbs with very few participial or subordinate constructions. In Latin the ideas are not expressed in this detached style, but one main idea is chosen and the subordinate ideas are grouped around it in participial and subordinate constructions. The English Style is called the Detached Style; the Latin Style is called the Periodic. In order to get a good idiomatic translation of a Latin sentence, it is often necessary to break it up into several detached sentences, and render Latin participles and subordinate verbs by principal verbs in English.

Exercises in Translation

A

His dimissis, et ventum et aestum uno tempore nactus secundum, dato signo, et sublatis ancoris, circiter millia passuum septem ab eo loco progressus, aperto ac plano litore naves constituit. —*Caesar* IV, 23.

Observe in the above extract:—

(*a*) There are five participles and one principal verb.

(*b*) The different movements are stated in the order of their occurrence.

(c) The one principal subject is maintained throughout.

Translation :—

The officers were then sent to their various posts ; and now as wind and tide were both favorable at one and the same time, he gave the signal, weighed anchor, and after proceeding about seven miles from that point, moored his ships on an open and level shore.

B

Quibus rebus cognitis, principes Britanniae, qui post proelium factum ad ea, quae jusserat Caesar, facienda convenerant, inter se colloquuti, cum equites et naves et frumentum Romanis deesse

58

intellegerent et paucitatem militum ex castrorum exiguitate cognoscerent,—quae hoc erant etiam angustiora, quod sine impedimentis
Caesar legiones transportaverat,—optimum factu esse duxerunt,
rebellione facta, frumento commeatuque nostros prohibere et rem
in hiemem producere, quod, iis superatis aut reditu interclusis,
neminem postea belli inferendi causa in Britanniam transiturum
confidebant.—*Caesar* IV, 30.

Observe :—

(*a*) The position of **quibus rebus cognitis** as the introductory words.

(*b*) The position of **principes Britanniae** as the subject, followed by
the **qui** clause connected with it, also **colloquuti** describing the mode of
operation.

(*c*) The **cum** clauses, giving the reasons for the action, placed before
the principal verb.

(*d*) **duxerunt**, the sole principal verb.

Translation :—

On learning these facts, the chiefs of Britain who after the battle had
assembled to carry out Caesar's orders, held a conference. They
perceived that the Romans lacked cavalry, ships and grain. They
also ascertained the small number of our soldiers from the smallness of
the camp. This was even smaller for this reason because Caesar had
transported the legions without baggage. (Accordingly) they concluded
the best thing to do was to renew the war, keep our men from
(procuring) grain and supplies and prolong the campaign into winter,
because they were sure that if these were overcome or cut off from
return, no one would (ever) after cross over into Britain for the purpose
of carrying on war.

Consistency of Latin Style

Examine :—

(*a*) **Caesar, etsi nondum consilia eorum cognoverat, tamen
legiones in acie pro castris constituit.**

Although *Caesar* was not yet aware of their plans, nevertheless
he posted his legions in line of battle before the camp.

(*b*) **Barbari, consilio Romanorum cognito, nostros navibus egredi
prohibebant.**

When the plan of the Romans became known *to the barbarians, they*
tried to prevent our men from landing.

(*c*) Qua re impetrata, arma tradere jussi, faciunt.

This request was granted ; and on being ordered to hand over their arms they do so.

(*d*) Hunc illi e navi egressum, cum ad eos imperatoris mandata perferret, in vincula conjecerant.

When *he* had landed from the ship and was delivering to them the orders of his commander, they had thrown *him* into chains.

These sentences illustrate the *compactness, brevity* and *consistency* of Latin style as compared with the English.

Latin as far as possible throughout the period or sentence—

(*a*) Makes the real subject the grammatical subject of the principal verb ;

(*b*) Avoids change of subject ;

(c) Places the subject at or near the beginning, thereby giving emphasis and prominence to it ;

(*d*) Keeps a substantive in the same case.

NOTES

BOOK IV

Chapter 20

exigua parte—reliqua : abl. abs., equivalent to a concessive clause introduced by etsi, co-ordinate with the next clause : *"though but little of the summer remained, and in this district the winters set in early."*

Note that etsi occurs in Caesar with the pres., impf., and plupf. indic.; never with the subj.

ad septentriones vergit : Caesar means that the rivers of Gaul outside the Provincia, *i.e.,* in the part occupied by the Aquitani, Celtae and Belgae, have a northerly course.

septentriones: properly the seven stars which form the constellation of the Great Bear, from **septem,** *seven,* and -trio, = strio, *star* ; cp. stella = sterula ; German *Stern,* English *star*.

Britanniam : probably from the Celtic, brit or brith, *painted,* from the custom of the inhabitants staining their bodies with woad (*B.* V, 14). The name Albion given to it by Aristotle (De Mundo, 3) is perhaps from Celtic **alp, alb,** *high* or *white* ; cp. Alpin, Albany (an old name for Scotland), Latin **albus, Alpes.**

quod—intellegebat : cp. *B.* III, 9, where he mentions the fact that the Nannetes and the Veneti sent for aid to Britain to carry on their war against the Romans. Dion Cassius says that Caesar's motive in crossing to Britain was simply this, to be the first Roman who visited the island. Suetonius attributes the expedition to avarice, mentioning the rich pearl fisheries as the inducement.

bellis Gallicis : *"in the wars against the Gauls."* Either (1) abl. of Time When, or (2) Time 'within which,' H. L., 116, 3 : R. C., 159, or (3) Local abl. with in omitted, H. L., 119, 5.

subministrata sc. esse : *"had been secretly supplied."* Note the force of sub in composition.

si—deficeret : *"even though the time of the year should be insufficient for carrying on a regular campaign"*: subj. in a subordinate clause in Oratio Obliqua, H. L., 269, 8 : R. C., 408 (*a*). Caesar started on his first expedition to Britain near the end of August (see note on Chapter 23).

61

magno sibi usui fore (= futurum esse): *"it would be of great advantage to him"*: usui, dat. of Purpose, H. L., 228, 2 : R. C., 431. The clauses si—adisset—perspexisset—cognovisset are subjects of fore; the plupf. subj. represents the fut. pf. indic. in Oratio Recta, magno mihi usui erit, si adiero perspexero—cognovero, H. L., 269, 8 : R. C., 408 (a).

loca, portus, aditus : note the Asyndeton.

quae—incogn'ta : this statement is not correct.   Caesar himself says (*B.* III, 8) : naves habent Veneti plurimas, quibus in Britanniam navigare consuerunt.

neque enim quisquam : neque enim implies an ellipsis, " *and (we can readily imagine this) for nobody goes there without good reason.*" —temere, *at random, rashly,* opposed to consulto.

mercatores : may be either Greeks from Massilia (now *Marseilles*) or Romans from Provincia (now *Provence*) in Southern Gaul, who followed in the wake of the army to purchase booty and sell provisions.

Gallias : the divisions of Gaul—Belgica, Celtica, Aquitania.

neque : join with reperire poterat.

esset—incolerent—haberent—uterentur—essent : subj. in Indirect Question after reperire, H. L., 200, 4 : R. C., 408 (b).

Note that poterat implies repeated action ; potuit would have meant that he called the traders on a single occasion.

Chapter 21

ad haec cognoscenda : join with praemittit.

priusquam periculum faceret : "*before running the risk,*" "*before making the attempt.*" Note that the subj. mood expresses intention on the part of Caesar ; H. L., 260, 6 : R. C., 387, 2 (b). Observe the meaning of periculum, "*trial*" ; cp. experior, πειράομαι πειρα.

C. Volusenum ; his full name was Caius Volusenus Quadratus. He held the office of *tribunus militum* and was employed by Caesar on several occasions. He aided in putting down Commius, king of the Atrebates, and as *tribunus plebis* in 43 B.C. supported Marc Antony. In *B.* III, 5, Caesar speaks of him in the highest terms in connection with the battle of the Nervii—vir et magni consilii et virtutis : Commius is also mentioned, *B.* IV, 27 ; V, 22 ; VI, 6 ; VII, 76, 79.

navi longa : ships of war—naves longae—were long and narrow, fitted for swift sailing ; ships of burden—naves onerariae—were bulky, with round bottoms, fitted for carrying as large a cargo as possible.

mandat: *"he charges"*; **mando** implies confidence in the person intrusted with a commission.

Morinos: The Morini inhabited the sea coast of Gallia Belgica. Their name is from the Celtic **mor**, *"sea"*; cp. **Armorica**. They occupied the district from the Scaldis (now *Scheldt*) on the east to the Samara (now *Somme*) on the west. Their chief town was Gesoriacum, afterwards Bononia, whence the modern *Boulogne*.

The **brevissimus trajectus** was, of course, the Straits of Dover, which is 28 miles in width between Calais and Dover; see note *B.* IV, 23.

Veneticum bellum: this war was carried on in 56 B.C., in consequence of the revolt of the Veneti and other states of north-western Gaul. Owing to the difficulty of getting at them by land, Caesar attacked them by sea and defeated them (*B.* III, 8-16) in the bay of *Quiberon*. Their chief town was Vindana (now *St. Orient*).

ejus = **Caesaris**.

per mercatores: H. L., 292, 5 (*b*).

perlato: *"reported."*

qui polliceantur: *"to promise"*; **qui** *Final*, H L., 232, 2: R. C., 388.

dare: for **se daturos esse**. The pres. infin. after verbs expressing *hope, promise, undertake* is an irregularity in good prose. The comic poets Terence and Plautus, sometimes use the English idiom. The pres. infin. may convey the idea that the promise will be at once fulfilled.

quibus auditis: (1) abl. abs.; or (2) possibly dative after **pollicitus**; *"making kind promises to them after they were heard."*

ut—permaneret: *"to adhere to that resolution"*; Substantive Clause of Purpose, H. L., 240, 2: R. C., 424 (*a*).

Atrebatis superatis: the Atrebates, a people of Gallia Belgica, occupied what was once called *Artois* (probably a corruption of the name, but now called *Pas-de-Calais*). Others say that *Arras* (Flemish *Autrecht*) is a corrupt form of the word.

They were defeated by Caesar at the river Sabis (now *Sambre*) in 57 B.C. (*B.* H, 23). A portion of them, after this defeat, crossed over to Britain and settled in the valley of the Thames, probably in Berkshire. The fact that Commins was king of the Atrebates on the continent may have influenced Caesar in sending him to treat with his countrymen in Britain.

magni—habebatur: *"was considered of great value"*; **magni**, gen. of Value, H. L., 290, 4.

huic=Commio.

imperat—civitates : construe imperat (ut) adeat civitates quas possit, *"he orders him to visit (all) the states he can"* ; **adeat,** Substantive Clause of Purpose, H. L., 240, 2 : R. C., 424; **possit,** subj. in Oratio Obliqua, H. L , 265, 2 : R. C., 408 (*b*). Primary Sequence, H. L , 198, 4, 5 : R. C., 587. The ᵘᶠ is sometimes omitted with the verbs of ' command' : *B.* III, 3, huic mandat, Remos reliquosque Belgas adeat.

eo : *"thither"*=in Britanniam.

ut—fidem sequantur : *"to be loyal to,"* literally, *"to accept the protection of."*

seque : construe imperatque huic ut nuntiet se (Caesarem) celeriter esse venturum.

perspectis regionibus : *"after ascertaining the character of the country"* ; so also cognoscere regiones, *B.* III, 7.

quantum potuit : *"as far as his opportunity allowed him,"* literally, *"as much (of) opportunity as could be afforded him."*—facultatis, Partitive gen., H. L., 287, 4 : R. C., 174.

qui—auderet : *"inasmuch as he did not dare."* Causal rel. and subj., H. L., 252, 4.

navi egredi : Caesar uses both navi egredi and ex navi egredi.

perspexisset : subj. in Indirect Question after Historic Present.— **quae,** acc. neut. pl. of quis, quae, quid.

Chapter 22

dum—moratur : dum, meaning 'while,' always takes the indicative in Caesar, except in *B.* VII, 82.

qui—excusarent—pollicerentur : *"to excuse themselves—and to promise"*; qui Final, H. L., 232, 2 : R. C., 388.

temporis : Descriptive Gen., H. L., 288, 5. This refers to the events mentioned in *B.* III, 28. After the rest of Northern Gaul had submitted to Caesar, the Menapii and Morini suddenly attacked the Romans.

homines barbari : *"as barbarous people,"* *"being (as they were) barbarians."*

nostrae consuetudinis : he refers to the mercy shown by the Romans to those who submitted to their sway.

populo : dat. : the construction of bellum facere populo Romano is formed on the analogy of bellum inferre populo Romano, H. L., 229, 4.

fecissent : Virtual Oratio Obliqua, H. L., 253, 6 : R. C., 408.

seque : construe pollicerentur se facturos ea quae imperasset : pollicerentur is co-ordinate with qui excusarent—imperasset : plupf. subj. in O.O. representing the fut. pf. indic. in O.R., 'what you shall have ordered, we shall do,' H. L., 269, 8.

hoc—arbitratus : "*Caesar thinking that this was a tolerably good streak of luck.*" Note that the pf. part. of a deponent verb is usually translated into English by a pres. part., H. L., 163, 2 (*b*), 3 : R. C., 31?

quod—volebat—habebat—judicabat : indic. as giving Caesar's own reasons, H. L., 252, 2.

has—anteponendas. "*that occupation with such trifling matters should take precedence over (his expedition to) Britain.*"—anteponendas (esse), H. L., 189, Gerundival Infinitive.—sibi : dat. of Agent, H. L , 188, 4 : R. C., 354.—Britanniae : dat after a compound verb, H. L., 229, 5, Note.—Britanniae=bello Britannico. This condensed mode of comparison is sometimes found in poetry : Shakespeare, Coriolanus, Act II, Sc. 2, 21 : *His ascent is not as easy as those who*=*His ascent is not so easy as that of those who, &c.*

iis—numerum imperavit : impero in the sense of "*command*" takes a dative of person "*commanded*": meaning "*levy, demand from,*" it takes dative of person and acc. of thing.

quibus : refers to the hostages ; eos, to the Morini.

in fidem recepit : "*he received under his protection*"; see B. IV, 21.

coactis contractisque : the first participle implies that the ships were collected under compulsion : the second that they merely assembled : "*having been pressed into service and brought to one place.*" They probably assembled at *Boulogne,* which was also the rendezvous of the French under Napoleon I when he intended to attack England in 1802 A.D.

duas legiones : the 7th and the 10th.

quicquid—navium longarum=omnes naves ; for Partitive gen., see H. L., 287, 4. For this use of quicquid, cp. Livy, III, 9 ; per quicquid deorum est=per omnes deos.

ab millibus—octo : "*at a distance of eight miles.*" The transports were at *Ambleteuse* eight miles north of *Boulogne.*

quominus=ut eo minus : "*so that . . . not*"; H. L., 248, 8, 9.

deducendum dedit : for the gerundive with do, see H. L., 187, 9.

Sabino et—Cottae : both highly esteemed legati of Caesar. They both fell in the ambuscade planned by Ambiorix, king of the Eburones, *B. V*, 37

Menapii : a people of Gallia Belgica, who inhabited both sides of the Rhine. Their chief town was Castellum Menapiorum (now *Kessel*).

Chapter 23

· his constitutis rebus : express this in various ways ; H. L., 204, 6 : R. C., 304.

tertia vigilia : the time between sunset and sunrise was divided into four watches, each of which was about three hours long. Caesar set out with the infantry for Britain at midnight, August 26th, from Port Itins which is generally supposed to be *Boulogne* at the estuary of the *Somme*.

solvit : "*he set sail*" : we find solvere or solvere naves, "*to set sail*"· for the former see also *B*. IV, 28 ; for the latter *B*. IV, 36 : V, 8.

ulteriorem portum : further north than *Boulogne* : cp. IV, 28, where it is called portus superior. The cavalry were detained wind-bound at *Ambleteuse*, eight miles north of *Boulogne*.

naves conscendere ; we also find in naves conscendere, "*to embark*." The cavalry did not start till three days afterwards, *i.e.*, August 30th.

a quibus—administratum : "*as his orders were carried out somewhat slowly by them*."·

ipse : notice that this pronoun when used alone generally refers to Caesar.

hora—quarta : as sunrise at this time of the year would be about 5 a.m. and sunset about 7 p.m., and an hour would be 1 hour and 10 minutes of our time, Caesar would arrive in Britain about 10 a.m.

expositas : here = instructas, "*drawn up*."

haec : "*the following*." **natura** : "*the character*."

adeo : join with angustis, "*so precipitous*." This statement applies to *Dover Cliffs*.

in litus : "*upon the beach*" = "*to the water's edge*"; cp. Celsus (Dig. 50, 16, 96), litus est quousque maximus fluctus a mari pervenit. Distinguish litus, the part of the shore washed by the water ; ripa, the bank of a river ; ora, the land on the shore.

ad egrediendum : sc. ex navibus, "*for disembarking*" ; see note *B.* IV, 21.

nequaquam idoneum : "*by no means suitable,*" "*altogether unsuited.*"

dum—convenirent : for subj.; see H. L., 259, 7.: R. C., 408 (*a*).

in ancoris exspectavit : "*waited at anchor.*"

legatis -convocatis : as the *imperator, tribuni militum*, and first centurions, *primipili*, formed the council of war, Caesar may mean that this was held.

quae—cognosset, quae—vellet : subj. in Indirect Question, H. L., 200, 3 : R. C., 408 (*b*).

monuitque—administrarentur : the first and second ut = 'as'; the third ut is closely connected with quae = cum ea or quippe quae, "*inasmuch as these,*" so that ut connecting monuit with administrarentur is omitted : "*and warned them that all his orders should be carried out at a nod and at the right moment, as the method of military tactics (and) especially as naval tactics demanded, inasmuch as these involved rapid and uncertain movements.*" For the omission of ut after monuit, see note on **imperat—adeat**, *B.* IV, 21.—**postularent** is subj. in Virtual Oratio Obliqua after monuit.—**haberent** is Causal subj., H. L., 252, 4 : R. C., 397.

sublatis ancoris :. "*having weighed anchor.*"

septem—progressus : Caesar may have gone either N. E. or S. W. of *Dover.* The former course would land him between *Deal* and *Walmer Castle;* the latter at *Hythe* or *Lymne.*

Chapter 24

at : generally denotes a transition in the narrative.

praemisso—essedariis : praemisso agrees with equitatu, the nearest word, though it applies also to essedariis.—The word essedum or esseda is said to be from the Celtic ess, 'a chariot.' The essedarii included the aurigae, 'drivers' (*B.* IV, 33), who were the nobles, and the clientes, 'retainers,' who were the fighting men ; cp. Tacitus (Ag. 12) · **auriga honestior ; clientes propugnant.** This was the reverse of the Homeric custom, where the driver was a mere attendant, and the warrior was the important man. In each chariot there were usually six warriors and the driver.

quo—genere : "*a kind of fighting force which.*" This statement does not harmonize with that of Tacitus (Ag. 12): **in pedite robur ; quaedam nationes et curru proeliantur.**

consuerunt = consueverunt.

reliquis copiis = cum reliquis copiis : Caesar and Livy often omit pre, osition with abl. of Accompaniment; II. L., 293, 3, (b).

egredi prohibebant : note that prohibeo takes acc. with infin.

militibus—desiliendum (erat) : "*the soldiers had to leap down.*"— militibus ; dat. of Agent, H. L., 187, 3 ; 188, 4, (b) : R. C., 354.

illi : this pronoun is regularly used to represent "*the enemy.*"

"*The soldiers moreover, ignorant of the locality, with their hands encumbered and burdened with the great and heavy weight of armor had at one and the same time to leap down from the ships, and get a firm footing amid the waves, and fight with the enemy, whereas they either from dry ground or after advancing a short distance into the water, with all their limbs unencumbered, and on ground quite familiar to them, kept boldly hurling their darts, and spurring on their horses trained (to such warfare.)*" For the abl. abs. see H. L., 159, 4, (b) : R. C., 303-5.

hujus—imperiti : "*wholly unskilled in this kind of fighting.*"

uti ; utebantur : "*employ,*" "*display.*"

Chapter 25

et – et : "*both . . . and.*"

specie : "*appearance*" embracing shape, size, color.

inusitatior : "*somewhat unfamiliar*": for force of comparative see II. L., 88, 6.

motus—expeditior : "*movement in actual service less difficult.*" The naves onerariae were unwieldly compared with the naves longae, as the former were broader and heavier.

naves longas : join with jussit removeri—incitari—constitui.

remis incitari : "*to be rowed rapidly forward.*" **ad latus apertum :** "*on the exposed flank,*" i.e., the 'right.' Their left was protected by their shields.

fundis—tormentis : the slingers (funditores) and bowmen (sagittarii) belonged to the light-armed infantry (velites), see p. 14 : for tormenta, see p. 15.

propelli ac summoveri : "*to be driven off and dislodged.*"

quae res : "*this movement.*"

usui nostris : for the two datives see H. L., 228, 2 : R. C., 430.

paulum modo : "*a short distance only,*" "*just a little*" : R. C., 436.

atque : rarely found at the beginning of a new sentence, marking a contrast between what precedes and what follows : *"and then."*

nostris—cunctantibus : *"while our men were wavering"* : abl. abs., H. L., 160 (c) : R. C., 303-5.

qui—aquilam ferebat=aquilifer : see p. 17.

decimae legionis : Caesar's favorite legion : *B.* I, 40 ; Huic legioni Caesar et indulserat praecipue et propter virtutem confidebat maxime. The legions were numbered according to the order of enlistment.

contestatus deos : *"appealing to the gods."* The Romans seldom entered upon any important undertaking without an appropriate prayer to the deity or deities likely to aid them.

ea res : *"this undertaking," "this action."*

legioni : dat. of Indirect Object, H. L , 284, 1 : R. C., 39.

nisi—vultis : to lose the standard was looked upon as most disgraceful, especially to the standard-bearer, since this would be a violation of the military oath (sacramentum) which bound the soldier *"*not to desert the standard through a desire to escape or through fear, nor to leave the ranks." To arouse the soldiers, the standard was sometimes thrown into the midst of the enemy.

ego certe officium praestitero : *"I, at least, shall have done my duty."* The fut. pf. is used because the eagle-bearer looks on his duty as having been completed by the act.

aquilam ferre : = *"to advance."*

inter se : *"each other," "one another."* Latin has no reciprocal pronoun corresponding to the Greek ἀλλήλων.

dedecus : *i.e.*, the loss of the eagle.

hos—conspexissent : *"likewise when those on board the nearest ships had observed these"* ; with **ex proximis navibus**, cp. **ex equo (equis) pugnare**, *"to fight on horseback."*

Chapter 26

pugnatum est : H. L., 155, 5.

acriter : note the emphatic position.

nostri : join with **perturbabantur**.

Note throughout the chapter the frequent use of the impf. to express repeated or continuous action.

atque alius alia ex navi : **quod** is still understood after **atque** : *"and further because one from one ship and another from another."*

qvibuscumque—**occurrerat**—**aggregabat** : *"kept joining themselves to whatever standards they met."* The verbs are sing., agreeing with **alius**.—For the tenses expressing repeated action in the past, see II. L., 263, 8.—**signis** : dat. with a compound of **ob** (**oc**), H. L., 229, 4.

ubi—**conspexerant** : *"whenever they saw"*; cp. **occurrerat** above.

ex litore : cp. **ex arido** (*B.* IV, 24).

singulares : *"in scattered bodies."*

plures : *"a large number."*

alii—**conjiciebant** : *"others on the exposed flank (right side) kept hurling their darts on the massed forces (of the Romans)."*

ab latere aperto : see note on **ad litus apertum** (*B.* IV, 25).—For the force of **ab** ; cp. **a fronte**, 'in front'; **ab oriente sole**, 'on the east.'

speculatoria navigia : *"spy boats"* of light construction used for scouting purposes, and hence quick-sailing craft.

quos conspexerat : *"(all) whom he saw in distress"*; for tense see **occurrerat** above.

suis—**consecutis** : *"after all their comrades joined them."*

neque—**potuerunt** : *"but they were not able to pursue (the enemy) any great distance."*

longius : for force of comparative see H. L , 88, 6.

quod—**potuerunt** : they were wind-bound at *Ambleteuse.*

ad : *"in accordance with."*

Caesari : for dat., see H. L., 229, 4 ; 208, 8 : R. C., 39. *"This was the only break in Caesar's habitual good fortune."*

Chapter 27

daturos : the full form would be **se daturos esse.**

imperasset : = **imperavisset** ; Oratio Obliqua representing fut. pf. indic. in Oratio Recta, H. L., 269, 8.

supra demonstraveram : *B.* IV, 21. The perf. would be more usual.

praemissum : sc. **esse.**

cum—**deferret** : *"though he was delivering to them the orders of his commander in the character of an ambassador (or spokesman)."*—**cum** Narrative, H. L., 204, 4 ; or Concessive, 255, Note : R. C., 397.

ut (sibi) ignosceretur : *"that it should be pardoned to them"* = *"to be pardoned"* : subj. in Substantive Clause of Purpose, H. L., 240, 2 : R. C., 424.—For impersonal use, see H. L., 178, 2.

quod bellum intulissent : *"of their having commenced hostilities"* ; Virtual O.O., H. L., 253, 6 : R. C., 408 (*a*).

cum—petissent: *"though they had of their own accord sent ambassadors to the continent and had sought peace from him."*

ignoscere : sc. **se.**

arcessitam : *"after they had been summoned."*

remigrare in agros : *"to return to their own lands."* **agri** may mean either '*districts*' or '*farm lands*.'

Chapter 28

his rebus : either *"on these terms"* or *"by these means."*

post diem quartum quam: **post** is regarded as a prep. governing **diem** ; but really goes with **quam**, forming **postquam**. The simpler but less usual form would be **die quarto postquam**. Since, in reckoning time, the Romans counted inclusively, this in English would be *"three days after."*

est ventum : used impersonally ; sc. **Caesari** = **Caesar venit** : *"after Caesar's arrival in Britain."*

supra demonstratum est : see previous note ; *"mention has been made above."*

superiore portu : *Ambleteuse*, north of *Boulogne*, called **portus ulterior** in *B.* IV, 23.

solverunt : *"set sail,"* *"started,"* applied absolutely to **naves** after the analogy of **solvere naves** used transitively ; see *B.* IV, 23.

sed aliae—referrentur ; aliae—dejicerentur : the **ut** Consecutive is still understood with these clauses, H. L., 203, 1, 2 : R. C., 371.

propius solis occasum : *"further west,"* literally *"nearer the sunset."* Caesar is said to have been the first to use **propius** as a preposition.

magno sui cum periculo : *"at great danger to themselves"* ; **sui** is Objective Gen., H. L., 287, 3 : R. C., 429 (*d*).

quae—petierunt : *"These, nevertheless, cast anchor, but, since they were being filled by the waves, of necessity they put out to sea in the face of night and made for the continent.'*

tamen : means in spite of the storm raging. Evidently the anchors prevented the boats from riding the waves and so they were in danger of being swamped.

adversa nocte : some render "*though the night was stormy*" or "*in a foul night*" ; abl. abs.; though possibly abl. of Time When.

Chapter 29

eadem nocte : the night of 30th Aug., 55 B.C.

maritimos aestus : spring tides occur a day after full moon, and new moon. The spring tides at *Dover* are said to rise to the height of 19 feet ; at *Boulogne*, to the height of 25 feet.

incognitum : in the Mediterranean there are no tides or very slight ones at certain points. One would have supposed that Caesar's soldiers would have observed the phenomena of tides in the war against the Veneti fought the previous year (*B*. III, 12). The influence of the moon on tides was known to Cicero (De Divin. 2, 14): quid de fretis aut de maritimis aestibus dicam ? quorum accessus et recessus (flow and ebb) lunae motu gubernantur. This work was not published till 44 B.C., eleven years after Caesar's first expedition to Britain.

uno tempore : "*at one and the same time.*"

exercitum—curaverat : "*had had his army brought over.*" For this use of the Gerundive, see H. L., 187, 9 : R. C., 449.

subduxerat : naves subducere, "*to haul vessels on shore,*" "*to beach,*" opposed to naves deducere. "*to launch vessels.*"

et—adflictabat : "*and the storm kept dashing the transports about which were riding at anchor.*"—onerarias, sc. **naves**. Note the force of the imperfect frequentative **adflictabat**.

aut—auxiliandi : "*either of managing (their own ships) or of lending aid (to others).*"

compluribus—inutiles : "*since several vessels were wrecked and since the rest were unfit for sailing owing to the loss of their cables, anchors, and the rest of their tackling.*" The first abl. abs. is Causal, and co-ordinate with the Causal cum clause. The second abl. abs. is also Causal.

id quod necesse erat accidere : "*as was unavoidable.*"

quibus—possent : quibus : abl. of Means and Final Relative, hence **possent**. H. L., 232, 2 : R. C., 385.

usui : dat. of Purpose, H. L., 228, 2 : R. C., 431.

quod—oportere : "*because it was understood by all that the winter ought to be passed in Gaul.*" omnibus constat: we also find inter omnes constat ; omnibus is dat.—hiemari oportere : literally "*it ought to be wintered.*"—in hiemem : "*for the winter*" ; Time Prospective, H. L., 117, 6.

Chapter 30

For the translation of this chapter see p. 59. quibus rebus cognitis : express this in different ways.

principes : subject to duxerunt ; see end of Chapter 27.

ad ea facienda : in how many ways may this be expressed ? See H. L. 232, 3.

optimum factu : supine in -u ; H. L., 180, 3 : R. C., 470 (b).

his superatis—interclusis : Conditional abl. abs. = si hi superati et interclusi essent.

ac—deducere : "*and withdraw their men secretly from the country,*" *i.e.*, from the interior to the sea coast.

Chapter 31

ex eventu navium suarum : "*from what had happened to his ships*" : Objective Gen., H. L., 287, 3 : R. C., 429 (d).

ex eo quod : "*from this fact that,*" defined by the clause following.

fore—suspicabatur : "*he began to suspect that this would happen which actually did happen.*"

ad—comparabat : "*he made provision for all emergencies.*" subsidia (plural) elsewhere in Caesar means "*reserves*"; (the singular) "*the act of bringing aid.*"

cotidie : "*daily,*" implying repetition : in dies, in diem, "*daily,*" implying increase or diminution.

quae—naves earum = earum navium quae : the antecedent is expressed in the relative clause.

aere : "*metal*" ; the word aes seems to be a general word for all metals, except gold or silver; bronze or copper was generally employed in shipbuilding as these did not corrode.

quae—erant : the antecedent is ea understood. usui : see note Chapter 25.

cum—administraretur: *"since the work was carried on with the greatest zeal on the part of the soldiers"*; cum Causal, H. L., 252, 3.

duodecim navibus amissis: *"though twelve ships were lost"*: concessive abl. abs.

reliquis effecit: *"he so arranged matters that the voyage could be conveniently made with the rest"*: literally *"he brought it to pass that it could be sailed."*—reliquis, abl. of Means or Instrument.—Note with a pass. infin. **navigari** that **posset** is impersonal.

Chapter 32

dum geruntur: see note Chapter 22.

ex consuetudine: *"in accordance with custom," "as was the custom."* The foraging was generally done by the 7th legion : the severe fighting, by the 10th.

frumentatum: supine: H. L., 180, 2 : R. C., 470 (a).

neque ulla—interposita: *"and though no suspicion of war up to the present had arisen"*: Concessive abl. abs.—Note that Latin requires **neque ullus**, not **et nullus** for *"and no."*

cum pars hominum: *"since some of the people,"* i.e., the Britons.

in agris: *"on their lands."*

pars—ventitaret: *"(while) others were coming and going to the camp (i e., of the Romans)."*

in statione: *"on sentry duty."* For the gates of a Roman camp see page 18. The sentries at the gates of the camp were called **stationes**; **excubiae** were day or night guards; **vigiliae** were night guards only; **custodiae**, guards of the fortifications. The night guard was inspected every three hours by **circuitores**, who were changed at the end of every watch.

quam consuetudo ferret: *"than custom admitted of," "than usual."* The subj. is either (1) in a subordinate clause in Oratio Obliqua, or (2) the clause is Consecutive.

in ea parte—in quam partem: the repetition of the antecedent in the relative clause is frequent in Caesar. In English omit the antecedent in the relative clause.

id quod erat: *"the actual state of affairs," "what really was the fact."*

aliquid consili: *"some new design had been formed"*: Part. Gen., H. L., 287, 4: the inf. clause is in apposition to **id**: R. C., 174 (a).

cohortes : join this with **jussit.**

in stationibus : "*on the outposts*," "*on guard*"; cp. **in statione,** page 74.

in stationem succedere : "*to take their place on guard*" :

Note the idea of motion conveyed by **succedere,** and hence the accus.

armari = se armare : the passive in Latin is sometimes used with a reflexive meaning corresponding to the Greek middle.

confestim : "*immediately*": note the emphatic position of the adverb · from the same root as **festino,** "*hasten.*"

aegre sustinere sc. **hostes,** "*with difficulty were keeping the enemy in check.*"

conferta legione : the abl. abs. is equivalent to a Causal clause giving the reason why the Romans were exposed to a cross-fire : "*since the legion was massed together*"

conjici : sc. **in eam.** Caesar might have written **in confertam legionem — conjici.**

nam quod : "*for since.*" Join **nam** with **deli

uerant,** and **quod** with **erat.**

"*for, because, the corn having been reaped from all other parts, one part was left, etc.*" = "*for, since the corn had been reaped from all parts but one, the enemy, suspecting that our men would come there, had concealed themselves in the night-time in the woods.*"

dispersos — occupatos : sc. **nostros** : "*then having attacked our men while scattered, with their arms laid down (piled up), and while engaged in reaping.*"

incertis — ordinibus : Causal abl. abs.: "*since their ranks were in confusion.*" The Romans were scattered and could not take their places in the line.

circumdederant : sc. **nostros.**

Chapter 33

genus — pugnae : "*the following is their mode of fighting on war chariots.*" — **pugnae = pugnandi.** With **ex essedis pugna,** cp. **ex equis pugnare,** "*to fight on horseback.*"

per omnes partes, i.e., up and down between the two armies.

ipso terrore equorum : "*by the sheer terror caused by their horses*": Subjective Gen., H. L., 287, 2 : R. C., 429 (c).

cum—insinuaverunt : "*when once they work their way.*"

For **cum** with pf. indic. in the subordinate clause expressing a repeated act in the present see H. L., 263, 9.—The British charioteers drove into the spaces between the cavalry squadrons of their own troops. The warriors (**essedarii**) would then dismount, and the drivers (**aurigae**) retreat to the rear.

desiliunt : sc. **essedarii**, *i.e.*, "*the warriors*" : see note on **praemisso essedariis**, *B.* IV, 24.

praestant: "*display*," "*combine.*"

tantum—efficiunt : "*they become so expert by daily experience and practise.*"

in—loco : "*when the ground is sloping and even steep.*" This construction where **in** with the abl. is used with the same force as an abl. abs. is sometimes called the Prepositional abl. abs. This arises from the want of a present participle of the verb **sum**.

brevi : sc. **tempore** : "*in a moment.*"

per temonem : "*along the pole.*"

Chapter 34

quibus rebus: either (1) abl. of Cause "*owing to these tactics*," "*wherefore*" ; or (2) abl. abs. "*when matters were in this state*," "*under these circumstances*" ; or (removing the commas and considering **nostris** dat. instead of abl. abs.) (3) abl. of Means with **perturbatis** "*to our men confused by these tactics from the fact that the mode of fighting was new.*"

namque = Greek καὶ γάρ : "*and (this was evident) for*" ; **namque** in Caesar and Cicero is usually used before a vowel and is always the first word of its clause.

quo—facto : "*though this was done*" ; Concessive abl. abs.

ad lacessendum : "*for skirmishing with the enemy.*"

alienum : "*unfavorable*" : **alienus** is rarely applied to things and when it is, it is opposed to **suus** or **opportunus** ; cp. **locus suus**, "*ground of his own choosing*," hence "*favorable*" : **tempus suum**, "*time chosen by himself.*" **suo loco** = in **suo loco** ; the prep. **in** is often omitted with **locus**.

quae—continerent : subj. of Result = **tantae ut continerent** : "*so great that they kept our men inside the camp.*"—**castris** : see **suo loco**, previous note.

praedicaverunt: "*they openly boasted*": distinguish in meaning praedīco and praedĭco.

quanta facultas—daretur: "*what a fine opportunity was being offered them*"; subj. in Indirect Question, H. L., 200: R. C., 362.

praedae faciendae: "*of securing booty*"; facere praedam does not occur elsewhere in Caesar.

in perpetuum: "*forever.*"

sui liberandi: with the genitives mei, tui, sui, nostri, vestri, the Gerund or Gerundive form in -di is used, without reference to the gender or number of the pronoun, H. L., 187, 8.

si expulissent: "*if they succeed in driving out*"; subj. in Virtual O.O. representing the fut. pf. indic.—si expuleritis—in O.R., H. L., 269, 8: R. C., 408.

his rebus: "*by these representations.*"

Chapter 35

etsi: join with videbat: see note B. IV, 20.

idem: subject of foré and explained by the appositive ut clause.

ut—effugerent: "*that they would escape owing to their speed.*" The Britons were armed with a long sword and a light buckler. What was the armor of the legionary soldier? See page 16.

si essent—pulsi: subj. in Virtual O.O., representing the fut. pf. indic.—si erunt pulsi—in O.R., H. L., 269, 8: R. C., 408.

diutius: join with non; "*they could not for any length of time withstand.*"

quos—potuerunt: "*and pursuing them over as great a distance as (=as far as) their strength and speed allowed.*"—tanto spatio: abl. where we would have expected the acc. of Extent of Space.—cursu et viribus: abl. of Instrument.

occiderunt: sc. nostri milites.

Chapter 36

his—numerum—duplicavit: = his duplicem numerum imperavit; his is dat. of Indirect Object.

quem—imperaverat: see B. IV, 27.

propinqua die aequinoctii: Causal abl. abs.; "*as the day of the equinox was near.*" This was the period of equinoctial gales. As Caesar

landed in Britain on Aug. 27th, and left (according to Napoleon III)
probably Sept. 11th or 12th, we can see how stubbornly the Britons
must have resisted his landing, since he got no farther than the shore in
his first expedition.—dies is fem. in the sing. when it refers to a fixed
or set day.

infirmis—navibus: Causal abl. abs.; "*since his ships were unsea-
worthy.*"

hiemi—existimabat: "*he did not think that the voyage ought to be
exposed to (the risk of) a storm.*"--hiemi: dat. with a compound of sub—,
H. L., 229, 4.—subjiciendam: sc. esse; Gerundival infin., H. L., 189.

naves solvit: see note on solvit, *B*. IV, 23.

eosdem portus capere: "*to make the same ports,*" see note on tertia
vigilia, *B*. IV, 23.

infra: "*further,*" down the channel, *i.e.*, below *Boulogne.*

Chapter 37

essent expositi: The full phrase is milites ex navibus in terram
exponere. This clause refers to the duae onerariae, referred to at the
end of the preceding chapter.

proficiscens: "*on his departure.*"

pacatos: see *B*. IV, 22.

non ita magno numero: "*with not a very large number*"; this use
of ita is confined to negative sentences.

circumsteterunt: sc. nostros milites, which is also to be supplied as
the object of jusserunt.

si—nollent: subj. in Virtual O.O. after jusserunt.

orbe facto: in cases of extreme danger, the Roman soldiers formed a
circle with their faces to the enemy and their baggage in the centre.
We should say "*forming a hollow square.*"

celeriter: note the emphatic position of the adverb.

suis auxilio: for the two datives, see H. L., 228, 1, 2: R. C., 431.

horis: abl. of Comparison after amplius; cp. amplius octingentos
equites habere, *B*. IV, 12; amplius, plus, minus, longius, may or
may not affect the syntax of the accompanying words.

paucis—acceptis: "*with trifling loss.*"

Chapter 38

qui rebellionem fecerant : "*who had recommenced hostilities*"; "*who had renewed the war.*"

siccitates : either (1) "*continued droughts*" or (2) "*droughts in several localities.*"

quo se reciperent non haberent : "*had no place to betake themselves to.*" **quo reciperent** ; Final Rel. Adv. and Subj., H. L., 232, 2 : R. C., 388.—It might mean "*did not know where to betake themselves*" ; **habeo**, like Greek ἔχω, sometimes has this meaning; **reciperent** would then be subjunctive in Indirect Question, representing a deliberative subjunctive—**quo nos recipiamus**—in O.R.

quo—usi : **quo** is attracted into the case of **perfugio** ; "*which they had used as a refuge.*"

omnino : "*in all.*"

ex litteris : "*in accordance with a despatch from Caesar.*"

BOOK V

Chapter 1

Lucio Domitio Appio Claudio consulibus : The **et** is often left out between the names of the consuls in a phrase of this kind. The year was 54 B.C. The consuls entered office on January 1st. Lucius Domitius Ahenobarbus belonged to the **optimates**. He fell at Pharsalia, 48 B.C., by the hand of Marc Antony. Appius Claudius was brother of the notorious Clodius, killed by Milo. He was also one of the **optimates**.

ab hibernis : these winter camps were among the Belgae (*B.* IV., 38).

in Italiam = in Galliam Cisalpinam : Italy proper did not till 27 B.C. include Gallia Cisalpina, Liguria, and Illyricum, though as here it was often applied to the country south of the Alps. Caesar during his Gallic wars usually spent the winter at Luca or Ravenna.

consuerat = consueverat.

legatis—curarent : "*he orders his staff officers, whom he had appointed over the legions, to have as many ships as possible built during the winter, and the old ones repaired.*" Note the sequence **imperat—uti—curarent,**

is imperat is an historical present.—possent : Virtual O.O.   For the gerundive with curo, see H. L., 187, 9.

modum formamque : *"the size and style."*

subductiones : *"hauling up"* on land, or *"beaching"* (cf. *B.* IV., 29). The plural is used because more than one vessel is referred to.   Explain naves subducere, naves deducere.

humiliores : sc., naves : *"lower."*   The vessels had less elevation above the water.

quam quibus = quam (eas naves) quibus.

in nostro mari : the Mediterranean.

id eo magis : sc. facit : *"and he does this the more (= and all the more) for the following reason."*

propter crebras commutationes : he refers to the varying currents in the Channel.

ad onera : sc. transportanda from the transportandam following.— transportandam agrees with the nearest noun.

in reliquis maribus : the different parts of the Mediterranean were known under different names.

actuarias : *"furnished with oars"* as well as with sails.   Note that impero can be used with acc. and inf. when the infinitive is passive. What would be the more usual construction ? retrahi imperat : cp. *B.* V, 7.

usui : dat. of Purpose, H. L., 228, 1 : R. C., 431.

ad armandas naves : *"for equipping vessels."*   Spain supplied metal, cables, rigging, etc.

conventibus : Caesar as proconsul held assizes or courts at the chief cities of Northern Italy.

Galliae citerioris = Galliae Cisalpinae.

a Pirustis : the Pirustae were a tribe occupying the modern *Herzegovina.*

qui doceant : *"to inform him"*; Final Rel. and Subj , H. L., 232, 2 : R. C., 388.

paratos satisfacere = paratos (esse) ad satisfaciendum : the infin. after paratos esse is on the analogy of velle which takes the infin.

percepta : *"having been listened to."*

ad certain diem : *"by a stated day"*; Time Prospective, H. L., 117, 6.

nisi—fecerint: subj. of Virtual O.O. in Primary Sequence, representing fut. pf. indic.—**nisi feceritis**—in O.R., H.L., 269, 8 : R. C., 408.

arbitros: "*assessors*," "*arbitrators*."

qui—aestiment—constituant: see **qui doceant**, page 80. — **litis aestimatio** in criminal law is the assessment of the amount of damages which a convicted person has to pay.

Chapter 2

citeriorem Galliam = **Galliam Cisalpinam.**

revertitur: give the principal parts ; generally **revertor** is to return before completing one's journey : **redeo**, after completing it.

ad exercitum : after wintering in Belgium : *B.* IV, 38.

inde = **ex Gallia citeriore**: Long estimates that Caesar must have travelled over 2,000 miles. In the beginning of the year he left the army in Belgium, passed through Transalpine Gaul, held court in Cisalpine Gaul, went to Illyricum, settled disputes there, and returned to Belgium in May or June.

circuitis omnibus hibernis : "*after inspecting all the winter quarters.*"

in—inopia : "*though in the greatest need of all kinds of material*": see note on **in—loco**, *B.* IV, 33.

cujus: **quod** would be more usual. The attraction of the relative to the case of the antecedent (common in Greek) is not often met with in Latin.

instructas : "*fully rigged.*"

neque abesse—possint: "*and they were not far from being able to be launched within a few days,*" literally, "*and they were not much short of that point that they might be launched.*"

deduci : see note on **subduxerāt**, *B.* IV, 29.

quid—velit: Indirect Question, H. L., 200 : R. C., 362.

portum Itium : see note on **tertia vigilia**, *B.* IV, 23.

circiter triginta : Caesar is remarkably accurate in distances. The Roman mile was 1,618 yards, or 142 yards shorter than the English mile. The distance from Calais to Dover is 28 miles : from Boulogne to Folkestone 29 miles. Thirty Roman miles would be about 27½ English miles.

huic rei : "*for carrying out this purpose,*" *i.e.*, collecting a fleet at Portus Itius.

expeditis: "*in fighting trim*," "*ready for action*," *i.e.*, without heavy baggage.

concilia: a general council of the Belgic Gauls which Caesar held at Samarobriva (now *Amiens*).

Chapter 3

plurimum—valet: the genitive after the neuter of pronouns and adjectives arises from their partitive sense. For the excellence of the cavalry of the Treviri, cp. *B*. II, 24: equites **Trevirorum, quorum inter Gallos virtutis opinio est singularis.**

ut—demonstravimus: *B*. III, 11 ; IV, 10. ·

Indutiomarus was opposed to the Romans. Caesar ordered the leading men of the state to take sides with Cingetorix, the son-in-law and rival of Indutiomarus. The latter took up arms against the Romans but was defeated and slain by Labienus. (*B*. V, 7).

alter: Cingetorix.—**simul atque**: H. L., 259, 4.

in officio: "*in allegiance*," "*loyal*."

quae—gererentur: subj. in Indirect Question, H. L., 200: R. C., 362.

at: used to contrast the doings of two persons. Caesar has been speaking of Cingetorix ; he now turns to describe the course of Indutiomarus.

Indutiomarus: join with **instituit** at the end of the chapter.

iisque: -que joins **cogere** with **bellum parare.**

iis: join with **abditis**: "*and he decided to prepare for war, after those who, owing to their age, were not able to take the field had been hid in the Ardennes wood.*"

per aetatem: they were either too young or too old.

abditis in silvam, really means "*having been removed to the forest and hidden there.*" The accusative after **abdo** involves the idea of removal as well as of concealment.—**ingenti magnitudine**: abl. of Description : H. L., 293, 6 : R. C., 383 (*a*).

privatim: "*privately*," *i.e.*, for their own private security.

petere: used absolutely, "*to make requests*."

quoniam—possent: Virtual O.O. since Caesar is not stating their real motive, but merely what they said was their motive, H. L., 253, 6 · R. C., 408. Distinguish **virum consulere, viro** (dat.) **consulere, in virum consulere.**

veritus ne : what construction accompanies verbs of *fearing* ? H. L., 242, 243.

sese : often the introducing verb to O.O. is not directly expressed ; **dixit** is implied in **legatos mittit**.

idcirco—laberetur : "*that he was unwilling to leave his followers, and to come to him (Caesar) for this reason that he might the more easily keep the state loyal, lest by the defection of all the nobles the common people might revolt from thoughtlessness,*" literally "*fall off*" from its allegiance. —**quo facilius** : see H. L., 233, 4.

imprudentiam : derive this word.

in sua potestate : "*in his power*"; "*under his control.*"

ejus fidei permittere : "*to put under his protection.*"

Chapter 4

dicerentur : Indirect Question ; H. L., 200 : R. C., 362.

eum : Indutiomarus

ab instituto consilio : "*from carrying out the plan he had formed (or his original plan).*"

filio propinquisque : in apposition to **his** in **his adductis**.

nominatim : "*by name,*" "*expressly.*"

consolatus : "*he sympathised with him*" in regard to the enforced exile of his son and relatives who were to go to Britain with Caesar

nihilo tamen secius : **secius** is comparative of the adv. **secus** literally "*less by nothing*" : **nihilo** being abl. of Measure of Difference : translate the phrase "*still,*" "*however.*".

singillatim : "*one by one,*" "*individually.*"

principibus convocatis, hos—conciliavit : regularly = **principes convocatos conciliavit** : a noun or pronoun should not be put in abl. abs. when it is already the subject or object of another verb, H. L., 163, 5 ; 164 : R. C., 298.

quod—perspexisset : "*for he was both aware that this was done according to the deserts of the latter (Cingetorix) and he considered that it was of great importance that the influence of that man among his people should be as great as possible whose very marked good-will towards himself he had observed.*"

quod : rel. pron. acc., subject of **fieri**, acc. with infin.—**merito** : abl. of Cause or Manner.—**magni interesse**, see H. L., 289, 3 ; 290, 4.

—tam egregiam : tam is often attached to an adjective to give it
additional force ; cp. the frequent use of tantus for simple magnus.
—perspexisset : subj. in O.O. ; but cujus perspexisset may be Causal
Rel. and Subj., H. L., 252, 4.

graviter tulit : "*was annoyed at.*"

et qui—exarsit : "*and whereas he had been of an unfriendly dis-
position toward us even before, he was still more exasperated through
resentment at this act (or through this grievance).*"—qui fuisset : Concessive Rel. and Subj., H. L., 255, Note.—inimico animo : abl. of
Description, H. L., 293, 6 : R. C., 383 (b).

Chapter 5

Meldi or Meldae, a people of Gallia Belgica dwelling between the
Sequana (*Seine*) and the Matrona (*Marne*) near the modern town of
Meaux, a corrupt form of Meldi.

revertisse : conjugate this verb.

cursum tenere : compare cursum capere, *B.* IV, 26.

atque : "*but*" : rather adversative than connective here.

eodem : "*to the same spot*" = in eundem locum.

equitatus : the nobility who served as cavalry.

numero : abl. of Respect : H. L., 293, 7 : R. C., 414.

perspexerat : "*he had observed.*"

obsidum loco : "*instead of hostages,*" "*as hostages*" : when found with
a genitive loco has a semi-prepositional force. We also find in loco.
The gen. is Objective (H. L., 287, 3) after the analogy of gratia, causa,
with genitive.

cum—abesset : "*on account of his absence*" ; cum Causal : or "*while
he personally was absent*" ; Virtual O.O. representing fut. indic. of the
actual thought.

motum = rebellionem : "*an uprising.*"

Chapter 6

Dumnorix had conspired against the Romans 58 B.C., but was
pardoned owing to the entreaties of his brother Divitiacus (*B.* I, 20).
For fear that he might a second time stir up strife, Caesar desired to
take him to Britain.

ante : *B.* I, 3, 18.

magni animi, magnae auctoritatis : Descriptive genitives, H. L., °88, 5 : R. C., 383.

quod—cognoverat : explain the syntax of **quod** : H. L., 252, 2 : R. C., 256.

accedebat huc quod : **accedit** may take (1) an **ut** clause of Result with subj. or (2) a substantive clause introduced by **quod** with indicative.

graviter ferebant : the Aedui annually elected a magistrate called *Vergobretus* or "*judge*," and were naturally annoyed that the right of ' election had been taken out of their hands (*B.* I, 16). Caesar (*B.* VII, 33) states that the person holding this office could not leave the state during his term of office, and that no one could be elected if a living member of the family held the post.

neque—audebant : "*and yet they did not dare to send ambassadors to Caesar for the purpose of objecting or petitioning against (the appointment).*"

omnibus precibus : "*by all kinds of entreaties.*"

quod—timeret : "*because, being unaccustomed to sailing, he was, as he said, afraid of the sea*"; the subjunctive **timeret** implies that the reason given was not the real one ; H. L., 252, 1, 2 : R. C., 408 (b).

religionibus : "*by religious scruples.*"

impediri sese diceret : **diceret** by mistaken analogy with **timeret** is itself put in the subj. We should have expected, **quod impediretur** or **quod sese impediri dicebat**. Sometimes in Causal clauses a verb of 'saying' is inserted parenthetically merely introducing the statement.

id : the request to be left behind.

sollicitare depends on **coepit**.—**sevocare singulos** : "*to call them aside individually*"; "*to hold secret meetings with persons individually.*" Note that **coepit** means here "*he began*"; H. L., 219, 2.

territare : either (1) Historical infin. or (2) depending on **coepit**. Note the intensive or iterative force of the frequentative **territo**.

non—fieri : supply 'saying' from **territare** ; cp. note on **sese**, *B.* V, 3.—**non—ut** : "*it was not without a reason that.*"—**fieri** is impersonal ; **fit ut** = "*it happens that*"; cp. **accidit ut**.

id—necaret : "*(saying) it was the policy of Caesar to transport into Britain and murder there all those whom he was afraid to kill (in sight of Gaul) before the eyes of the Gauls.*"

interficere—vereretur : note that verbs of '*fearing*' may take an infinitive in the sense of "*to be afraid,*" "*not to have the courage*" to do a thing. — **interficere**, "*to kill*" in any manner ; **necare** implies cruelty or injustice.

For **traductos necaret** see H. L., 164 (c) Note.

fidem—interponere: "*he pledge l* (oi to pledge) *his worl to the rest*,"
i.e, to those not in Caesar's power.—**interponere**: Historical infinitive,
or after **coepit**, as **territare** above; so also **poscere.**

jusjurandum, civil oath: **sacramentum**, oath taken by the military.

ex usu: cp. **usui.**—**communi consilio**: as a unite *l* people.

Chapter 7

Caesar: join with **statuebat**.

quod—**tribuerat**: H. L., 252, 2: R. C., 256.

coercendum—**statuebat**: "*determinel that Dumnorix should be
checkel and restrainel by whatever means he coull.*"—**coercendum,
deterrendum (esse),** Gerundival Infin, H. L., 189; the dat. of the
Agent (**sibi**) is omitted, H. L, 188, 4 (b): R. C., 351.—**posset**: sc.
Caesar eum coercere et deterrere: subj., in Virtual O.O.

longius: "*too far.*"

prospiciendum: sc. **statuebat**: "*he male up his mind that he must
take piec utions.*"—the dat. of the Agent (**sibi**) is omittel; see **coercendum** above.

What difference is there between the use of **coercendum** aul **deterrendum (esse),** and of **prospiciendum (esse)**? H. L., 188, 5 (c).

ne—**posset**: "*that he might not be able to do any haim to himself
(Caesar) or the state.*"—**ne**, see H. L., 233, 5.—**quid**: A l verbial acc.,
H. L., 283, 9.

commoratus: "*having lelayed*"="*being letainel,*" "*since he had to
wait.*"

Corus: written also **Caurus, Chorus**, the N.W. win l. This woull
be unfavorable to any one sailing from *Boulogne* to *Britain*. Note the
apposition as in urbs **Roma,** flumen **Rhenus.**

partem: acc. of Extent, H. L., 283, 10: R. C., 231.

omnis temporis: "*of every season.*"

dabat operam: "*he took pains,*" "*he did his best.*"—**contineret**—
cognosceret; subj. in Final Clause, H. L., 240, 8: R. C., 386.

milites = **pedites**; the infantry formed the main strength of the
Roman army.

conscendere in naves: we also find **conscendere naves.**

impeditis animis : *"while the minls of all weie occupiel," "while the attantion of all was distracted "* with the embaikation ; cp. IV, 34, nostris omnibus occupatis.

insciente Caesare : *"without Caesar's knowlelge,"* H. L., 159, 4 (b) · R. C., 305.

domum : H. L., 119, 4, 5.

intermissa—postpositis : *" lelaying his lepaiture and in fact disregarling eveiything else."*

retrahi imperat : see note on actuarias, *B.* V, 1.

si—pareat : subjunctive in Viitual O O. : in direct narration this woull be : si vim faciet neque parebit, (eum) interfice ; see H. L. 269, 8 : R. C., 408.

pro sano : *"like a sensible man," "rationally."*

praesentis : praesens takes the place of the present participle of adsum which is wanting.

qui—neglexisset : *"inasmuch as he had lisregailel his commanl when piesent."* Causal Rel. and Subj., H. L., 252, 4.

manu : *"by foice,"* or, *"in a hanl to hanl fight"* : Livy II, 46 · pugna jam ad manus venerat.

liberüm—civitatis : wiite this in O.R.

Chapter 8

Labieno : Titus Annius Labienus was perhaps the most trustel of Caesar's geneials in the Gallic war. He seivel Caesar for eight yeais through all the campaigns in Gaul, and was intiustel with most important duties. He joinel the sile of Pompey at the outbieak of the civil war and, fought at Phaisalia 48 B.C. against Caesar, and finally fell at Munda in Spain 45 B.C.

portus : probably *Boulogne* and *Ambleteuse.*

consiliumque caperet : *"and alopt a policy to suit the time and circumstances."*

pari numero—quem—reliquerat = numero pari (ei numero) quem reliquerat : literally *"with a numbei of cavaliy equal to that (numbei) which he had left"; "with the same numbei of cavaliy as he had left."* Caesar took with him half of his whole cavaliy foice, *i.e.,* 2000 (see Chapter-5).

ad solis occasum : *"about sunset"*; July 20th or 21st.

Africo : called by the Greeks Λίψ, as it blows from Libya. The S.W. wind is still said to be called by the modern Italians *Affrico* or *Gherbino*.

intermisso : "*having calmed down.*"

longius : probably Caesar went as far north as the North Foreland, the ebb-tide carrying his ships from the shore.

eam partem insulae : see note on **septem**—**progressus**, *B.* IV, 23.

admodum—**laudanda** : "*the pluck of the soldiers was highly praise-worthy.*"—**admodum** properly "*according to measure,*" *i.e.,* "*in as great measure as can be.*" In combination with numerals it denotes *approximation,* and often occurs in Livy and Curtius ; Cicero uses it in the phrase **nihil admodum** : "*in reality nothing at all.*"

non — **labore**: "*since there was no relaxation in their exertion in rowing.*" The abl. abs. is Causal.

accessum—**navibus** : "*all the ships reached.*"

cum : "*though*" : Concessive.

cum annotinis, sc. **navibus** : "*added to the ships used in the previous year.*" In *B.* V, 1, these are called **veteres**.

quas—**fecerat** : "*which each one had built for his own service.*"—**commodi** either (1) genitive governed by **causa** understood, or (2) s̄ui **commodi** is Descriptive Genitive depending on **quas**.

quae —**amplius octingentae** : "*of which more than eight hundred*"; see note on **horis** : *B.* IV, 31.

se —**abdiderant**: see note on **abditis in silvam,** *B.* V, 3.

Chapter 9

exposito exercitu: see note on **essent exppositi**, *B.* IV, 37.

castris idoneo : "*suitable for a camp.*" What adjectives govern a dative case ? H. L., 286, 10.

consedissent : Indirect Question ; H. L., 200 : R. C., 362.

cohortibus decem : probably the two best from each of the five legions.

qui—**essent** ; the pronoun generally agrees with the nearest ante-cedent : Final Rel. and Subj., H. L., 232, 2 : R. C., 388.—For the two datives, see H. L., 228, 1, 2 : R. C., 431.

de tertia vigilia: **de** in such expressions of time means 'starting from that point'; hence the meaning is : "*after the third watch was set.*"

veritus navibus: dative of Indirect Object after verbs of fearing, metuo and timeo, is common ; but not common with **vereor** : "*for his ships.*"

molli : "*shelving*," or "*sandy*" ; where there were no dangerous rocks : cp. *B.* IV, 23, at the end.

praesidio navibusque : dat. after a compound of **prae—**, H. L., ᶜ29, 4 : R. C., 431 (a).

equitatu atque essedis : usually **cum** would be expressed with abl. of Accompaniment without an adjective : H. L., 293, 3.

ad flumen : the Great Stour near Canterbury. The north bank is said to be higher than the south and so would form a natural defence.

in silvas abdiderunt : see note on **abditis in silvam**, *B.* V, 3.

et natura et opere : "*both naturally and artificially.*"

opere : explained afterwards by **crebris arboribus succisis**.

ipsi—propugnabant : "*they themselves in small bands rushed out of the woods to fight*," or "*they themselves here and there hurled missiles from the woods.*"

ingredi prohibebant : note that **prohibeo** takes acc. and inf., not **quominus** with subjunctive.

testudine facta : "*having formed a testudo.*" This movement was done by the soldiers of the inner files locking their shields above their heads while the outer files protected the sides. The resemblance of the locked shields to a tortoise shell (**testudo**) gave this formation its name.

eos fugientes : **eos** is governed by **vetuit** and **fugientes** governed by **prosequi**.

Chapter 10

postridie ejus diei = **postero die**, "*on the next day*," literally "*on the morrow of that day*" : **postridie** = **posteri die**, a locative of time : **ejus diei**, Descriptive Gen.

expeditionem : 'the rapid march of a flying column.'

aliquantum itineris: "*some distance*": **aliquantum** : acc. of Extent ; **itineris** : Partitive Gen.

extremi : "*the rear guard*" of the enemy. Others take it "*the rear*" of the expeditionary force of Caesar. In that case **jam in conspectu** means "*still in sight of Caesar*" who remained behind in the camp.

qui nuntiarent : "*to announce*" : **qui** Final, H. L., 232, 2 : R. C., 388.

afflictas atque ejectas esse : *"had been shattered and thrown up on the beach."*

quod —subsisterent—possent : subj. of Virtual O.O. ; H. L., 253, 6 : R. C., 408 (*a*).

co concursu : *"the consequent collision."*

Chapter 11

legiones = pedites : see note on milites, *B* V, 7.

revocari : *i.e.*, from pursuing the enemy.

resistere : *"to halt."*—revertitur : see note, *B*. V, 2.

coram perspicit : *"he sees with his own eyes."*

sic ut : literally "to *the extent that.*" The construction is somewhat irregular. Regularly sic ut would be omitted, and the acc. with the infin. in the clause reliquae—viderentur would be used. The only justification for Caesar's mode of expression would be that the regular construction would have three infinitives coming together.

amissis—navibus : Concessive use of abl. abs. *"though about forty ships had been lost."*

magno negotio ; *"though with great trouble."*

fabros deligit : usually a corps of *"wrights"* under the direction of praefectus fabrum was attached to each legion. Here in the absence of such a corps, Caesar calls for volunteers out of the legion.

Labieno scribit = Labieno imperat, hence the ut clause following, H. L., 240, 2.

possit : Virtual O.O.

iis legionibus : abl. of Instrument : H. L., 18, 2 (1) : R. C., 145 (*a*).

multae operae ac laboris : Descriptive Gen. : H. L., 288, 5 : R. C., 383.

subduci : see note on subduxerat, *B*. IV, 29.

ne nocturnis—intermissis : translate freely, *" not allowing the work of the soldiers to cease even in the night time."*

praesidio—navibus : H. L., 228, 2 : R. C., 431.

eodem : *"to the same place,"* i.e., to the camp by the river.

summa administrandi : *"the supreme command and entire conduct of the war,"* literally *"the whole of the command and the whole (of th)conduct of the war."*

communi consilio : *"by common consent"*: cp. publico consilio.

circiter—octoginta : reckoning from Deal to the point where he crossed the Thames.

huic—intercesserant : "*constant wars had occurred between this man and the other states.*"—huic : H. L., 229, 4 : R. C., 39.

Chapter 12

quos —dicunt : quos natos (esse) is acc. with infin. after proditum (esse) which is infin., used impersonally after dicunt ; "(*in regard to whom) they themselves state there is a tradition that they were born in the island.*"—memoria proditum esse : literally "*it has been handed down by tradition.*" The inhabitants of Britain belonged to the great Celtic family, not indigenous, but following an earlier Iberian race. However, the belief that people were autochthonous was general among the ancients : Tacitus (Ag. 2) : ceterum qui mortales initio coluerint, indigenae an advecti, ut inter barbaros, parum compertum.

pars : sc. incolitur.

ab iis : so Tacitus (Ag. 11) : proximi Gallis et similes sunt.

iis nominibus civitatum = nominibus earum civitatum : "*by the names of those states.*" Caesar means that there were tribes in Britain and on the Continent with the same names, as Atrebates and Belgae.

quibus—ex civitatibus : for the repetition of the antecedent in the relative clause, compare quo ex portu, B. V, 2.

hominum : "*of the population.*"

fere Gallicis consimilia : sc. aedificiis.

aere : "*bronze*": a mixture of copper and tin, different from brass which was a mixture of copper and zinc.

taleis ferreis : "*iron bars.*"—ad certum pondus examinatis : literally "*weighed to a definite weight*"; cf. examen, "*the tongue of a balance.*" Translate, "*of definite weight.*"

plumbum album : "*tin.*" Caesar here reverses the facts. The tin mines are found chiefly on the coast, chiefly in Cornwall, Devon and Wales, while iron is found in Stafford, Shropshire, Derby, parts of York and Durham. Long before Caesar's time the Phoenicians worked tin mines in the Scilly Islands, which were called by the Greeks Cassiterides, 'Tin Islands.'

ejus : refers to iron.

praeter fagum ac abietem : probably Caesar did not meet with these trees and so denies their existence. Both are abundant in Britain.

haec : sc. animalia.

animi : *" sentiment."*

loca : *"climate"*; cp. frigidissimis locis, *B.* IV, 1.

Chapter 13

natura : *" in shape."* Caesar may have gained his knowledge of the shape of Britain from the natives or from the then extant works of the Greek writers, since the island was not circumnavigated by the Romans till 84 A.D., more than a century after Caesar's time ; cp. Tacitus (Ag. 10); hanc oram novissimi maris tum primum Romana classis circum-venta insulam esse Britanniam affirmavit. Strabo (IV, 5, 1) mentions the fact that Britain is triangular and says that its longest side is parallel to Celtica, and is 4.300 stadia, or about 500 miles in length. Celtica was a term applied to the country generally between the mouth of the Rhine and the Pyrenees. Pomponius Mela (III, 6) compares Britain in shape to Sicily, and says one side faces Gaul, and another side Germany.

Cantium : now Kent, which is said to be from the Celtic *Kenn,* 'headland,' or *Can ;* cp. Kenmore, Canmore, Cantire.

quo—appelluntur : *"at which almost all the ships from Gaul put in."*

inferior, sc. angulus, *i.e.*, Land's End, off the Coast of Cornwall. The distance from North Foreland to Land's End is said to be 344 British or 374 Roman miles. Strabo's statement is evidently taken from Caesar. The indentations of the coast may be taken into account by Caesar.

alterum, sc. latus : cp. Tacitus (Ag. 10) Britannia in orientem Germaniae, in occidentem Hispaniae obtenditur : *" Britain lies opposite Germany on the east, opposite Spain on the west."* Tacitus (Ag. 34) also says that Ireland is between Britain and Spain. The word Hibernia is derived from the Celtic *Erin* or *Iveriu,* meaning *" Western"* (Max Müller, *Science of Languages,* Vol. I, 284).

dimidio minor : *" a half smaller"*; literally *" less by a half"*; abl. of Amount of Difference, H. L., 88, 5. Great Britain is said to contain 84,000 square miles ; Ireland 36,000 square miles.

pari spatio transmissus : literally *" but of the same interval of space across as from Gaul to Britain."*—pari spatio : abl. of Description, H. L., 293, 6. transmissus : gen. depending on pari spatio.

The distance from Carnsore Point in Southern Ireland to St. David's Head in Wales is 53 miles ; from the Mull of Cantire in Scotland to Fairhead in Northern Ireland is 13 miles ; from Dover to Calais 28 miles.

cursu : "*passage.*"

Mona : some have supposed that the *Isle of Man* is meant as it answers the description, but (1) *Mona* in Tacitus (Ag. 14; Ann. XIV, 29) can refer only to Anglesey ; (2) Caesar may have been informed wrongly as to the position of Anglesey ; (3) the *Isle of Man* is properly called *Monopia*, not *Mona*. According to Taylor's *Words and Places Mona* is from the Celtic *Monn*, "*a district*"; cp. *Maine*, *Mayence* in France ; *Mantua* in Italy ; *La Mancha* in Spain ; *Mansfie'd*, *Manchester*, *Menai* straits in England. · Others say it is from the Welsh *mon*, "*alone*"; or *menedh*, "*an island*."

subjectae : "*adjacent,*" Caesar no doubt refers to the Hebrides, Orkney and Shetland Islands, but wrongly places them in the Channel between Britain and Ireland.

nonnulli : probably some Greek geographers whose works have perished.

sub bruma : bruma = brevima = brevissima, sc. dies ; Dec. 21st.

nisi = nisi quod : "*except that.*"

certis—mensuris : "*by exact measurements made by the water clock.*" The *clepsydra* is meant. The water-clock was said to have been invented by the Babylonians, and was constructed on the principle of the hour-glass.

ut fert opinio : "*according to their belief*" : referring to the **nonnulli scriptores.**

septingentorum millium : 700 Roman miles would represent 643 English miles. The western coast of Britain is said to be about 670, not allowing for indentations. Caesar is not far from the mark.

tertium : sc. latus.—**septentriones** : see note, *B.* IV, 20· This side Caesar places on the north. It faces the east.

passuum octingentorum : 800 Roman miles would be about 735 English miles. This is probably not far from the truth, not allowing for the indentations of the Frith of Forth and Moray Firth.

angulus : Kent.

vicies—passuum : 2,000 Roman miles would be 1,839 English miles. The actual circumference of Britain, not counting indentations, is said to be 1,668 miles. Caesar's figures are fairly accurate.

Chapter 14

humanissimi: *"most civilized"*: cp. Shakespeare, *Henry VI*, Second Part, I, 4, 7 :

> " Kent, in the commentaries of Çaesar writ,
> Is termed the civil'st place in all the isle."

interiores plerique : *"the majority of the people of the inland districts."*

lacte ac carne vivunt : **vivo** follows the analogy of **vescor** and takes the ablative of Means : H. L., 136, 7, 8. ·

vitro : *"woad,"* produced from the plant *Isatis tinctoria*, or Dyer's Woad (akin to *Shepherd's Purse*), by fermentation, and much used till indigo took its place. The *Picts* are said to have got their name from *painting* their bodies (**picti,** *"painted"*).

hoc : *"by this,"*—horridiore—aspectu : *"of rather terrible appearance"* : abl. of Description, H. L., 293, 6 : R. C., 383.

promisso—capillo : abl. of Description, H. L., 293, 6 : R. C., 383.

quo : adverb, literally : *"whither,"* = *"to whose house."*

virgo deducta est : *"was led home as a bride"* : cf. **ducere uxorem in matrimonium.**

Chapter 15

essedarii : see note on praemisso—essedariis : *B.* IV. 24.

tamen (ita conflixerunt) ut—fuerint : *"still (they fought in such a way) that our men were victorious in every quarter."* Note that ut—fuerint is Consecutive ; H. L., 203 : R. C., 386 (b) ; and that the perf. subj. expresses a single fact ; H. L., 203, 2 (b).—omnibus partibus : Local abl., H. L., 119, 5.

compluribus interfectis : abl. abs. : *"after killing quite a number "*

cupidius : *"too eagerly."*

illi : *"the enemy."*

intermisso spatio : *"after a short interval."*

imprudentibus nostris : *"while our men were off their guard."*

se—ejecerunt : *"they sallied forth."* The impetuous character of the Celt was as strongly marked in Caesar's time as it was in later days.

in statione : see note on in statione, *B.* IV, 32.

subsidio : *"as a reinforcement"* : H. L., 228, 1, 2 : R. C., 431.

his primis : the first cohort of the legion regularly contained the finest troops.

cum—constitissent : "*when they took up their position with a very small space between them.*"

per. medios : *i.e.*, through the space between the two cohorts.

Chapter 16

dimicaretur : subjunctive (1) after cum Causal, meaning "*since*," H. L., 204, 4 ; and (2) subordinate clause in O.O. after intellectum est. Note dimicaretur is impersonal, "*since the struggle took place*," H. L., 155, 5 : R. C., 397 (*a*).

sub oculis : "*before the eyes*" = in conspectu.

cedentes : acc. after insequi.

ab signis discedere : "*to leave the ranks.*"

equites autem dimicare : "*that the cavalry moreover fought*"; this clause is still after intellectum est.

illi : "*the enemy.*"

cederent—desilirent—contenderent : subj. in O.O. after intellectum est.

equestris—ratio : "*on the other hand the ordinary method of cavalry battle*"; as contrasted with the unfamiliar tactics described in the previous sentence.

et cedentibus et insequentibus : either (1) dat. after inferebat (H. L., 229, 4) with nostris militibus understood, "*to our men whether retreating or advancing*" or (2) abl. abs. with hostibus understood, "*(to our men) whether the enemy were retreating or advancing.*"

accedebat huc ut : "*to this was added the fact that*" = "*besides*"; see note, *B.* V, 6.

rari magnisque intervallis : "*in scattered bands and with wide spaces between the detachments.*"

alios alii : "*one another*"; see note on inter se, *B.* IV, 25.

exciperent : "*relieved.*"

integri : "*the unwounded.*"

Chapter 17

rari : "*in scattered bands.*"

lenius : = minus acriter, "*with less spirit.*"

proelio lacessere : "*to draw out to battle*": distinguish this from proelium lacessere, "*to skirmish.*"

tres legiones : this is an unusually large number to send on a foraging expedition. Perhaps the lesson they had learned on a previous occasion may have made them more guarded (*B.* IV, 32).

Caio Trebonio : Caius Trebonius was one of Caesar's **legati** and distinguished himself by his personal bravery when the winter quarters of Cicero were attacked by the German horse (*B.* VI, 40).

advolaverunt, sc. hostes.

sic uti—absisterent = tam celeriter advolaverunt ut—absisterent · "*so impetuously did they rush forward that they did not stop short of the companies of the legions.*"—**signis legionibusque = signis legionum** (by *hendiadys*). The **signa** were the standards of the **manipuli** ; see p. 17.

subsidio sc. **legionum** : "*the support of the legions.*"—**fido** and **confido** take (1) dat. of person, (2) abl. of thing, H. L., 176, 6.

praecipites : "*in headlong flight.*"

sui colligendi : "*of recovering themselves,*" "*of rallying*" ; for syntax see H. L., 187, 8.

protinus : put here, as usually, after the expression it limits "*immediately after that rout.*"

quae : antecedent is **auxilia.**—**unquam** and **usquam** are usually used in sentences either negative or virtually negative.

summis copiis : "*with their full strength,*" "*in full force.*"

Chapter 18

fines Cassivelauni : embraced Middlesex, Hertfordshire and Buckingham.

uno omnino loco : where Caesar crossed is a matter of doubt. Sunbury, Conway Stakes near Walton, Kingston, Westminster are advocated by different authorities.

hoc : agrees with **loco** understood.

ad alteram ripam : "*on the opposite bank.*"

praefixis : driven into the sloping bank ; on the north side of the Thames.—**defixae** refers to those in the bed of the river. ·

perfuga : said of a deserter with reference to those to whom he flees ; **transfuga** with reference to those from whom he has fled.

ea celeritate—ierunt : *"but our soldiers advanced with such speed and such force, though they had only their heads above water that,"* etc. cum, Concessive.

capite solo : abl. of Amount of Difference, H. L., 88, 5.

Chapter 19

ut—supra : *B.* V, 17.

contentionis : *"of continuing the war."*

amplioribus copiis : *".the most of his forces."*

millibus—quattuor essedariorum : if each chariot contained six men besides the driver, as it seems it did, there would be about 600 chariots.

servabat = observabat : *"kept watching"* : note the force of the imperfects all through this chapter.

locis = in locis : Local abl., H. L., 119, 5.

eis regionibus : *"throughout that district"* : Local abl., H. L., 119, 5 · R. C., 98.

cum—ejecerat : cum, ' whenever ' : H. L., 263, 8.

viis semitisque : via is a regular road ; semita, a by-path.

et – configebat : *"and attended with these he was wont to engage with great danger to our cavalry."*—nostrorum equitum : Objective Gen. : H. L., 287, 3.

hoc metu : *"through fear of this"* : the danger of being cut to pieces by the British charioteers : cp. hoc dolore, *B.* V, 4.

relinquebatur—poterant : *"the consequence was that Caesar did not allow too far a departure from the line of march of the legions, and that only so much harm was inflicted on the enemy by laying waste the lands and by setting fire to the buildings as. the soldiers of the legions could cause by a toilsome march."*—discedi : impersonal infin.

noceretur : impersonal : governs hostibus : H. L., 178, 2 : R. C., 357.

labore et itinere = labore itineris (by hendiadys).

Chapter 20

Trinobantes : occupied Essex and Suffolk. Their chief town was Camalodunum, afterwards a Roman colony under the name of *Colonia Castrorum :* now *Colchester.* The proper way to translate this sentence is to divide it into four English sentences :—

"*Meanwhile the Trinobantes, about the most powerful state of that district, send ambassadors to Caesar, and promise to surrender (themselves) to him, and obey his orders. From that (state) the youthful Mandubratius, who had attached himself to Caesar, had come to him in continental Gaul. Immanuentius, the father of this (Mandubratius), had held sovereign power in that state and had been slain by Cassivellaunus, (while) he himself (Mandubratius) had escaped death by flight. They (the Trinobantes) ask (Caesar) to defend Mandubratius from all wrong-doing on the part of Cassivellaunus and to send (a man) to the state to rule it and to exercise sovereign power.*" See page 58.

ex qua, sc. civitate.

Caesaris fidem secutus, "*having accepted the protection of*," "*having attached himself to*," said of an inferior. The superior was said **recipere in fidem**.

ab injuria Cassivelauni "*from all wrong doing on the part of Cassivelanus*": Subjective Gen. 287, 2 : R. C., 420.

qui praesit : Final Rel. and Subj. : H. L., 232, 2 : R. C., 388.

ad numerum : "*to the required amount.*"

Chapter 21

The **Cenimagni** probably occupied *Bedford* and *Cambridge*; the **Segontiaci**, *Berks*; the **Ancalites**, *Oxford* and *Buckingham*; the **Bibroci**, *Berks*; the **Cassi**, *Hertfordshire*, though this is largely conjecture. The defection of the Trinobantes was ruinous to the British cause.

oppidum=Verulamium, now *St. Albans*.

satis magnus, "*quite a large.*"

convenerit : "*mustered*" : subjunctive in Virtual O.O. H. L., 253, 6 : R. C., 408 (a).

autem : "*now.*"

cum—munierunt : "*whenever they fortify*" : note the tense, H. L., 263, 9 : see note on cum—insinuaverunt, *B.* IV, 33.

natura atque opere : "*by its natural position and especially by its fortifications*," cp. natura et opere, *B.* V, 9.

oppugnare : "*to storm*" : **expugnare**, "*to take by storm.*"

multi, sc. Britanni.

Chapter 22

in—locis : about St. Albans.

ad mare : "*on the sea coast.*"

quibus regionibus : "*over which district.*"

castra navalia : see note on subduxerat, *B.* IV, 29: a camp on shore protected by a mound and ditch adjacent to the ships which were beached.

imperat uti adoriantur : Explain the mood and tense : H. L., 240 2, 3.

constituisset—superesset—intellegeret : explain the subjunctives; and for distinction between tenses, see H. L., 204, 4 (*b*).

id—posse : "*that this might easily be wasted,*" by further delay. The experience of the previous autumn is evidently in Caesar's mind.

quid—penderet : "*what tax Britain should pay.*"—vectigalis : Partitive Gen.: H. L., 287, 4 : R. C., 174 ; for Indirect Question see H. L., 200. — tributum money paid through the tribe on the value of property held by the individual ; vectigal, taxes levied in any other way ; stipendium, war tax. Caesar left no garrison, and probably no tribute was collected. For nearly a hundred years the Romans left Britain unmolested, for it was not till 43 A.D., that the next conquest took place under the Emperor Claudius, and not till 81 A.D., under Domitian, that the part of Britain south of the Frith of Forth was reduced to the rank of a Roman Province. According to Napoleon III, Caesar's second visit lasted from July 20th till September 21st.

interdicit et imperat : "*he prohibits and charges.*"

Chapter 23

his deductis : supply navibus with his : see note on subduxerat, *B.* IV, 29.

duobus commeatibus : "*in two relays*" : abl. of Means.

sic accidit ut : "*it so happened that.*"

neque desideraretur : "*neither in this nor in the preceding year was a single ship at all which carried soldiers lost.*"—quae portaret ; subj. in a clause of Characteristic : H. L., 237, 1 ; or perhaps merely subj. by Attraction.

inanes : of two kinds, (1) those of the first relay which returned to the continent and landed their cargo and were sent back ; (2) those that Labienus had had built.

et prioris commeatus : "*both those of the former relay after the troops were landed*" : sc. eae, in apposition to quae, both before prioris and quas following.—prioris commeatus : Descriptive Gen. 288, 5 : R C., 385.

ne—excluderetur : "*that he might not be prevented from sailing by the time of the year.*"

acquinoctium suberat : Dec. 21st.

necessario—collocavit : "*he of necessity stowed his soldiers in narrower space than was usual.*"

solvisset : see note on solvit, *B.* IV, 23.

secunda vigilia : from 9 p.m. to 12 p.m.

EXERCISES IN LATIN PROSE.

NOTE.—The exercises are based on the chapters of Caesar, both as regards Vocabulary and Constructions. Before attempting an exercise, the student is supposed to have carefully read the chapter of Caesar, noting each word, phrase and construction, and also to have looked up the grammatical references. The exercise should then be done without reference to the text. Each exercise is divided into two parts. The first part is intended to test the pupil's knowledge of the ordinary inflections and vocabulary, and does not involve a knowledge of the subjunctive mood. Consequently the first part of each exercise may be taken up in order before the second part is attempted. For the second part of each exercise, a knowledge of the subjunctive is implied. It is only by constant drill that a knowledge of this mood can be obtained.

The references are to the pages and sections of the New First Latin Book by Henderson and Little, and to sections only in Robertson and Carruthers' Latin Lessons for Beginners.

EXERCISE I

Caesar iv, 20

A

1. A small part of the summer was left for carrying on war.
2. In almost all the Gallic wars, the Britons had furnished aid to our enemies.
3. He was aware that the winters are early.
4. The sea coast and the districts opposite Gaul were known to the merchants.
5. He ascertained that the Britons were carrying on war.
6. We knew nothing about the island, for no one but the merchants go to it.
7. He decided to go to Britain in person at the end of the summer.
8. Can the merchants tell us anything about the island?
9. How large is the island? Did he call the merchants to him from all sides?

101

B

Subordinate Classes in Oratio Obliqua : H. L., *268; 269 :* R. C., *408* (a)

Indirect Question : H. L., *200 ; 234 :* R. C., *362.*

Conditional Clauses : H. L., *249; 250 :* R. C , *475-479.*

1. Caesar thought it would be of great service to him, if he ascertained what harbors of the island were suitable for landing.
2. He thought that he would find out the size of the island, and the character of the tribes that inhabited it.
3. The merchants did not know what experience in war the Britons had.
4. If the Britons had been able to tell Caesar the extent of the island, he would not have gone to Britain.

EXERCISE II

Caesar iv, 21

A

1. Thinking him to be a suitable person, they sent him ahead with a warship.
2. They themselves set out with all their forces into the territory of the Morini.
3. He ordered the ships, which he had built the previous summer, to assemble at this point.
4. When his plan became known, the ambassadors, who had come from several states of the island to him, promised to give hostages.
5. After hearing the ambassadors, he made liberal promises, and sent them back home.
6. After the conquest of the Atrebates, Commius, whom Caesar considered faithful to himself, was made king of that state.
7. They announced that they would soon come there.
8. They did not dare to land from the ship, and five days after returned to the continent.

B

Temporal clauses with **pruisquam** *:* H. L., *259, 8.*

Substantive Clauses of Purpose : H. L., *239 ; 240 :* R. C., *424.*

Indirect Question : H. L., *200 ; 234 :* R. C., *362.*

Cum, *meaning since :* H. L., *204, 3 :* R. C., *397.*

Subordinate Clauses in Oratio Obliqua : H. L., *265, 2 :* R. C., *408* (a).

1. Before he set out for Britain, he ordered his lieutenant to cross the sea in a warship.
2. He instructed them to report to him the character and size of the harbors.

3. They soon returned, since they did not dare to intrust themselves to the barbarians.

4. He urged them to discover the size of the island, and return as soon as possible.

5. When he advised the ambassadors of the enemy to give hostages, they said that they would do what he had commanded.

6. After five days they returned, and reported to Caesar what they had observed there.

EXERCISE III

Caesar iv 22

A

Dum, *while* ; *H. L., 259, 5 : R. C., 273.*

1. While he is delaying here for the purpose of gathering forces, ambassadors were sent to him by the Morini.

2. They promised to do the work, and build the ships.

3. Thinking that the enemy did not wish to give hostages, he wished to have the means for carrying on war.

4. He thought twenty ships were sufficient for transporting the whole army.

5. He gave the rest of the legions to Cotta, to be led into those states from which ambassadors had not come to him.

6. He ordered them to hold the harbor with that guard which he considered to be sufficient.

B

Causal Subjunctive : H. L., 253, 6 : R. C., 256, 397

Final Relative : H. L., 232, 2 : R. C., 388.

Relative Clause in O.O. : H. L., 265, 2 : R. C., 408 (a).

Clause with **quominus** : *H. L., 248, 8.*

1. The barbarians excused themselves on the ground that they were unacquainted with our custom.

2. Deputies came to Caesar from the Morini, to promise to do what he had commanded.

3. Caesar said he did not wish to carry on war against the Gauls, because he wished to cross as quickly as possible to Britain.

4. The ships, in which the cavalry were being transported, were prevented by the wind from reaching the same harbor.

EXERCISE IV

Caesar iv, 23

A

1. After these matters were arranged, he ordered the cavalry to embark.
2. They themselves reached the island about the fourth hour of the day with all the ships.
3. They beheld the forces of the enemy drawn up on all the hills.
4. Javelins could be thrown from the higher ground upon the shore.
5. At last he obtained weather suitable for sailing.
6. He did not think this place at all suitable for disembarking.
7. He assembled the military tribunes. The lieutenants assembled. The soldiers were assembled.

B

Cum, *meaning since:* H. L., *204, 3:* R. C., *397.*

Consecutive Clauses: H. L., *236:* R. C., *371.*

Dum, *meaning until:* H. L., *259, 7:* R. C., *273.*

Indirect Question: H. L., *200, 234:* R. C., *362.*

Substantive Clauses of Purpose: H. L., *239, 240:* R. C., *424.*

1. Since the cavalry advanced a little too slowly into the further harbor, all the ships were not able to reach Britain at the same time.
2. The mountain was so high that the enemy were able to throw darts upon the shore.
3. Since he thought the weather by no means suitable for sailing, he waited for nine hours until the rest of the ships should assemble there.
4. They will point out both what they have ascertained from the messengers, and what they wish to be done.
5. He will warn them to disembark as quickly as possible.

EXERCISE V

Caesar iv, 24

A

1. The barbarians sent their cavalry ahead.
2. They were accustomed to use this kind of force.
3. They tried to prevent our men from landing from the ships.
4. Our men landed from the ships. Our men were landed from the ships. The soldiers embarked. He embarked the soldiers.

5. On account of their size, the ships could not approach the shore.
6. Our men must at once leap down from the ships, and fight with the enemy (188, 5).
7. Terrified by these circumstances, the enemy were willing to surrender.

B

Consecutive Clauses: H. L., 236 : R. C., 371.

Final Clauses: H. L., 197 : R. C., 386.

Quod, *because, with Indic.: H. L., 252, 2 : R. C., 256.*

1. The enemy were so terrified that they did not dare to advance into the water.
2. We could not land, because the ships were so large that they could not be moored except in deep water.
3. When the barbarians became aware of the plan of the Romans, they sent forward all their cavalry in order to prevent our men from landing.
4. The enemy advanced into the water, in order that they might be able to hurl their javelins upon the ships.

EXERCISE VI

Caesar iv, 25

A

1. I am accustomed. He was accustomed. They are accustomed. We were accustomed.
2. When Caesar observed this, he ordered his men to moor the ships at the exposed flank of the enemy.
3. The enemy were dislodged with slings and arrows.
'. This movement was of great service to our men.
. Alarmed at the size of the ships, the enemy retired.
6. While our soldiers were wavering, he who was carrying the eagle of the tenth legion leapt down from the ship into the water.

B

Subordinate Clauses in O.O.: H. L., 265, 2 : R. C., 408 (a).

Cum *narrative : H. L., 262, 4 : R. C., 397.*

Substantive Clauses of Purpose : H. L., 239, 240 : R. C., 424.

1. The eagle-bearer ordered the men to leap down from the ships if they did not wish to let the eagle fall into the hands of the enemy.
2. When the standard-bearer saw that our men were wavering he charged them not to betray the eagle to the enemy.

3. When he had proclaimed in a loud voice that he at least would do his duty to his country and commander, he began to advance against the enemy.
4. Our men exhorted one another to leap down from the ship and follow the standard.

EXERCISE VII
Caesar iv, 26
A

1. The battle was long and fierce.
2. Our men could not follow the standards closely.
3. The barbarians quickly threw our men into confusion.
4. They hurled darts upon them as they landed from the ships.
5. Caesar saw that his men were in trouble.
6. Spurring on their horses, they would assail our men while at a disadvantage.
7. As soon as our men got footing on dry land, they charged the enemy and soon put them to flight.
8. We were not able to pursue the enemy farther because the cavalry had not been able to reach the island.

B

Repeated acts in the past: H. L., 263, 8 : R. C., 119.

Cum *narrative: H. L., 262, 4: R. C., 397.*

1. Whenever we saw that our men were being attacked by superior numbers, we sent aid to them.
2. Whenever the enemy saw any disembarking singly, they kept hurling darts at them.
3. When Caesar saw that the enemy were assailing his men while at a disadvantage, he ordered the lieutenants to send up reinforcements.
4. When Caesar learned that the ships, in which the cavalry were being transported, had not been able to hold their course, he knew that he could not pursue the enemy far.

EXERCISE VIII
Caesar iv, 27
A

1. As soon as the enemy saw that the Roman forces were retreating into camp, they decided on an immediate attack.
2. We promised to give hostages, and not attack our neighbors.
3. We have shown above that these men were sent ahead.

4. We promised to send these men ahead.
5. When this man landed from the ship, he was seized and thrown into prison.
6. Although they had sent ambassadors of their own accord to Caesar, and had sought peace, yet they commenced hostilities at the beginning of spring.
7. Caesar said he would pardon them.
8. We have said that Commius came to Caesar along with these ambassadors.
9. The hostages, sent by the enemy, came to Caesar on the third day.
10. The chiefs began to assemble from all sides.
11. They assembled their forces on the following day.
   Five days after, the chiefs assembled, and intrusted themselves and their states to Caesar.

B

Cum *narrative : II. L., 262, 4 : R. C., 397.*

Conditional Clauses in O.O. : II. L., 268, 6 : R. C., 475-479.

V.O.O., or Causal Subj. : II. L., 253, 6 : R. C., 408.

Substantive Clauses of Purpose : H. L., 239, 240 : R. C., 424.

1. When this ambassador was landing from the ship, he was wounded by the darts of the enemy.
2. They promised to give hostages if Caesar would pardon them.
3. They intreated Caesar to pardon them.
   They earnestly asked to be pardoned (178, 3).
   We will ask him to pardon us.
   We will ask to be pardoned (178, 3).
4. Caesar complained that in seeking peace they had not promised to surrender their arms.
5. Caesar said he would pardon them if they surrendered their arms before he reached the walls of the town.
6. They said they would surrender to Caesar those who had thrown Commius into prison.

EXERCISE IX

Caesar iv, 28

A

1. How many chiefs assembled ? How large forces did they assemble ?
2. The eighteen ships, of which mention has been made above, reached Britain four days after setting sail from the continent.
3. We saw that the ships were approaching the shore at great risk.
4. One ship, being cast on the lower part of the island by the storm, was lost.

B

Cum *narrative: H. L., 262, 4 : R. C., 397.*

Consecutive clauses : H. L., 236 : R. C., 371.

1. Two ships were lost just as they were approaching the shore and could be seen from the camp.
2. Such a storm suddenly arose that the ships were not able to hold their course.
3. The storm was so great that many ships were carried back to the point from which they had set out.
4. When our men were coming into camp the enemy made such a sudden attack that a large part of the baggage was lost.

EXERCISE X

Caesar iv, 29

A

1. A full moon usually makes the tides very high.
2. The ships, in which the army had been transported, were being filled by the tide.
3. Many ships were shattered ; several were useless for sailing.
4. They had provided corn for winter.
5. The army must be transported.
6. Caesar had had the army transported in warships.
7. All things, which are of use for repairing ships, were wanting.
8. The baggage of the whole army had been lost.

B

Final Relative: H. L., 232,·2 : R. C., 388.

Final Clauses: H. L., 197 : R. C., 386.

Cum *meaning since : H. L., 204, 3 : R. C., 397.*

1. There were no other ships in which the army could be carried back.
2. Caesar had twenty warships built in which to transport the army.
3. He ordered them to beach the ships, that the baggage might not be lost.
4. Since many ships, which had been drawn up on dry land, were shattered by the storm, Caesar decided to send for workmen who should build new ships.

EXERCISE XI

Caesar iv, 30

A

1. On learning of the arrival of the legions, the Britons assembled to carry out Caesar's orders.
2. The Romans lacked cavalry and ships and grain.
3. The legions had been transported without baggage.
4. They learned that they had transported the army without baggage.
5. They thought that Caesar had crossed over to Britain with warlike intentions.
6. They began to leave the camp secretly and return to their own people.

B

When the chiefs, whom Caesar had called together for the purpose of ascertaining these things, perceived that the forces of the Romans were few and that they lacked corn, they thought the best thing to do was to retreat as far as possible from the sea coast because they were confident that the Romans would not dare to advance more than twenty miles from their camp.

EXERCISE XII

Caesar iv, 31

A

1. Although Caesar had not yet learned their plans, nevertheless he was suspecting that they would not give hostages.
2. He ordered his men to gather corn from the fields into the camp daily.
3. Very many ships had been very seriously shattered and twelve were lost.
4. They promised to give hostages and bring corn into the camp.
5. The materials, which were of use for repairing ships, were brought from the continent.
6. Caesar was suspecting that they would try to destroy the ships.

B

As soon as Caesar was informed that many ships had been shattered, he suspected that the enemy would gather all their forces and make an attack on the camp. In order that he might as soon as possible transport his army to Gaul, he ordered his men to build twenty new ships as soon as possible. In the meantime he kept his cavalry posted in front of the camp, and sent scouts to ascertain what the enemy were doing and how large forces they were assembling.

EXERCISE XIII

Caesar iv, 32

A

1. Two legions were sent to forage.
2. Those who were on guard before the gates of the camp reported to Caesar that they saw a great dust.
3. They saw a great dust in the direction in which the legions had gone.
4. Caesar suspected that the barbarians had formed some new plan.
5. Caesar ordered three legions to set out with him in the direction in which the soldiers had gone, and the rest to follow closely as soon as possible.
6. After advancing a little farther from the camp, they saw that the enemy were attacking our men vigorously, and that the legion could not hold out much longer.

B

Since Caesar had not been able to find out from the merchants how large forces of infantry and cavalry the barbarians had, nor where he could land his army, he sent Volusenus, whom he thought to be a suitable person, to urge the Britons to give hostages, and recognize the authority of the Roman people. But as this officer did not dare to land from his ship, he was not able to learn much about the island, and returned to Caesar after a few days. About the end of summer Caesar set out in person with a large army, and, after defeating the barbarians, demanded a large number of hostages from them.

EXERCISE XIV

Caesar iv, 33

A

1. Javelins were hurled from all sides by the enemy.
2. They generally try first to disorder the ranks.
3. After hurling their javelins, they leapt down from their horses and fought on foot.
4. Sometimes they withdrew from the battlefield.
5. Our cavalry were hard pressed by superior numbers of the enemy.
6. They were accustomed to rein in their horses at full speed.

B.

Repeated Acts in the Past: H. L., 263, 8: R. C., 119.

Consecutive Clauses: H. L., 203: R. C., 371.

Final Clauses: H. L., 197 ; 232: R. C., 386.

1. Whenever they were hard pressed by superior numbers, they would retreat as quickly as possible to their own men.
2. They could rein in their horses and retreat so quickly that our men could not surround them.
3. They used to ride through all parts and hurl their javelins, in order to throw our ranks into confusion.
4. Whenever they had thrown the squadrons of cavalry into confusion, they would leap down from their chariots and fight on foot.

EXERCISE XV

Caesar iv, 34

A

1. On Caesar's arrival, our men, who were greatly disordered owing to the new method of fighting, recovered from their fear and attacked the enemy vigorously
2. After the lapse of a short time, the legions were led back into camp.
3. Thinking the time to be unfavorable for engaging in battle, Caesar did not lead his legions out of the camp.
4. While these operations are going on, the rest of the enemy's forces scattered.
5. Owing to the storms, which followed for several successive days, the enemy were forced to remain in the woods.
6. A great host of cavalry and infantry were collected by these measures.
7. Messengers were sent by the enemy into all sections.
8. A great opportunity of making plunder was afforded the enemy.
9. Our men will drive the enemy out of the woods.
10. The barbarians will be driven out of the camp.
11. Owing to the small number of our forces, two cohorts were driven out of the camp and forced to surrender.
12. We have a great opportunity of freeing ourselves (187, 8) forever, if we engage in battle at once.
13. We gave you a great opportunity of freeing yourselves.
14. Thinking the ground to be unfavorable for attacking the barbarians, they kept themselves on their own ground.

B

English present part. with causal force: H. L., 204, 5: R. C., 273.

Consecutive Clauses—qui consecutive: H. L., 236, 2: R. C., 371.

Indirect question: H. L., 200: R. C., 362.

Oratio Obliqua: H. L., 269, 8, Note: R. C., 40s.

1. Seeing that his men were disarranged by the unusual tactics of the enemy and thinking that larger forces of cavalry and infantry were coming up, Caesar resolved to await the arrival of the tenth legion.

2. Storms followed such as to force the enemy to remain in camp and, prevent (190, note 2) our men from foraging.

3. Observing that the enemy had halted, Caesar pointed out to his men how easily they could defeat the enemy if they attacked them vigorously from all sides.

4. The messengers, sent by Caesar to discover what the enemy were doing, reported that infantry and cavalry were being collected and pointed out what a grand opportunity our men had of taking the town if they crossed the river at once.

5. Suspecting that the enemy would attack the camp in the night-time, Caesar sent three cohorts to prevent them from crossing the bridge.

EXERCISE XVI

Caesar iv, 35

A

1. Although Caesar saw that the enemy had been routed, still he knew that they would escape danger by their speed.

2. The legions were posted in line of battle before the camp.

3. The same thing happened on this day as had happened on previous days.

4. The enemy will not be able to withstand the assault of our men long.

5. Quite a few of them were slain. We will slay a large number of them. He had been slain. He slew him with his own hand.

6. They said that quite a large number of them had been slain.

7. After slaying quite a number, they set fire to all their buildings.

8. He knew that many had escaped. He thought that their leader would escape.

9. After pursuing them for ten miles, our cavalry saw that the infantry were not able to reach the top of the hill, and returned to camp.

B

Oratio Obliqua: H. L., 269, 8, Note · R. C., 408.

Final Clauses: H. L., 197, 1 : 232, 3 : R. C., 386.

Consecutive Clauses: H. L., 203 : R. C., 371.

Although Caesar saw that, if the enemy were defeated, they would escape into the woods and marshes, nevertheless, having assembled his officers, he announced that he would engage the enemy on the following day. As soon as the battle commenced, the enemy became aware that they could not bear up against the assault of our legions, and immediately fled. Caesar sent all the cavalry to pursue them, and ordered the infantry to follow closely. The enemy, however, being well acquainted with the locality,[1] got out of reach so quickly that our men killed very few of them. Accordingly, after burning all their villages and devastating their fields, they returned to camp.

EXERCISE XVII

Caesar iv, 36

A

1. The hostages, sent by the enemy to Caesar, arrived in camp on the following day.
2. Caesar ordered the rest of the hostages to be brought to the continent.
3. Caesar did not wish to remain longer in Britain, because his ships were weak, and winter was near at hand.
4. At last, having obtained suitable weather for sailing, he ordered all to go on board the ships.
5. All the ships reached the coast of Gaul in safety, but all were not able to reach the same harbor.
6. They reported that two merchantmen had not been able to reach the same harbor as the rest.
7. He demanded a large number of hostages from them, and ordered them to bring grain into the camp.
8. Caesar ordered his lieutenant to send the hostages, given by the enemy, to the continent.

EXERCISE XVIII

Caesar iv, 37

A

1. Caesar landed about three hundred soldiers from these ships. **A** thousand soldiers landed.
2. They immediately proceeded into camp.

---

[1] The places (being) well known : Abl. Abs.

3. At the time of his departure to Britain, Caesar left **the Morini at** peace.
4. But being inspired by the hope of plunder, they surrounded **our men** on all sides.
5. Lay down your arms if you do not wish to be killed.
6. Our men at once formed a circle and assumed the defensive.
7. Soon, however, about six thousand of the enemy assembled.
8. When this was reported to Caesar, he sent all the cavalry from the camp to the support of his men.
9. Meanwhile our men were able to withstand the assault of the enemy, and fought very valiantly for more than two hours.
10. They slew quite a number of the enemy. Very few of our men were slain.
11. After our cavalry came in sight, the enemy threw away their arms and fled.

B

Cum *narrative* : *H. L.*, *262, 4* ; *204, 3, 4* : *R. C.*, *397*.

Virtual, O.O.

1. When the three hundred soldiers, who had landed from these ships, were hastening into camp, suddenly the cavalry of the Morini surrounded them and ordered them to surrender if they wished to save their lives.
2. After our men had fought very valiantly for more than two hours and had killed quite a number of the enemy, Caesar was informed that about six thousand had surrounded the seventh legion and were hurling javelins upon it from all sides.

EXERCISE XIX

Caesar iv, 38

A

1. On the following day those legions, which had been brought back from Britain, were sent under Titus Labienus against the Morini.
2. They had availed themselves of the marshes as a place of refuge the previous summer.
3. After devastating all the fields and burning the buildings, the legions returned to Caesar.
4. The Menapii will all hide in the densest woods.
5. Caesar had established the winter quarters of two legions in the country of the Belgae.
6. Hostages were sent by only two states from Britain.
7. The Morini will betake themselves into the marshes.
8. Many states came into the power of Labienus.
9. Since all their crops were cut down, the Morini were willing to give hostages to Caesar.

B

cum, *meaning since* : *H. L., 204, 3, 4 : R. C., 397.*

Oratio Obliqua : H. L., 265, 2 : R. C., 408.

1. Since the woods had been burned, the enemy had no place to betake themselves to.
2. The enemy learned that Caesar had sent the three legions, which had been brought back from the island, against the Morini, because they had renewed the war.
3. Caesar informed the ambassadors that he would devastate the fields, and burn the dwellings of the Menapii, because they had hid in the woods and marshes.
4. Since you cannot retreat across the river, are you willing to allow the legions to winter in your territory ?

EXERCISE XX

Caesar v, 1

A

1. Caesar was accustomed to pass the winter in Italy.
2. They will place officers in command of the legions.
3. Labienus was placed in command of the tenth legion.
4. As many ships as possible were built during the winter.
5. The old ships had to be repaired.
6. Caesar provided for the construction of twenty ships.
7. He knew that the waves were not so large there.
8. They were accustomed to employ larger ships in that sea.
9. On account of the tides the ships were made larger.
10. The materials, which were of use for building ships, were brought from Spain.
11. The Pirustae were devastating the province.
12. They heard that Caesar had set out into Illyricum.
13. He levied three thousand soldiers from all the states.
14. The soldiers assembled at the stated place. They assembled the soldiers on the appointed day.
15. The soldiers were assembled at an appointed place.
16. When the Pirustae were informed of this matter, they sent ambassadors and promised to bring the hostages by the appointed day.
17. The hostages were brought by the day as he had commanded.
18. He made it clear that hostages had to be given.
19. We shall make it clear that we will devastate the province.

B

Substantive Clauses of Purpose: II. L., 239 ; 240 · R. C., 424.

Cum *narrative:* II. L., 204, 3, 4 : R. C., 397.

Qui *Final:* II. L., 232, 2 : R. C., 388.

Oratio Obliqua: H. L., 269 : R. C., 408.

1. Officers were sent to superintend the construction of a large number of ships.
2. He commanded his officers to see that all the materials, that were necessary for repairing the ships, were brought from Spain.
3. Caesar told his men that, unless more ships were built, they could not be taken back to Gaul.
4. The enemy were told that, unless hostages were given by the appointed day, our general would send cavalry to ravage their territory.
5. On their arrival at the larger camp, they learned that the cavalry, which had been sent into the territory of the Remi for the purpose of plundering and devastating, had not yet returned.
6. On learning that sufficient ships for transporting the army had been built, he departed at once for the sea-coast.

EXERCISE XXI

Caesar v, 2

A

1. These transactions were quickly concluded.
2. He will set out for the army.
3. The ships will be able to be launched within a few days.
4. He commended those who had been in charge of the work.
5. He left what he considered a sufficient force to perform these operations.
6. He had learned that all would assemble at Port Itius.
7. Owing to the wonderful enthusiasm of the soldiers the ships were all launched within a few days.
8. When this fact was reported to him, he at once set out in person with three legions ready for action into the territory of the Treviri because he heard that they would not obey him.

B

Cum *narrative:* H. L., 204, 3, 4: R. C., 397.

Indirect Question: H. L., 200: R. C., 362.

Clause with **quin**: H. L., 247, 4.

1. On his return to the army, he found that all the ships were able to be launched.
2. The ships were not far from being able to be launched within a few days.

3. He pointed out what he wished to be done. He asked the officers how many ships had been built.

4. He learned from merchants in what harbor he could most easily disembark the soldiers.

5. When he learned that his lieutenant had left camp with three hundred horse, he himself returned to Hither Gaul.

EXERCISE XXII

Caesar v, 3

A

1. We have shown above that this state is by far the strongest of all Gaul in cavalry.

2. Two chiefs were at the head of this state, of whom, one was very friendly to Caesar, the other was collecting forces of cavalry and infantry preparatory to engaging in war.

3. As soon as the legions arrived, this chief wished to come to Caesar and promise to continue loyal.

4. All who on account of their age were not able to bear arms were concealed in the Ardennes wood.

5. Many chiefs, alarmed at the arrival of Caesar and the legions, began to fear for their own interests.

6. I did not wish to leave my people and come to you because the common people through thoughtlessness wished to desert the friendship of the Roman people.

7. The state is under my control, and if you will allow me I shall come to you in the camp and intrust my fortunes and those of the state to your honor.

B

' *as soon as* ' : *H. L., 259, 4 : R. C., 119.*

' *after* ' : *H. L., 259, 4 : R. C., 119.*

quoniam, cum, ' *since* ' : *H. L., 252, 2, 3 : R. C., 307.*

Clauses with verbs of ' *fearing* ' : *H. L., 242 ; 243.*

quo *Final : 253, 4.*

O.O. : 265 ; 269, 8 : R. C., 408.

1. As soon as the chiefs of this state learned that Caesar and the legions had arrived, they sent ambassadors to assure him that they would continue loyal, and to report what the Treviri were doing.

2. After some chiefs had informed Caesar that Indutiomarus was
gathering forces of cavalry and infantry, the latter, fearing that
Caesar would put him to death, came to him to intreat (him) to
spare him.

3. He said that he was afraid that they would not be able to carry on
war longer.

4. Fearing that the soldiers would not be able to cross the river on
foot, he sent workmen ahead to build a bridge that he might
more quickly reach the camp of the enemy.

EXERCISE XXIII

Caesar v, 4

A

1. Though all preparations had been made for a war in Britain, he was
forced to spend the summer among the Treviri.

2. Why were those statements made ?   Why did he order the chief to
come to him ?

3. The two hundred hostages, which he had ordered to be brought to
him, arrived on the following day.

4. It was of great importance that hostages should be given.

5. He perceived that this chief had very great influence among his
people.

6. He was aware that Caesar wished to go to Britain this summer.

7. They were aware that this could not be done.

B

Indirect Question: H. L., 200 : R. C., 362.

Ne *Final: H. L., 233, 5 : R. C., 424.*

Oratio Obliqua: H. L., 265 : R. C., 408.

Substantive Clauses of Purpose: H. L., 239 ; 240: R. C., 424.

1. Although Caesar was aware why Dumnorix had said that he did not
wish to come to him, nevertheless, to avoid being forced to remain
in Gaul all summer, he ordered him to bring two hundred hostages
to him.

2. He urged this chief to continue loyal and announce to his people
that Caesar would return as soon as possible.

3. Inasmuch as all preparations had been made for a campaign in
Britain, he thought that it was of great importance to go to the
island this summer.

4. He knew why Dumnorix was summoning the chiefs to him and
urging them to remain in Gaul.

EXERCISE XXIV

Caesar v, 5

A

1. All these matters were already settled.
2. The forty ships, which had been built by the Meldae, were driven back by a storm.
3. These ships were not able to reach the harbor from which they had set out.
4. They will return to the same harbor from which they sailed.
5. All the rest of the ships were ready for sailing.
6. He found many ships shattered by the storm.
7. He ordered the cavalry of all-Gaul to assemble at the same point.
8. He determined to take with him those chiefs who were not friendly to him.
9. He left the rest of the chiefs in Gaul.
10. He feared an uprising of Gaul in his absence.
11. Very few chiefs were left in Gaul by Caesar.

B

1. When Caesar learned that many of his ships had not been able to hold their course and reach Port Itius; he was afraid that the barbarians would assemble all their forces and attack the naval camp.
2. Accordingly he ordered his lieutenants to collect as large a quantity of corn as possible, because he was afraid that in his absence the enemy would try to prevent our men from foraging.
3. On his arrival at the winter camp, he found it admirably fortified with a rampart and trench.

EXERCISE XXV

Caesar v, 6

A

1. He did not dare to leave Dumnorix in Gaul, because he knew him to be a man of great influence among his people.
2. All the Gauls are desirous of change.
3. Caesar had learned that Dumnorix had told the chiefs that he had determined to take them all with him to Britain.
4. They said that, being unused to sailing, they were afraid of the sea.

5. Alarmed by the approach of Caesar, the chiefs came to him, **and** promised to go with him to the island.
6. They saw that they would not obtain this request.
7. They knew that Caesar would not dare to kill these chiefs before the eyes of the Gauls.
8. They told their people that Caesar would take all the chiefs over to Britain; and put them to death there.
9. Several reported to Caesar that the Gauls were carrying out these plans with one common purpose.

B

Virtual O.O. : H. L., 253, 6 : R. C., 408.

Posteaquam, '*after*' : *H. L., 259, 4 : R. C., 119.*

Substantive Clauses of Purpose : H. L., 239 ; 240 : R. C., 424.

1. He begged of Caesar to allow him to remain in Gaul, because (as he said) he did not wish to leave his people, and he was afraid of the sea.
2. After he saw that he would not obtain his request to be left behind, he began to summon the other chiefs and urge them not to set out along with Caesar.
3. To this was added the fact that they did not dare to leave the camp lest Caesar should send cavalry to capture them and then put them to death.
4. They knew that Caesar, being afraid that these chiefs would stir up all the Gauls against him, had decided to take Dumnorix especially with him.

EXERCISE XXVI

Caesar v, 7

A

1. These facts were soon ascertained through scouts.
2. This wind was accustomed to hinder navigation.
3. Our men were not accustomed to go on board ships in the night-time.
4. We shall ascertain all their plans.
5. He ordered the cavalry and infantry to go aboard at midnight.
6. If he does not obey, kill him.
7. I am a free man and of a free state.
8. According to orders they killed the man.
9. The cavalry will advance ; the infantry will return to Caesar.
10. He returns. He returned. They said he would not return.

The Gerundive: H. L., 187; 188: R. C., 448-450.

11. We must ascertain these things. We must advance with all our forces.

12. All his plans must be discovered. A large part of the cavalry must be sent to overtake him.

13. This chief must be checked. The other had to be put to death.

Participles: H. L., 152-158: R. C., 271-273; 261, 312.

14. Having advanced; having delayed; having obtained suitable weather; having been sent; thinking; on being called back · shouting; having been killed.

Ablative Absolutes: H. L., 159-160: R. C., 304.

15. Having ascertained all his plans; without my knowledge; without our knowledge; a large part of the cavalry having been sent forward; in my absence; in our absence; in the presence of Caesar; in the presence of the consuls; while the minds of all were engaged.

B

1. Thinking that the cavalry would soon return, they ordered the soldiers to prepare for an attack on the enemy's camp.

2. Caesar took pains not only to ascertain all their plans, but also to collect as large forces as possible.

3. When the soldiers had gone aboard the ships, the chiefs in a body began to leave the camp for home.

4. After advancing about five miles, they suddenly turned back again, and seeing that our men had not yet landed from the ships, they made a fierce attack on our camp, and put the cavalry to flight.

EXERCISE XXVII

Caesar v, 8

A

1. Three legions and two thousand cavalry were left with Labienus on the continent.

2. He was unable to reach that part of the island where he had found a suitable harbor the previous year.

3. The endurance of the soldiers was very commendable.

4. The ships were not able to hold their course.

5. Caesar learned from captives that large bands of the enemy had assembled at this place.

6. Terrified by the large number of ships, the barbarians had concealed themselves in the uplands.

7. Leaving a large number of cavalry to guard the camp, they crossed the river and hastened into the territory of the Remi.

B

1. Thinking Labienus to be a suitable person, he left him on the continent to defend the camp and build ships and ascertain how large forces the enemy were gathering.
2. Setting out from the camp at daylight, he came up to the baggage-train of the enemy about mid-day, and knowing that their cavalry were still five miles distant, he sent one legion to seize the heights and prevent auxiliaries from coming to their aid.
3. As we have shown above, the Remi were coming to the aid of their neighbors, but hearing that these had been defeated by Caesar, they turned back and sought refuge in the forests.

EXERCISE XXVIII

Caesar v, 9

A

1. Caesar at once landed the army and chose a suitable place for a camp.
   The soldiers landed from the ships at daybreak.
2. The cavalry were landed a little later.
4. Ten cohorts and two hundred cavalry were left to guard the camp.
5. The enemy's forces had encamped on the heights.
6. The ships were left on an open shore.
7. Our men tried to keep the enemy from getting inside the fortifications.
8. The soldiers of these two legions made a fierce attack and drove the enemy out of the camp.
9. With trifling loss our men withstood the assault of the enemy for more than three hours and killed quite a large number of them.
10. Caesar did not allow his men to leave the camp.
11. Caesar was not able to pursue the fleeing enemy further because the cavalry had not been able to hold their course and reach the island.
12. No time was left for fortifying the camp.

B

Ubi, "*when*": *H. L., 259, 4 : R. C., 119.*

Indirect Question: H. L., 200 : R. C., 362.

Qui *Final: H. L., 232, 2 : R. C., 424.*

1. When Caesar learned through scouts that the forces of the enemy had encamped on a high hill, he sent his lieutenant to find out by what route he could most easily and quickly reach them.
2. He left two cohorts to serve as a guard for the bridge.

3. Being informed of these facts, he sent forward the cavalry to aid the allies, (while) he himself with the rest of the forces made a quick march of five miles and attacked the enemy while they were crossing the river.

4. The cavalry, being defeated by the enemy, retreated to the camp, but the infantry, having obtained a position admirably fortified, held out for more than three hours.

EXERCISE XXIX

Caesar v, 10

A

1. On the morning of the following day the cavalry were sent to pursue those who had fled.
2. We will pursue those who ravaged our lands and burned our villages.
3. Cavalry reported to Caesar that on the previous night a great storm had arisen.
4. The storm shattered nearly all the merchant ships.
5. After advancing some distance, they saw that cavalry were coming from Caesar.
   No ship could endure such a storm.
6. All the ships were shattered and many were cast up on shore.

B

1. On the following day Caesar ordered the cavalry to set out along with him for the purpose of laying waste the fields of the enemy.
2. When the rear of the enemy came in (= into) sight, our general sent forward the cavalry to attack the enemy, and ordered his lieutenants to lead the rest of the forces against the Remi who were coming up to their aid.
3. Ambassadors came to promise to give hostages and to do what Caesar had commanded.
4. Caesar knew that, if a storm should arise, the vessels would be shattered and great damage sustained.

EXERCISE XXX

Caesar v, 11

A

1. The legions were recalled and ordered to halt on the march.
2. As has been shown above, about forty ships were lost.
3. The rest of the ships could not be repaired.
4. He ordered all the ships to be beached.
5. He ordered the workmen, whom he had chosen from the legions, to build as many ships as possible.

6. The legions returned to the same place from which they had set out.
7. After beaching the ships and strongly fortifying the camp, these two legions returned to the hills.
8. Three cohorts and two hundred horse were left to guard the ships.
9. The territory of this chief was eighty miles distant from the sea.
10. They will place him in command of the legion.
11. This man's brother had been in command of two legions.

B

When Caesar learned that so many ships had been lost, he concluded that it was not safe for his men to advance farther into the enemy's country. Accordingly the legions and cavalry were recalled, and he himself returned to the seacoast as fast as he could. On his arrival there, he at once gave instructions to his officers to build as many ships as possible, and warned them not to allow the soldiers to go outside the fortifications. Since he knew that very large forces of Britons had assembled there, he was afraid lest they should make an attack on our camp when he himself was absent.

EXERCISE XXXI
Caesar v, 15
A

1. Our cavalry engaged in a fierce battle with the cavalry and charioteers of the enemy.
2. When the cavalry and charioteers were routed, the infantry fled into the woods and hills.
3. After routing their infantry, our men pursued the charioteers too far and lost some of their own men.
4. While the enemy were off their guard, our men suddenly rushed out of the camp.
5. The enemy made a fierce attack upon those who were posted on sentry duty before the camp.
6. Two cohorts were sent as a reinforcement to our men.
7. All our men got back to the camp in safety.
8. Inasmuch as our men were terrified by these unusual tactics, the enemy very boldly burst through our line.
9. Two military tribunes were among the slain in that engagement.

B
Consecutive Clauses: H. L., 203: R. C., 371.

Conditional Clauses: H. L., 249; 250: R. C., 477-478.

1. Our cavalry engaged so fiercely in battle with the enemy's cavalry that two thousand of the latter were slain and the rest driven into the woods and hills.

2. Our men would not have lost so many of their number if they had not pursued so eagerly.

3. If two cohorts had not been sent up as a reinforcement, the enemy would not have been defeated.

4. If Caesar defeats the enemy, they will escape into the woods.

5. If the enemy should take up their position on that hill, Caesar would attack them.

6. If our men had not been so terrified, the enemy would not have got off in safety.

7. If they make an attack on those posted before the camp, they will easily win a victory.

8. Our men were so terrified by the horses and chariots of the enemy, that they did not fight as boldly as usual.

EXERCISE XXXII
Caesar v, 16
A

1. The battle took place in front of the camp.
2. Our men could not pursue the retreating enemy far.
3. They will not dare to go far away from the standards.
4. The enemy sometimes retreated purposely.
5. Our men advanced across the marsh at great risk.
6. They tried to draw our men away from the legions.
7. It was their custom to leap down from the chariots and fight on foot.
8. They will never fight in close order and will relieve one another in turn.
9. Our men being weary were not able to defeat the fresh and vigorous (troops of the) enemy.
10. Shall we contend in unequal combat?
11. Did not the enemy leap down from their chariots?

B

Causal Clauses: H. L., 252, 1, 2: R. C., 397.

Repeated Acts in the Past: H. L., 263, 8: R. C., 119.

Conditional Clauses: H. L., 249; 250: R. C., 477-478.

1. Caesar perceived that our men fought at great risk, because the enemy sometimes retreated purposely, in order that they might draw our men away from the legions.

2. Whenever our men departed from the standards, the enemy would attack them more boldly.

3. The enemy used to leap down from their chariots whenever they drew off our men a little from the standards.

4. If our men had been able to pursue the enemy with cavalry, they would have slain a great number of them.

5. If our men dare to leave the standards, the charioteers will try to surround them.

6. If the enemy would not retreat purposely, our men would soon defeat them.

EXERCISE XXXIII

Caesar v, 17

A

1. On the following day; on the day before; at mid-day; in the morning; at midnight; in the previous summer.

2. For the purpose of plundering and foraging; an opportunity of sending hostages; for the purpose of freeing themselves, (1) ad ; (2) causa; a reason for departing; an opportunity of rallying—of halting—of leaping down from chariots; an end of pursuing.

3. At daybreak our men will take up their position on the top of the hill.

4. The enemy soon began to attack our cavalry and more fiercely than on the day before.

5. Three legions and all the cavalry were sent by Caesar for the purpose of devastating.

6. The enemy made a fierce attack and our men were driven from the hill.

7. Trusting to the support of the infantry, the cavalry drove the enemy from the hills, on which they had taken up their position the previous day.

8. Auxiliaries will assemble from all sides.

9. Caesar will assemble auxiliaries from all the states.

10. We engaged the enemy with all our forces.

B

Consecutive Clauses : H. L., 236 : R. C., 371.

Cum, *meaning since : H. L., 204, 3 : R. C., 397.*

Dum, Quoad, *meaning until : H. L., 259, 7.*

Cum, *narrative : H. L., 262, 4 : R. C., 397.*

1. Since we see that the infantry are following closely, we shall not stop pursuing the enemy nor shall we give them any opportunity of halting, until we drive them out of our territory.

2. Since our men gave the enemy no opportunity of rallying, a large number of them were slain.

3. When the enemy had made a fierce attack on our legions, and had killed quite a number of them, they leaped down from their chariots, and drove our men in headlong flight.

4. Our men were so hard pressed by the enemy's cavalry, that Caesar sent the tenth legion to their support.

EXERCISE XXXIV

Caesar v, 18

A

1. On learning their plan, Caesar ordered the lieutenants to lead the army back into camp.
2. This river could be crossed at one place only on foot.
3. All the forces of the enemy were drawn up on the other bank.
4. When Caesar got this information from the captives, he sent forward the cavalry, and ordered the legions to follow closely.
5. The enemy will not be able to withstand the assault of our legions.
6. With difficulty he crossed the river at this point.
7. After leading his army into their territory, he saw that the enemy would not long remain in their towns and villages.
8. He will send forward the cavalry. The legions will follow closely.
9. He thought that the legions would follow closely
10. The soldiers were not able to cross the river on foot.

B

On his arrival at the river bank, he learned from the cavalry, whom he had sent ahead, that large forces of the enemy had been led into the territory of our allies for the purpose of devastating their lands. Accordingly he left one legion and two hundred cavalry to guard the camp, and he himself set out with the rest of the forces to a place where he knew the river could be crossed on foot. Though the soldiers advanced with great speed, the enemy heard of their arrival, and, leaving all their baggage behind, consigned themselves to flight.

EXERCISE XXXV

Caesar v, 19

A

1. We have shown above that this chief had disbanded the greater part of his forces.
2. About four thousand charioteers were left.
3. They kept withdrawing a little from the road by which they had learned we would march.
4. Our cavalry frequently scattered over the country for the purpose of plundering and devastating.
5. Our cavalry could engage with the enemy only at great risk.
6. The charioteers of the enemy prevented our men from wandering too widely.

7. Caesar did not allow his men to go away far from the line of the legions.

8. We shall not allow you to harm our neighbors.

9. We shall do harm to the enemy's lands. They have injured us.

B

Repeated Acts in the Past: H. L., 263, 8: R. C., 119.

Substantive Clauses of Result: H. L., 244, 1: R. C., 424.

1. Whenever our cavalry withdrew a little from the road, they would hide in woody places.

2. Whenever Caesar sent cavalry ahead to plunder and forage, they would send charioteers against them from the woods.

3. The result of this was (244, 1 (*b*)) that our men did not go far away from the line of the legions.

4. The result of this was that the soldiers could not do the enemy much harm by devastating their fields.

5. When Caesar saw that his cavalry were engaging with the enemy's cavalry at great risk, he did not allow them to advance farther.

EXERCISE XXXVI

Caesar v, 20

A

1. In the meantime this tribe, which was the strongest in that district, sends ambassadors to Caesar.

2. One chief had come to him on the continent.

3. His father had for a long time held sovereign power in that state.

4. They will surrender to him. He surrendered to me. Many surrendered.

5. They promise to surrender to him and obey his orders.

6. They will promise to send ambassadors.

7. Caesar protected this chief and sent him into the state.

8. He was long at the head of this state.

9. They will be in command of this legion.

10. He will demand forty hostages from them.

11. They very quickly carried out his orders.

12. They sent the required number of hostages and corn for the army.

B

Substantive Clauses of Purpose : H. L., 239 ; 240 : R. C., 424.

Qui *Final : H. L., 232, 2 : R. C., 424.*

Dum, *while* : *H. L., 259, 5 : R. C., 273.*

1. While Caesar is marching into the territory of this tribe, this young man, whose father had long held sovereign power in this state, came to our camp.

2. He said that his father had been killed by Cassivelaunus, who was secretly gathering forces in order to drive the Romans out of that district.

3. They intreated Caesar to protect them and send an army into that district to prevent the enemy from destroying their towns.

4. Caesar sent a young man into the state to be at its head and hold the sovereign power.

5. They were advised to send the requisite number of hostages and at once surrender to Caesar.

EXERCISE XXXVII

Caesar v, 21

A

1. They had already surrendered to him. Many promised to surrender.

2. Embassies will be sent. Embassies had been sent.

3. Their town was not far distant from our camp.

4. Into this town, which was no more than three miles distant, a very large number of people had assembled.

5. They are assembling. We will assemble. Many had assembled.

6. This place was fortified with a rampart and trench.

7. They were in the habit of assembling at this place for the purpose of avoiding an attack.

8. He set out there immediately with two legions.

9. The place was admirably fortified both naturally and artificially.

10. After delaying a short time, the enemy fled into the woods and marshes.

11. They reported that the place was splendidly fortified.

12. Word was brought that a large number had been caught in flight and killed.

B

Although Caesar found the place strongly fortified, nevertheless he determined to assault it from two quarters. As soon as the legions had been drawn up in front of the walls, the enemy saw that they could not long withstand the assault of our men and at once rushed out of another part of the town. From those, who were captured in flight, Caesar learned that there was a fortified town about three miles distant and that many had fled there so as to avoid (233, 5) being captured and put to death.

EXERCISE XXXVIII

Caesar v, 22

A

1. Four kings held sway over these districts.
2. They collected all their forces, and attacked the naval camp unexpectedly.
3. Our men made a sally, killed a large number of them, even took their leader prisoner, and brought back their own men in safety.
4. We returned to the camp in safety.
5. They will send ambassadors to treat for surrender.
6. Since so many losses had been sustained, and his territory had been devastated, he determined to at once surrender.
7. Alarmed by the sudden arrival of our army, they threw away their arms and fled.
8. Caesar decided to spend the winter in Gaul.
9. He was aware that the enemy would attack the naval camp.
10. He was informed that they had collected all their forces.
11. When news of this battle reached them, the chiefs decided to surrender.

B

1. On their arrival at the camp, they decided on an immediate assault.
2. Since they were aware that Caesar was anxious to return to the continent, they determined to collect all their forces, and not allow our men to leave the place.
3. He decided how many hostages they should give, and where they should send them.
4. The lieutenants issued orders to their men not to leave the camp.
5. These chiefs advised their neighbors not to give hostages to Caesar, since they knew that he could not stay much longer on the island.

EXERCISE XXXIX

Caesar v, 23

A

1. The army was led back to the seacoast.
2. The ships had already been repaired.
3. These ships were launched ; the others were beached.
4. Neither this nor the previous year was a single ship lost.
5. These ships were sent back to him empty, after the soldiers had been landed from them.
6. The soldiers were soon landed.   He quickly landed the soldiers.
7. How many soldiers landed from these ships ?
8. Labienus superintended the construction of these ships.
9. The officers took charge of the landing of the soldiers.
10. Caesar waited for these ships for quite a while.
11. He set sail at the beginning of the second watch.
12. All the ships reached the contiuent in safety at daybreak.
13. The rest of the ships were driven back.
14. After landing the soldiers, he fortified the camp with a rampart and trench.

B

1. When these vessels were launched, he decided to leave part of the army in Britain, because so many of the vessels. whose construction Labienus had superintended, had been lost tnrough the storm.
2. It so happened that almost all the ships, which had soldiers on board, reached the continent in safety.
3. Caesar waited for these ships for some time in vain, but at last fearing (243, 2) that he might be forced to spend the winter in Britain, he set sail in person with twenty ships and ordered his lieutenants to follow with the rest as soon as they could.

SIGHT TRANSLATION

Introduction

BOOK I

Before resigning his consulship at the end of 59 B.C., Caesar was invested with proconsular power for five years over the two Gauls and over Illyricum. The Gauls were always a turbulent people, torn by factions and dissensions, and were also a constant menace to the Romans of the Province (Provincia) which occupied the southern part of the Rhone valley. The dangers, however, which threatened the Romans at this time did not come so much from the Gauls, as from two other quarters, namely, from the Helvetii, a tribe which occupied what is now Switzerland, and from the German chief Ariovistus.

The events in *B.* I naturally fall into two divisions :

(1) The campaign against the Helvetii : chap. 1-30 ;

(2) The campaign against Ariovistus : chap. 31 to end.

The Helvetii were old foes of the Romans. In 107 B.C. they had joined forces with the Cimbri and had defeated the Romans. The latter were fully aware that this might happen a second time. As early as 61 B.C. news reached Rome of the intended migration of the Helvetii, but their departure was delayed by the death of their leader, Orgetorix. At last in 58 B.C. they made full preparations for setting out from their homes and moving into southwestern Gaul. They gathered provisions, burned their villages, and with their whole population were on their way to the rich plains of Aquitania. Of the two routes which they might take, the more difficult lay through the territories of the Sequani ; the other, easier and more direct, was through the Roman Provincia. The Helvetii decided to go by the latter route, and by the end of March were already starting on their journey. Within a week Caesar was at Genâva (*Geneva*), levied an army in the *Provincia* and broke down the bridge over the Rhine. He thus hemmed in the Helvetii between Mt. Jura and the Lake of Geneva. Checked by works that Caesar constructed, they turned into the territory of the Sequani, who allowed them to pass ; and they then attempted to enter the territory of the Haedui. The Haedui had been

132

friendly to the Romans, and Caesar, deciding to defend his allies, cut to pieces one canton of the Helvetii. Caesar was, however, hampered by lack of provisions. The Haedui had promised grain but it had not yet arrived, and they were constantly putting off Caesar by fair promises which naturally aroused his suspicions. He soon found out that politics were at the bottom of this delay. The Haeduan state was torn by rival parties, one led by Dumnorix, and the other by his brother Divitiacus, a high official. Caesar, for the present, reprimanded Dumnorix, and provisions were obtained. Finally Caesar overtook the Helvetii and signally defeated them at Bibracte (*Autun*).

After the defeat of the Helvetii, the Haedui invited Caesar to assist them in driving out the Germans under Ariovistus. Two factions stirred up Gaul, one led by the Haedui, friendly to Rome, the other headed by the Arverni and Sequani, opposed to Rome. The two latter tribes had invited Ariovistus, a German chief, to assist them in the conquest of Gaul. After fruitless negotiations between Caesar and Ariovistus, the two armies met near *Basle*, and Ariovistus was defeated.

Gaul and its divisions (*B.* I, 1).

Gallia est omnis divisa in partes tres; quarum unam incolunt[1] Belgae, aliam Aquitani, tertiam, qui ipsorum lingua Celtae, nostrā Galli appellantur. Hi omnes linguā, institutis, legibus inter se differunt. Gallos ab Aquitanis Garumna flumen, a Belgis Matrona[2] et Sequana[3] dividit. Horum omnium fortissimi sunt Belgae, propterea quod a cultu[4] atque humanitate[5] provinciae longissime absunt, minimeque ad eos mercatores saepe[6] commeant[7] atque ea, quae ad effeminandos animos[8] pertinent, important; proximique sunt Germanis, qui trans Rhenum incolunt, quibuscum continenter bellum gerunt. Quā de causā Helvetii quoque reliquos Gallos virtute praecedunt, quod fere cotidianis[9] proeliis cum Germanis contendunt, cum aut suis finibus eos[10] prohibent, aut ipsi in eorum finibus bellum gerunt.

---

[1]inhabit. [2]the Marne. [3]the Seine. [4]mode of life. [5]civilization. [6]minimē saepe = very seldom. [7]go, resort. [8]to weaken their courage. [9]daily. [10]the Germans.

II

Orgetorix, chief of the Helvetii, persuades his countrymen to leave their homes (*B.* I, 2).

Apud Helvetios longe nobilissimus et ditissimus fuit Orgetorix. Is, Marco Messala et Marco Pisone consulibus, regni cupiditate inductus, conjurationem[1] nobilitatis fecit et civitati persuasit ut de suis finibus cum omnibus copiis exirent : (dixit) perfacile esse, cum virtute omnibus praestarent, totius Galliae imperio potiri. Id hoc facilius eis persuasit, quod undique loci natura Helvetii continentur[2] : una ex[3] parte flumine Rheno, latissimo atque altissimo, qui agrum Helvetiorum a Germanis dividit : altera ex parte monte Jura altissimo, qui est inter Sequanos et Helvetios ; tertia, lacu Lemanno et flumine Rhodano, qui Provinciam nostram ab Helvetiis dividit.

---

[1]league, in which the members swear fidelity to each other (con, together, and juro, swear). [2]are confined by the character of their country. [3]on.

III

Caesar overtakes a part of the Helvetii and defeats them (*B.* I, 12).

Flumen est Arar[1], quod per fines Haeduorum et Sequanorum in Rhodanum influit, incredibili lenitate ita ut oculos in utram partem[2] fluat judicari non possit. Id Helvetii ratibus ac lintribus junctis transibant. Ubi per exploratores Caesar certior factus est, tres jam copiarum partes Helvetios id flumen transduxisse, quartam vero partem citra flumen Ararim reliquam esse, de[3] tertia vigilia cum legionibus tribus e castris profectus ad eam partem pervenit quae nondum flumen transierat. Eos impeditos et inopinantes[4] aggressus magnam eorum partem concidit[5]: reliqui fugae sese mandaverunt atque in proximas silvas abdiderunt.

---

[1]the Saône. [2]direction. [3]in the course of. [4]off their guard. [5]concīdō, ere, -cīdī, -cīsum, cut to pieces.

IV

Caesar meets with a reverse and follows the Helvetii cautiously (*B.* I, 15).

Postero die castra ex eo loco movent. Idem facit Caesar equitatumque omnem ad numerum quattuor millium, quem ex omni provincia et Haeduis atque eorum sociis coactum[1] habebat, praemittit qui videant quas in partes hostes iter faciant. Qui cupidius[2] novissimum agmen[3] insecuti alieno[4] loco cum equitatu Helvetiorum proelium committunt; et pauci de nostris cadunt. Quo proelio sublati[5] Helvetii, quod quingentis equitibus tantam multitudinem equitum propulerant, audacius subsistere nonnunquam et novissimo agmine nostros lacessere coeperunt. Caesar suos a proelio continebat, ac satis habebat in praesentia[6] hostem rapinis,[7] pabulationibus[8] populationibusque[9] prohibere. Ita dies circiter quindecim iter fecerunt uti[10] inter novissimum hostium agmen et nostrum primum[11] non amplius quinis aut senis millibus passuum interesset.[12]

[1]cōgō, -ere, coēgī, coactum, collect. [2]too eagerly. [3]the rear. [4]unfavorable. [5]elated: perf. part. pass. of tollō, -ere, sustulī, sublātum. [6]held it sufficient for the time being. [7]plundering. [8]foraging. [9]raiding. [10]uti=ut. [11]primum sc. agmen, the van. [12]intersum, -esse, -fuī, be between.

V

Caesar advances against the enemy (*B.* I, 21).

Eodem die ab exploratoribus certior factus hostes sub monte consedisse[1] millia passuum ab ipsius castris octo, qualis esset natura[2] montis et qualis ascensus[3], qui cognoscerent, misit. Renuntiatum est facilem esse. De[4] tertia vigilia Titum Labienum legatum cum duabus legionibus et iis ducibus,[5] qui iter cognoverant, summum jugum[6] montis ascendere jubet;

quid sui consilii sit osténdit. Ipse de quarta vigilia eodem itinere, quo hostes ierant, ad eos contendit, equitatumque omnem ante se mittit. Publius. Considius, qui rei militaris peritissimus habebatur[7] et in exercitu Lucii Sullae et postea in Marci Crassi fuerat cum exploratoribus praemittitur.

[1]consīdō, -ere, -sēdī, -sessum, encamp.   [2]character.   [3]ascent.   [4]after. [5]guides.   [6]ridge.   [7]was considered.

VI
Caesar prepares for battle with the Helvetii
(B I, 24).

Postquam id animadvertit[1], suas copias Caesar in proximum collem subducit[2], equitatumque qui sustineret[3] hostium impetum misit. Ipse interim in colle medio triplicem aciem instruxit legionum quattuor veteranarum[4], ita uti[5] supra se in summo jugo duas legiones, quas in Gallia citeriore proxime conscripserat[6], et omnia auxilia collocaret[7], ac totum montem hominibus compleret[8]; interim sarcinas[9] in unum locum conferri et eum ab his qui in superiore acie constiterant[10] muniri jussit. Helvetii cum omnibus suis carris[11] secuti impedimenta in unum locum contulerunt; ipsi confertissimā[12] acie, rejecto[13] nostro equitatu et phalange[14] facta, sub primam nostram aciem successerunt[15].

[1]animadvertō, -ere, -vertī, -versum, notice.   [2]lead up.   [3]sustineō, -ere, -tinuī, -tentum, check.   [4]veterānus, -a, -um, veteran.   [5]so that (uti = ut) join with collocāret.   [6]con-scrībō, enrol.   [7]place.   [8]com-pleō, -plēre, -plēvī, -plētum, fill.   [9]sarcina, -ae, baggage carried by individual soldiers = packs; impedīmenta, baggage of legion not carried by the soldiers.   [10]con-sistō, -sistere, -stitī, no sup, take up position.   [11]carrus, ī-, cart.   [12]confertus, -a, -um, dense, closely crowded.   [13]re-jicio, -jicĕre, -jēcī, -jectum, drive back, repel.   [14]phalanx, phalangis, F., solid mass in close order.   [15]succēdō, -cēdere, -cessī, -cessum, advance.

BOOK II

Belgic Campaign, 57 B.C.

The campaign of 57 B.C. is marked by the signal defeat of the tribes of the Belgic confederacy. The Belgae occupied northeastern Gaul, *i.e.*, the country between the Sequana *(Seine)* and the Rhenus *(Rhine)*, roughly speaking, part of France bordering on Belgium, the whole of Belgium, and part of Holland west of the Rhine. In the time of Caesar that part of Europe was covered by extensive swamps and impenetrable forests. It was, however, peopled by a race fond of freedom and, therefore, difficult to conquer. The tribes inhabiting this district were rather of Germanic than of Celtic origin.

Caesar estimates the number of the fighting force of the enemy at about 250,000 men, while his own force opposed to them, numbering eight[1] legions, would hardly be more than one tenth that number.

In a hurried march from Cisalpine Gaul, Caesar set out against them. Only the Remi were friendly and these were attacked by the other tribes but were relieved by Caesar. Advancing to the Axona *(Aisne)* he left six cohorts to guard the bridge. He occupied successively Bibron, Noviodunum and Bratuspantium. After these towns were captured, he fought one of his severest battles against the Nervii, near the river Sabis, in which the defeat of the Roman army was prevented by the personal courage and coolness of the general. Finally the Aduatuci were reduced to submission.

---

[1] In the year 58 B.C. in his first campaign against the Helvetii and Ariovistus, Caesar had *six* legions: the 10th he formed in Gaul: the 11th and 12th he enrolled in the *Provincia*: three he obtained from Aquileia in northeastern Gallia Cisalpina, the 7th, the 8th, the 9th ; in 57 B.C. he enrolled the 13th and the 14th in Cisalpine Gaul.

VII

Caesar marches against the Belgae *(B. II, 2)*.

His nuntiis litterisque commotus[1] Caesar duas legiones in citeriore Gallia novas conscripsit, et inita[2] aestate in interiorem Galliam qui deduceret Quintum Pedium legatum misit. Ipse, cum primum pabuli[3] copia esse inciperet[4] ad exercitum venit. Dat negotium[5] Senonibus reliquisque Gallis qui finitimi Belgis erant, uti[6] ea quae apud eos gerantur cognoscant seque de

his rebus certiorem faciant. Hi constanter omnes nuntiave-
runt manūs cogi[7], exercitum in unum locum conduci. Tum
vero dubitandum[8] non existimavit quin ad eos proficisceretur.
Re frumentariā comparatā castra movet, diebusque circiter
quindecim ad fines Belgarum pervenit.

---

[1]com-moveō, -movēre, -mōvī, -mōtum, influence.   [2]in-eō, -īre,
-iī (-īvī), -itum, enter into : perf. part. pass. ; translate : *"in the
beginning of summer."*   [3]pabulum, -ī, fodder.   [4]in-cipiō, -cipĕre, -cēpī,
-ceptum, begin.   [5]task.   [6]uti = ut.   [7]cōgō, cogere, coegī, coactum,
muster.   [8]supply sibi esse : *"that he should delay."*

VIII

Caesar marches to relieve the Remi (*B*. II, 7).

Eo[1] de[2] mediā nocte Caesar iisdem ducibus usus qui nuntii
ab Iccio[3] venerant, Numidas et Cretas sagittarios[4] et fundi
tores[5] Baleares subsidio[6] oppidanis[7] mittit ; quorum adventu
et Remis studium propugnandi[8] accessit[9], et hostibus eadem
de causa spes potiundi[10] oppidi discessit. Itaque paulisper[11]
apud oppidum morati[12] agrosque Remorum depopulati, omnibus vicis[13] aedificiisque quos adire potuerant incensis, ad
castra Caesaris omnibus copiis contenderunt et ab millibus
passuum minus duobus[14] castra posuerunt ; quae castra, ut
fumo[15] atque ignibus significabatur,[16] amplius millibus passuum octo in latitudinem patebant.

---

[1]to that place, thither.   [2]after.   [3]a nobleman of the Remi.   [4]Crēs
Crētis, a Cretan, a native of Crete.   [4]sagittārius, -ī, bowman.
[5]funditor, -ōris, slinger.   [6]subsidium, -ī, help.   [7]oppidān-us, -ī, (pl.)
townspeople (of Bibron).   [8]eagerness for a defence.   [9]ac-cēdō, -cēdere,
-cessī, cessum, come to : trans. was inspired in the Remi.   [10]gerun
dive : potior, potīrī, potitus sum, gain.   [11]for a short time.   [12]moror,
-ārī, -ātus, delay.   [13]vīcus, -ī, village.   [14]less than two miles off.
[15]fūmus, -ī, smoke.   [16]significō, show.

IX

Caesar marches against the Nervii, a tribe in the north-east of Gallia Transalpina (*B.* II, 16).

"That day he overcame the Nervii."—*Shakespeare.*

Cum per eorum fines triduum[1] iter fecisset, inveniebat ex captivis Sabim[2] flumen ab castris suis non amplius millia passuum decem abesse; trans id flumen omnes Nervios consedisse adventumque ibi Romanorum exspectare una cum Atrebatibus et Veromanduis, finitimis suis (nam his atrisque persuaserant uti eandem belli fortunam experirentur)[3]; exspectari etiam ab his Aduatucorum copias atque esse in itinere; mulieres quique per aetatem ad pugnam inutiles viderentur in eum[4] locum conjecisse[5], quo[6] propter paludes[7] exercitui aditus non esset.

---

[1]three days. [2]Sabis, -is, a river in north-eastern Gaul, now the *Sambre*. [3]ex-perior, -perīrī, -pertus, try. [4]a. [5]station; supply **eos** as subject. [6]whither=to which. [7]palus, -udis, marsh.

X

Caesar's soldiers equal to an emergency (*B.* II, 20).

NOTE:—Carefully read the uses of the gerundive, H. L., p. 187.

Caesari omnia uno tempore erant agenda; vexillum[1] proponendum[2] (quod erat insigne[3] cum ad arma concurri[4] oporteret), signum tubā[5] dandum, ab opere revocandi milites, ii qui paulo longius aggeris petendi causā[6] processerant arcessendi,[7] acies instruenda, milites cohortandi.[8] Quarum rerum magnam partem temporis brevitas et incursus[9] hostium impediebat. His difficultatibus duae res erant subsidio,[10]— scientia[11] atque usus[12] militum, quod superioribus proeliis

exercitati, quid fieri oporteret ipsi sibi praescribere[13] poterant;
et quod ab opere singulisque legionibus singulos legatos Caesar
discedere nisi munitis castris vetuerat[14].

[1]banner.   [2]pro-pōnō, -pōnere, -posui, -positum, hang out: supply
fuit. [3]insigne, -is, N. signal.   [4]con-curro, -currere, currī, -cursum,
rush.   [5]trumpet.   [6]for the purpose of seeking material for the mound.
[7]arcesso, -ere, arcessivī, arcessitum, summon.   [8]co-hortor, -hortārī,
-hortātus, address.   [9]onset.   [10]subsidium, -ī, help.   [11]skill.   [12]ex-
perience.   [13]praescribō, -ere, -scripsī, -scriptum, give directions.   [14]veto,
are, -uī, -itum, forbid.

XI

A thanksgiving is decreed at Rome in honor
of Caesar (B. II; 35).

His rebus gestis, omni Galliā pacatā,[1] tanta hujus belli ad
barbaros opinio[2] perlata[3] est uti[4] ab his nationibus quae trans
Rhenum incolerent mitterentur legati ad Caesarem qui se
obsides daturas, imperata facturas pollicerentur.   Quas
legationes Caesar, quod in Italiam Illyricumque properabat,
initā proximā aestate[5] ad se reverti[6] jussit.   Ipse, in Carnutes,
Andes, Turonesque, quae civitates propinquae his locis erant
ubi bellum gesserat, legionibus in hiberna deductis[7], in
Italiam profectus est.   Ob easque res ex litteris Caesaris dies
quindecim supplicatio[8] decreta[9] est, quod ante id tempus
accidit nulli.

[1]pācō, -āre, -āvī, -ātum, pacify.   [2]impression.   [3]per-ferō, -ferre,
-tulī, -lātum, spread.   [4]uti = ut.   [5]See VII.   [6]revertor, revertī, dep.
in present tenses, perf. revertī, reversum, return.   [7]dē-duco, -dūcere,
duxī, -ductum, withdraw.   [8]thanksgiving.   [9]decerno, -ere, -crēvī,
-crētum, decree.

BOOK III (56 B.C.).

The third campaign in Gaul (56 B.C.) naturally falls into three divisions: (1) the campaign against the Alpine tribes (chapters 1-6); (2)
the Venetic War (chapters 7-19); (3) the campaign against the Aquitani (chapters 20-29).

The valleys of the Alps leading to Italy were inhabited by predatory
tribes who gained a scanty living by working the mines, and exacting

tolls from people passing through their lands. From the days of Hannibal to those of Caesar these wild mountaineers had been a constant menace to the Roman armies who had occasion to pass from Italy to Gaul. Already two legions under Quintus Pedius (*B.* II, 2), had been attacked. The present expedition was undertaken to strike terror into the hearts of the barbarians in order to prevent the recurrence of a similar attack.

The Veneti were a people of Brittany, in north-western France. They were a nation of hardy mariners. They were fond of freedom and adventure. Their country was rugged, rocky and precipitous, with bold headlands on which their towns were perched. To subdue them, Caesar caused a fleet to be built at the mouth of the Loire. They were finally defeated in a naval battle fought in the Bay of Quiberon.

The campaign against the Aquitani seems to have been fought simply to complete the conquest of Gaul, for they had been, so far, a peaceable people.

XII

A new route to Italy (*B.* III, 1).

Cum in Italiam proficisceretur Caesar, Servium. Galbam cum legione duodecima et parte equitatus in Veragros misit, qui ab finibus Allobrogum ad summas Alpes pertinent. Causa mittendi fuit quod iter per Alpes, quo magno cum periculo magnisque cum portoriis[1] mercatores ire consueverant, pate-fieri[2] volebat. Huic permisit, si opus esse[3] arbitraretur, uti[4] in eis locis legionem hiemandi causā collocaret. Galba, secundis[5] aliquot proeliis factis castellisque[6] compluribus eorum expugnatis, missis ad eum undique legatis obsidibusque datis et pace facta, constituit cohortes duas ibi collocare et ipse cum reliquis ejus legionis cohortibus in vico Veragrorum[7], qui appellatur Octodurus, hiemare ; qui vicus positus in valle, non magna adjectā[8] planitie, altissimis montibus undique continetur.

---

[1]portōrium, -ī, N. (generally in plural) toll. [2]pass. of **pate-faciō**, open. [3]to be necessary. [4]uti = ut. [5]secund-us, -a, -um, successful. [6]castellum, -ī, N., fortress. [7]Veragrī, -ōrum, N. pl. Veragri, an Alpine tribe. [8]adjectus, -a, -um. (perf. part. of adjiciō) used as an adj., adjacent.

XIII

The Romans saved by a sortie (*B.* III, 5).

Cum jam amplius horis sex continenter[1] pugnaretur, ac non solum vires[2] sed etiam tela nostros deficerent[3], atque hostes acrius instarent[4], languidioribusque[5] nostris vallum[6] scindere[7] et fossas complere-coepissent, resque esset jam ad extremum perducta casum[8], Publius Sextus Baculus, quem Nervico proelio compluribus confectum vulneribus diximus, et item Caius Volusenus, vir et consilii magni et virtutis, ad Galbam accurrunt atque unam esse spem salutis docent, si eruptione[9] factā extremum auxilium[10] experirentur. Itaque, convocatis centurionibus, celeriter militibus imperat ut paulisper inter-mitterent[11] proelium, ac tantummodo[12] tela missa exciperent[13] seque ex labore reficerent; post, dato signo, ex castris erum-perent atque omnem spem salutis in virtute ponerent.

---

[1] without interruption. [2] pl. of **vis**, strength. [3] dēficiō, 3, -fēcī, -fec-tum, fail. [4] instō, 1, -stitī, -stātum, press on. [5] as our men grew feebler. [6] palisade, rampart. [7] scindō, -ere, scidī, scissum, tear down. [8] and when the battle had been brought to a final crisis. [9] ēruptiō, -ōnis, sally. [10] last resource. [11] discontinue. [12] merely. [13] *i e.*, on their shields.

XIV

Caesar's motives for making war (*B.* III, 10).

Erant hae difficultates belli gerendi quas supra diximus, sed multa Caesarem tamen ad id bellum incitabant[1]: injuriae retentorum equitum[2] Romanorum, rebellio[3] facta post dedi-tionem, defectio[4] datis obsidibus, tot civitatum conjuratio, in primis ne[5], hac parte[6] neglectā, reliquae nationes ĭdem sibi licēre[7] arbitrarentur. Itaque cum intellegeret omnes fere Gallos novis rebus studere[8] et ad bellum celeriter excitari,

omnes autem homines naturā libertati studere[8] et condicionem
servitutis odisse, priusquam plures civitates conspirarent[9],
partiendum[10] sibi ac latius distribuendum[11] exercitum putavit.

[1]urged. [2]wrongs done by detaining the cavalry. [3]renewal of
hostilities. [4]revolt. [5]supply timor. [6]district. [7]licet, licēre, licuit
(impersonal), it is allowed, "*the same course was lawful for them.*"
[8]to be eager for. [9]formed a league. [10]partior, -īrī, -ītus sum, divide.
[11]distribuo, -ere, -tribuī, -tribūtum, distribute.

XV

The naval battle against the Veneti (*B.* III, 14).

Compluribus expugnatis oppidis, Caesar, ubi intellexit
frustra[1] tantum laborem sumi[2], hostium fugam captis oppidis
non reprimi[3], statuit exspectandam classem. Quae ubi convenit ac primum ab hostibus visa est, circiter ducentae et
viginti naves eorum paratissimae atque omni genere armorum
ornatissimae[4], profectae ex portu, nostris adversae constiterunt[5]; neque satis Bruto, qui classi praeerat, constabat[6] quam
rationem pugnae insisterent[7]. Una erat magno usui res
praeparata a nostris—falces praeacutae[8]. His cum funes[9] qui
antennas[10] ad malos[11] destinabant[12] comprehensi adductique[13]
erant, navigio[14] remis incitato, praerumpebantur[15]. Quibus
abscissis[16], antennae necessario concidebant; ut, cum omnis
Gallicis navibus spes in velis armamentisque[17] consisteret, his
ereptis omnis usus[18] navium uno tempore eriperetur.

[1]in vain. [2]sūmo, -ĕre, sumpsī, sumptum, expend. [3]re-primō,
-primere -pressī, -pressum, check. [4]fully equipped. [5]con-sistĕ, -sistere,
-stitī, take position. [6]and it was not very clear to Brutus. [7]in-sistō,
-sistĕre, -stitī, adopt. [8]falx, falcis, hook, translate: hooks sharpened to
a point. [9]ropes. [10]yardarms. [11]mālus, -ī, F. mast. [12]made fast.
[13]draw tight. [14]ship. [15]break off. [16]abscīdo, -ĕre, abścīdī, abscīsum,
tear away. [17]tackle. [18]control.

XVI

Disastrous defeat of the Gauls (*B.* III, 19).

Locus erat castrórum editus[1] et paulatim ab imo acclivis[2] circiter mille passus. Huc magno cursu hostes contenderunt, ut quam minimum spatii[3] ad se colligendos[4] armandosque Romanis daretur exanimatique[5] pervenerunt. Sabinus suos hostatus signum dat. Impeditis hostibus propter ea quae ferebant onera, subito duabus portis eruptionem fieri jubet. Factum est[6] opportunitate loci, hostium inscientiā ac defetigatione, virtute militum et superiorum pugnarum exercitatione, ut ne unum quidem nostrorum impetum ferrent ac statim terga verterent. Quos integris viribus milites nostri consecuti magnum numerum eorum occiderunt; reliquos equites nostri consectati[7] paucos reliquerunt. Civitates omnes se statim dediderunt. Nam ut ad bella suscipienda Gallorum alacer ac promptus est animus, sic mollis ac minime resistens ad calamitates perferendas mens eorum est.

---

[1]high. [2]sloping. [3]as little time as possible, subject of **daretur.** [4]colligō, 3, -lēgī, -lectum, form into a body. [5]out of breath. [6]the result was. [7]consector, 1, follow.

BOOK IV (55 B.C.).

The fourth campaign, 55 B.C., naturally falls into two divisions: (1) the campaign against the Germans : (chapters 1-19): and (2) the first expedition against Britain.

The tribes on the Gallic frontier, the Usipetes and the Tencteri, had been hard pressed by their more powerful neighbors the Suevi, and had crossed the Rhine into northern Gaul. Caesar comes forward, as he had done in the war against Ariovistus, as the defender of the Gauls. He drove back the invaders, builds a bridge, which was a marvel of engineering skill, in the incredible short space of ten days, crosses over into Germany, recrosses the Rhine and breaks down the bridge.

XVII

Customs of the Suevi (*B.* IV, 1).

Suevorum gens est longe maxima et bellicosissima Germanorum omnium. Hi centum pagos[1] habere dicuntur, ex quibus
quotannis singula millia[2] armatorum bellandi causā ex finibus
ducunt. Reliqui, qui domi manserunt, se atque illos alunt[3].
Hi rursus in vicem anno post in armis sunt, illi domi remanent
Sic neque agri cultura nec ratio atque usus[4] belli intermittitur[5].
Sed privati ac separati agri apud eos nihil est, neque longius
anno remanere, uno in loco colendi[6] causa licet.   Neque
multum frumento sed maximam partem lacte et pecore vivunt
multumque sunt in venationibus[7] ; quae res et cibi genere et
cotidianā exercitatione et libertate vitae et vires alit et
immani corporum magnitudine homines efficit.

---

[1]district, canton.   [2]each a thousand.   [3]alō, -ĕre, aluī, altum, main-
tain.   [4]ratiō, theory ; usus, practice.   [5]is interrupted.   [6]of tilling the
soil.   [7]they are much given to hunting.

XVIII

The Ubii, tributaries of the Suevi (*B.* IV, 3).

Publice[1] maximam putant esse laudem quam latissime a[2]
suis finibus vacare agros ; hac re significari magnum numerum
civitatum suam vim sustinere non posse.   Itaque unā ex
parte a Suevis[3] circiter millia passuum sexcenta agri vacare
dicuntur.   Ad alteram partem succedunt[4] Ubii quorum fuit
civitas ampla atque florens ut est captus[5] Germanorum : ei
paulo sunt, quam ejusdem generis sunt ceteri, humaniores
propterea quod Rhenum attingunt multumque ad eos mercatores ventitant et ipsi propter propinquitatem Gallicis sunt
moribus adsuefacti.[6]   Hos cum Suevi multis saepe bellis

experti[7] propter amplitudinem gravitatemque civitatis finibus expellere non potuissent, tamen vectigales[8] sibi fecerunt ac multo humiliores infirmioresque redegerunt.[9]

---

[1]as a nation. [2]on the side of. [3]from the country of the Suevi in one direction. [4]come next. [5]according to German ideas; **captus, -us**, literally, "what may be grasped." [6]conformed. [7]tried. [8]tributary. [9]**redigō -ĕre redēgī, redactum,** render.

XIX
Fickle character of the Gauls (*B.* IV, 5).

His de rebus Caesar certior factus et infirmitatem[1] Gallorum veritus, quod sunt in consiliis capiendis mobiles[2] et novis plerumque rebus student, nihil his committendum[3] existimavit. Est enim hoc Gallicae consuetudinis[4] uti[5] et viatores[6] etiam invitos[7] consistere cogant, et[8] quid quisque eorum de quaque re audierit aut cognoverit quaerant; et mercatores in oppidis vulgus circumsistat[9], quibusque ex regionibus veniant quasque ibi res cognoverint pronuntiare[10] cogat. His rumoribus atque auditionibus[11] permoti, de summis saepe rebus consilia ineunt.

---

[1]fickleness. [2]easily influenced. [3]no trust should be placed in them. [4]this is a characteristic of the Gallic custom. [5]**uti = ut**, introducing a number of result clauses in apposition with **hoc**. [6]travellers. [7]against their will. [8]Join to **quaerant**. [9]**circum-sistō, -sistĕre, -stitī,** surround. [10]tell. [11]hearsays.

XX
The course of the Rhine described (*B.* IV, 10).

Mosa[1] profluit[2] ex monte Vosego, qui est in finibus Lingonum, et parte[3] quādam ex Rheno receptā quae appellatur Vacalus[4], insulam efficit Batavorum, neque longius inde millibus passuum octoginta in Oceanum influit. Rhenus autem oritur ex Lepontiis, qui Alpes incolunt et longo spatio per fines multarum gentium[5] citatus[6] fertur; et ubi Oceano appropropropopropropropopproproproproproproproproproproproprop

proproquavit, in plures defluit partes[7] multis ingentibusque

insulis effectis, quarum pars magna a feris barbarisque
nationibus incolitur—ex quibus sunt qui piscibus[8] atque
ovis[9] avium[10] vivere existimantur,—multisque capitibus[11] in
Oceanum influit.

[1]Meuse. [2]flows. [3]tributary. [4]Waal. [5]tribes. [6]quickly. [7]branches.
[8]piscis, -is, fish. [9]ovum, -ī, egg. [10]avis, -is, bird. [11]mouths.

XXI
Gallant conduct of two brothers (*B.* IV, 12).

In eo proelio ex equitibus nostris interficiuntur quattuor
et septuaginta: in his vir fortissimus, Piso Aquitanus[1], amplissimo[2] genere natus, cujus avus[3] in civitate suā regnum
obtinuerat[4] amicus ab senatu nostro appellatus. Hic cum
fratri intercluso[5] ab hostibus auxilium ferret, illum ex periculo
eripuit[6], ipse equo vulnerato dejectus[7], quoad[8] potuit fortissime
restitit[9]; cum circumventus multis vulneribus acceptis ceci-
disset[10], atque id frater, qui jam proelio excesserat[11], procul
animadvertisset[12], incitato[13] equo se hostibus obtulit[14] atque
interfectus est.

[1]An Aquitanian, belonging to Aquitania, a division of Gaul.
[2]most illustrious. [3]grandfather. [4]had held sovereign power. [5]inter-
clūdō, -clūdere, -clūsi, -clūsum, cut off. [6]ē-ripiō, -ripĕre, -ripui,
-reptum, rescue. [7]thrown. [8]quoad, as long as. [9]re-sistō, -sistĕre,
-stitī, resist. [10]from cadō, fall. [11]had withdrawn. [12]governed by cum;
had noticed. [13]spurring on his horse. [14]he rushed against; literally,
he threw himself upon.

BOOK V (54 B.C.).

The fifth campaign naturally falls into two parts: (1) the second
expedition against Britain, and (2) the uprising in Gaul. We shall
deal with the second part.

The uprising in Gaul had been fostered by (1) the absence of Caesar
in Britain; (2) the distribution of the winter camps.

Caesar arrived in Gaul from Britain at the end of September. The
summer had been unusually dry, the crops failed and he was compelled
to separate his seven and a half legions[1] so far apart that it appeared to

[1] The fourteenth was divided, one half being drafted into other legions.

the Gauls possible to attack them individually before the one could lend aid to the other. The disturbance began with the murder of Tasgetius, a chief of the Carnutes who was friendly to Caesar. Then followed the attack upon the camp of Sabinus and Cotta stationed at Aduatuca, by Ambiorix, king of the Eburones. In the council of war divided councils prevailed. Cotta was for holding out till aid should come from Caesar. Sabinus was for starting out to try and reach the camp of Cicero. They were surrounded and cut to pieces, only a few escaping to carry the word to Labienus. Ambiorix by his success was able to rouse the Aduatuci, the Nervii and other tribes to attack the headquarters of Cicero. At length, after gallantly defending himself till his resources were almost exhausted, he was relieved by Caesar. By the prompt action of Caesar danger was openly averted; still the Treviri were secretly urging the Germans to aid them against the Romans. Caesar was compelled to spend the winter of 54-53 B.C. in Transalpine Gaul. He enrolled another legion, the fifteenth, in Gallia Cisalpina.

XXII

The murder of Tasgetius (*B.* V. 25).

Erant in Carnutibus summo loco natus[1] Tasgetius, cujus majores in suā civitate regnum obtinuerant. Huic[2] Caesar pro[3] ejus virtute atque in se benevolentia, quod in omnibus bellis singulari ejus operā[4] fuerat usus, majorum locum restituerat. Tertium jam hunc annum regnantem inimici multis palam[5] ex[6] civitate auctoribus[7] interfecerunt. Defertur[8] ea res ad Caesarem. Ille veritus, quod ad plures pertinebat[9], ne civitas eorum deficeret[10], Lucium Plancum cum legione ex Belgio celeriter in Carnutes proficisci jubet ibique hiemare, quorumque operā cognoverat Tasgetium interfectum, eos comprehensos ad se mittere. Interim ab omnibus legatis quibus legiones tradiderat[11] certior factus est, in hiberna perventum[12] locumque hibernis esse munitum.

---

[1]Compare **amplissimō genere nātus**, xvii. [2]indirect object of **restituerat**. [3]for. [4]assistance. [5]openly. [6]in. [7]auctor, -oris, abettor. [8]dēferō, -ferre, -tulī, -lātum, is reported. [9]per-tineō, -tinēre, -tinuī, -tentum, concern. [10]dēficiō, revolt. [11]trādō, hand over. [12]Supply **esse cōpiīs**, that the troops had reached the winter quarters.

XXIII

Cotta opposes leaving the camp (*B.* V, 28).

Itaque ad consilium rem deferunt[1] magnaque inter eos exsistit[2] controversia[3]. Lucius Cotta compluresque tribuni militum et primorum ordinum[4] centuriones nihil temere[5] agendum, neque ex hibernis injussu[6] Caesaris discedendum existimabant; quantasvis[7] copias etiam Germanorum sustineri posse munitis hibernis docebant; rem esse testimonio[8] quod primum hostium impetum multis ultrō[9] vulneribus illatis[10] fortissime sustinuerint; re frumentaria[11] se non premi; interea et ex proximis hibernis et a Caesare conventura subsidia; postremo, quid esse levius aut turpius quam auctore hoste[12] de summis rebus capere consilium?

---

[1] lay before. [2] ex-sistō, -sistĕre, -stitī, arise. [3] dispute. [4] ordō, inis, M., rank. [5] rashly. [6] without orders. [7] no matter how great. [8] what had happened (rem) was a proof of this. [9] even. [10] inflicted. [11] by a scarcity of corn. [12] on the suggestion of an enemy.

XXIV

The Romans decide to leave their camp (*B.* V, 31).

Consurgitur[1] ex consilio; orant milites ne dissentione[2] et pertinacia[3] rem in summum periculum deducant[4]; facilem esse rem, seu maneant seu proficiscantur, si modo unum omnes sentiant; contra in dissentione nullam se salutem perspicere. Res disputatione ad mediam noctem perducitur. Tandem dat Cotta permotus manus[5]; superat sententia Sabini. Pronuntiatur[6] se primā luce ituros. Consumitur vigiliis reliqua pars noctis, cum sua quisque miles circumspiceret, quid secum portare posset, quid ex instrumento[7] hibernorum relinquere cogeretur. Primā luce ex castris proficiscuntur.

---

[1] they rise : impersonal use of passive. [2] by disagreement. [3] obstinacy. [4] cause a most perilous situation. [5] dare manūs, yield. [6] word is given out. [7] equipment.

XXV

The massacre (*B.* V, 37).

Sabinus quos[1] in praesentia[2] tribunos militum circum se habebat et primorum ordinum centuriones se sequi jubet ; et, cum propius Ambiorigem accessisset, jussus arma abjicere, imperatum facit, suisque ut idem faciant imperat. Interim-dum de condicionibus[3] inter se agunt longiorque ab Ambiorige instituitur sermo, paulatim circumventus interficitur. Tum vero suo more victoriam conclamant atque ululatum[4] tollunt, impetuque in nostros facto ordines perturbant. Ibi Lucius Cotta pugnans interficitur cum maximā parte militum. Reliqui se in castra recipiunt unde erant egressi. Ex quibus Lucius Petrosidius aquilifer cum magna multitudine hostium pre-meretur, aquilam intra vallum projecit, ipse pro castris fortissime pugnans occiditur. Illi aegre[5] ad noctem oppugna-tionem sustinent ; noctu ad unum omnes, desperata salute, se ipsi interficiunt.

---

[1]quos....tribunos militum = eos tribunos militum quos.   [2]at that time.   [3]terms, *i.e.* of surrender.   [4]yell.   [5]with difficulty.

XXVI

The rival centurions (*B* V, 44).

Erant in eā legione fortissimi viri centuriones qui primis ordinibus[1] appropinquarent Titus Pulio et Lucius Vorenus. Hi perpetuas inter se controversias[2] habebant uter ante-ferretur[3] omnibusque annis[4] de locis[5] summis simultatibus[6] contendebant. Ex his Pulio, cum acerrime ad munitiones pugnaretur, Quid dubitas, inquit, Vorene ? Aut quem locum[7] tuae probandae virtutis exspectas ? Hic dies de nostris contro-versiis judicabit. Haec cum dixisset, procedit extra munitiones, quaeque pars hostium confertissima est visa, in eam irrumpit[8]. Ne Vorenus quidem se vallo continet sed omnium veritus existimationem⁹ subsequitur. Mediocri spatio relicto, Pulio pilum in hostes immittit atque unum ex multitudine procurrentem trajicit; quo percusso¹⁰ et exanimato, hunc scutis protegunt, in bostem tela universi conjiciunt neque dant regrediendi facultatem¹¹.

¹rank. ²disputes. ³should have the preference. ⁴all their life. ⁵position. ⁶rivalry. ⁷opportunity. ⁸irrumpo, -ere, -rupī, -ruptum, rush. ⁹opinion. ¹⁰percutiō, -ere, -cussī, -cussum, strike. ¹¹opportunity.

XXVII

The rival centurions (*continued*).

Transfigitur¹ scutum Pulioni et verutum² in balteo³ defigitur⁴. Avertit⁵ hic casus⁶ vaginam⁷ et gladium educere conanti⁸ dextram moratur manum, impeditumque hostes circumsistunt⁹. Succurrit¹⁰ inimicus illi Vorenus et laboranti subvenit. Ad hunc se confestim¹¹ a Pulione omnis multitudo convertit¹²; illum veruto arbitrantur occisum. Gladio comminus¹³ rem gerit¹⁴ Vorenus et uno interfecto reliquos paulum propellit; dum cupidius instat, in locum dejectus inferiorem, concidit¹⁵. Huic rursus circumvento fert subsidium Pulio atque ambo incolumes, compluribus interfectis, summa cum laude sese intra munitiones recipiunt. Sic fortuna in contentione et certamine utrumque versavit¹⁶ ut alter alteri inimicus auxilio salutique esset, neque dijudicari¹⁷ posset, uter utri virtute anteferendus videretur.

¹transfīgō, -fīgere, -fixī, -fixum, pierce. ²dart. ³balteus, sword belt. ⁴dēfīgō, -ere, -fixī, -fixum, fasten. ⁵avertō, -ere, -vertī, -versum, turn aside. ⁶accident. ⁷scabbard. ⁸literally, "*to him attempting to draw his sword,*" "*as he was attempting to draw his sword.*" ⁹circumsistō, -ere, -stitī, no sup., surround. ¹⁰succurro, -ere, -currī, -cursum, runs to his aid (dat.). ¹¹immediately. ¹²convertō, -ere, -vertī, -versum, turn. ¹³hand to hand. ¹⁴carries on the fight. ¹⁵stumbling into a hollow place, he falls. ¹⁶changed the positions of both. ¹⁷to be decided.

XXVIII

News conveyed to Caesar's camp by a Gallic slave
(*B*. V, 45).

Quanto erat in dies gravior atque asperior oppugnatio,[1] et
maxime quod, magna parte militum confectā vulneribus[2], res ad
paucitatem defensorum. pervenerat,[3] tanto crebriores litterae·
nuntiique ad Caesarem mittebantur ; quorum pars deprehensa
in conspectu nostrorum militum cum cruciatu[4] necabatur..
Erat unus intus[5] Nervius nomine Vertico, loco natus honesto,
qui a prima obsidione ad Ciceronem perfugerat suamque ei
fidem praestiterat[6].   Hic servo spe libertatis magnisque
persuadet praemiis ut litteras ad Caesarem deferat[7].   Has ille
in jaculo illigatas[8] effert et Gallus inter Gallos sine ullā
suspicione versatus ad Caesarem pervenit.   Ab eo de periculis
Ciceronis legionisque cognoscitur.

---

[1]the fiercer and more desperate the siege became from day to day.
[2]worn out with wounds.   [3]the fighting (rēs) now devolved on few de-
fenders.   [4]cruciātus, -us, ₥. torture.   [5]inside the camp.   [6]praestō, -āre,
-stitī, -stātum, show.   [7]dēferō, carry.   [8]illigō, -āre, -āvī, -ātum, tie to.

XXIX
Prompt measures of relief (*B*. V, 46).

Caesar acceptis litteris horā circiter undecimā diei statim
nuntium ad M. Crassum quaestorem mittit, cujus hiberna
aberant ab eo millia passuum viginti quinque ; jubet media
nocte legionem proficisci celeriterque ad se venire.   Exit cum
nuntio Crassus.   Alterum ad Caium Fabium legatum mittit
ut in Atrebatium fines legionem adducat, quā sibi scit iter
faciendum.   Scribit Labieno[1] si reipublicae commodo facere
posset cum legione ad fines Nerviorum veniat.   Reliquam
partem exercitus, quod paulo aberat longius, non putat expec-
tandam ; equites circiter quadringentos ex proximis hibernis
colligit[2].

---

[1]supply **ut** ; join with **veniat** ; scrībit has an analogous construction
to imperat.   [2]colligō, -ere, -lēgī, lectum, muster.

XXX
An "armed council" of the Gauls is summoned
(*B.* V, 56).

Indutiomarus, ubi intellexit Nervios bellum Romanis parare neque sibi voluntariorum copias defore[1] armatum concilium indicit[2]. Hoc more[3] Gallorum est initium belli, quo[4] lege communi omnes puberes[5] armati convenire consueverunt; qui ex iis novissimus convenit, in conspectu multitudinis omnibus cruciatibus affectus necatur. In eo concilio Cingetorigem, alterius principem factionis, generum suum, quem supra demonstravimus Caesaris secutum fidem ab eo non discessisse, hostem judicat bonaque ejus publicat[6]. His rebus confectis in concilio pronuntiat[7] arcessitum[8] se compluribus Galliae civitatibus; se iturum per fines Remorum eorumque agros populaturum[9]; ac priusquam id faciat[10] castra Labieni oppugnaturum. Quae fieri velit[11] praecipit[12].

---

[1] = dēfutūrās esse, fut. infin. of dēsum, -esse, dēfuī, fail (with dative). [2]proclaims. [3]mōs, mōris, M., custom. [4]adv. to·which. [5]pūbēs, pūberis, M., adult. [6]confiscate. [7]declares. [8]arcesso, -ere, arcessīvī, arcessītum, invite. [9]populor, -ārī, populātus sum, devastate. [10]Subord. clause in O.O.; H. L., 265, 2 (*b*). [11]Indirect Question; H. L., 200, 4. [12]praecipio, -ere, -cepī, -ceptum, inform.

XXXI
Death of Indutiomārus (*B.* V, 58).

Interim Indutiomārus ad castra Romana accedit atque ibi magnam partem diei consumit[1]; equites Gallorum tela conjiciunt et magnā cum contumeliā[2] nostros ad pugnam evocant[3]. Nullo ab nostris dato responso, sub vesperum[4] dispersi ac dissipati[5] discedunt. Subito Labienus duabus portis[6] omnem equitatum emittit; praecipit ut, territis hostibus atque in fugam conjectis, unum omnes peterent[7] Indutiomarum.

---

[1]consūmō, -ere, consumpsī, consumptum, spend. [2]insulting language. [3]challenge. [4]towards evening; note use of sub in expression of time; sub noctem, towards night, just before nightfall; sub prīmam lūcem, just before daybreak. [5]in scattered and straggling bands. [6]abl. of Route by Which: H. L., 294, 3. [7]attack, make for.

XXXII

Death of Indutiomārus (*continued, B. V, 58*).

Interdicit Caesar ne quis[1] quem[2] prius vulneret quam
Indutiomarum interfectum viderit, quod spatium nactum[3]
illum effugere nolebat; magna proponit iis qui occiderint
praemia; submittit[4] cohortes equitibus subsidio. Probat consilium hominis fortunā; et, cum unum omnes peterent, in ipso
fluminis vado deprehensus Indutiomarus interficitur caputque
ejus refertur in castra; redeuntes equites quos possunt con-
sectantur[5] atque occidunt. Hāc re cognitā, omnes quae convenerant copiae discedunt; pauloque habuit post id factum
Caesar quietiorem Galliam.

---

[1] that no one; H. L., 233, 5. [2] anyone. [3] nanciscor, nanciscī,
nactus sum, obtain. [4] sends. [5] consector, -arı, -ātus ·sum, overtake.

BOOK VI (53. B.C.).

Early in the spring of 53 B.C. Caesar suddenly appears in the territory of the Nervii and the Menapii, whom he subdues. Meanwhile
Labienus, his trusty lieutenant, defeated the Treviri, and placed Cingetorix, who had always been loyal to the Romans, in supreme power.
After uniting his own forces with those of Labienus, Caesar led his
army across the Rhine by a new bridge built near the modern city of
Berne. The Suevi had mustered to oppose his advance, but subse-
quently withdrew to the end of their territories without coming to an
engagement. Caesar takes occasion to describe the habits and customs
of the Galli, their religion, and priests. He then describes the Germans, the Hercynian Wood, and the wild animals found in it. He
returns to Gaul, cuts down part of the bridge, and scatters the forces of
Ambiorix, chief of the Eburones. In the late summer, the Sigambri, a
German tribe, cross the Rhine and attack Aduatuca (*Tongres*), where
Cicero was stationed. Cicero nearly met with a severe defeat. After
ravaging the country of the Eburones, Caesar holds an assembly of the
Gauls at Durocortorum (*Rheims*), at which the rebellious chiefs were
condemned. Acco, the leader of the rebellion among the Carnutes
and Sennones, is put to death; the other condemned chieftains fled.
Caesar then felt safe to go to Italy.

XXXIII

The Treviri stir up war (*B.* VI, 2).

Interfecto Indutiomaro, ut docuimus, ad ejus propinquos[1] a
Treviris imperium defertur. Illi finitimos Germanos sollicitare et pecuniam-polliceri non desistunt[2]. Cum ab proximis
impetrare[3] non possent, ulteriores temptant.[4] Inventis
nonnullis civitatibus, jurejurando inter se confirmant[5]; Ambiorigem sibi societate et foedere[6] adjungunt. Quibus rebus
cognitis Caesar, cum undique bellum parari videret, Nervios,
adjunctis Cisrhenanis omnibus Germanis, esse in armis,
Senones ad imperatum non venire et cum finitimis civitatibus
consilia communicare,[7] a Treviris Germanos crebris legationibus sollicitari, maturius[8] sibi de bello cogitandum[9] putavit.

---

[1]near relatives. [2]dēsistō, -ere, -stitī, -stitum, cease from. [3]to
obtain their wish. [4]try those farther off. [5]they bind themselves
mutually by an oath. [6]by alliance and treaty. [7]were forming common
plans. [8]earlier than usual. [9]Gerundival Infinitive ; H. L., 189.

XXXIV

Caesar quells the Nervii and summons a council at Paris (*B.* VI, 3).

Itaque, nondum bieme confectā[1], proximis quattuor coactis
legionibus, de improviso[2] in fines Nerviorum contendit, et
priusquam illi aut convenire aut profugere possent, magno
pecoris atque hominum numero capto atque ea praedā militibus
concessa vastatisque agris, in deditionem venire atque obsides
sibi dare coegit. Eo celeriter confecto negotio, rursus in
hiberna legiones reduxit. Concilio Galliae primo vere, ut
instituerat[3], indicto[4], cum reliqui praeter Senones, Carnutes,
Treverosque venissent, initium belli ac defectionis[5] hoc esse
arbitratus, ut omnia postponere videretur[6], concilium Lutetiam
Parisiorum[7] transfert. Confines[8] erant hi Senonibus civitat-
emque patrum memoriā conjunxerant ; sed ab hoc consilio.

afuisse[9] existimabantur. Hac re pro suggestu[10] pronuntiatā, eodem die cum legionibus in Senones proficiscitur magnisque itineribus eo pervenit.

---

[1]before winter was quite over. [2]unexpectedly. [3]arranged. [4]havin been proclaimed. [5]revolt. [6]that he might make it appear that he wa postponing the whole matter. [7]to Lutetia of the Parisii = to Paris The council before met at Samarobriva (*Amiens*). [8]neighbors. [9]to b averse. [10]suggestus, -us, tribunal, or platform.

XXXV
Caesar crosses the Rhine a second time
(*B.* VI, 9).

Caesar postquam ex Menapiis in Treveros vēnit, duabus de causis Rhenum trānsire constituit: quarum una erat quod Germani auxilia contra se[1] Treviris miserant; altera, ne ad eos Ambiorix receptum haberet[2]. His constitutis rebus, paulo supra[3] eum locum quo ante exercitum traduxerat facere pontem instituit. Magno militum studio paucis diebus opu efficitur. Firmo in Treveris ad pontem praesidio relicto, ne quis ab his subito motus oriretur[4], reliquas copias equitatumque traducit. Ubii, qui ante obsides dederant atque in deditionem venerant, purgandi sui[5] causā ad eum legatos mittunt qui doceant neque auxilia ex suā civitate in Treveros missa neque ab se fidem laesam[6] : petunt atque orant[7] ut sibi parcat, ne communi odio Germanorum innocentes pro nocentibus poenas pendant[8]; si amplius obsidum velit dari, pollicentur.

---

[1]se = ipsum, *i.e* , Caesar. [2]that Ambiorix might not find refuge with them. [3]the former bridge was built near *Bonn*, 55 B.C. (*B.* IV, 17) ; the present one was built farther up the stream, near *Andernach.* [4]orior, orīrī, ortus sum, arise ; "*to prevent any sudden rising taking place among them.*" [5]of clearing themselves ; H. L., 187, 8. [6]laedō, -ere, laesī, laesum, break ; with fidem, to break their word. [7]they beg and pray, *i.e.*, they earnestly beg. [8]pay the penalty.

XXXVI

Factions among the Gauls (*B.* VI, 11).

Quoniam ad hunc locum[1] perventum est,[2] non alienum[3] esse
videtur de Galliae Germaniaeque moribus et quo differant hae
nationes inter sese proponere[4]. In Galliā non solum in
omnibus civitatibus atque in omnibus pagis[5] partibusque, sed
paene etiam in singulis domibus factiones[6] sunt; earumque
factionum principes sunt, quorum ad arbitrium summa
omnium rerum redeat[7]. Ita ejus rei causā antiquitus[8] insti-
tutum esse videtur, ne quis ex plebe contra potentiorem
auxilii egeret[9]; suos enim quisque[10] opprimi et circumveniri
non patitur[11], neque, aliter[12] si faciat, ullam inter suos habeat
auctoritatem.

[1]*place* (in my narrative). [2] = **pervēnī.** [3]amiss, out of place; literally,
foreign (to my subject). [4]to lay before (my readers)=to explain.
[5]cantons. [6]political parties. [7]the final decision of all matters is
referred. [8]in former times. [9]that no one from the common people
should be at a loss for aid against any one more powerful than himself.
[10]*i.e.* each party leader. [11]refuses to allow. [12]otherwise.

XXXVII

Rival factions in Gaul (*B.* VI, 12).

Cum Caesar in Galliam venit, alterius factionis[1] principes
erant Haedui, alterius Sequani. Hi[2], cum per se minus
valerent,[3] quod summa auctoritas antiquitus[4] erat in Haeduis
magnaeque eorum erant clientelae[5], Germanos atque Ariovistum
sibi adjunxerant eosque ad se magnis jacturis[6] pollicitationi-
busque[7] perduxerant. Proeliis vero compluribus factis secundis
atque omni nobilitate Haeduorum interfectā, tantum potentiā
antecesserant[8] ut magnam partem clientium[9] ab Haeduis ad se
traducerent obsidesque ab iis principum filios acciperent et

publice jurare cogerent nihil se contra Sequanos consilii inituros[10], et partem finitimi agri per vim occupatam possiderent[11], Galliaeque totius principatum obtinerent.

---

[1]factiō, -ōnis, F. political party.   [2]the latter.   [3]were not sufficiently strong of themselves, valeō, -ēre, -uī, -itum, be strong.   [4]in ancient times.   [5]clientēla, -ae, F., the relation of *patrōnus* and *cliens* : dependant.   [6]jactūra, -ae, F., sacrifice.   [7]pollicitātiō, -ōnis, F., promise.   [8]they (Sequani) so far excelled in power (the Haedui).   [9]cliens, -tis, M., dependant.   [10]consilium inīre, to enter upon a plan, to undertake.   [11]possideō, -ēre, possēdī, possessum, possess.

XXXVIII

Caesar supports the Aedui and Remi (*B.* VI, 12).

Necessitate adductus[1] Haeduus Divitiacus auxilii petendi causa Romam ad senatum profectus imperfectā re[2] redierat. Adventu Caesaris factā commutatĭone[3] rerum, obsidibus Haeduis redditis, veteribus clientelis restitutis, novis per Caesarem comparatis, quod hi, qui se ad eorum[4] amicitiam aggregaverant, meliore condicione atque aequiore imperio se uti[5] videbant, eorum gratiā dignitateque amplificatā, Sequani principatum dimiserant.[6]   In eorum locum Remi successerant[7]; quos quod adaequare[8] apud Caesarem gratiā intellegebatur, ii qui propter veteres inimicitias nullo modo cum Haeduis conjungi poterant se Remis in clientelam dĭcabant[9].   Hos illi diligenter tuebantur; ita novam auctoritatem tenebant.   Eō tum statu res erat, ut longe principes haberentur Haedui, secundum locum dignitatis Remi obtinerent.

---

[1]forced by necessity.   [2]without accomplishing his purpose.   [3]commūtātiō, -ōnis, F, change.   [4]*i e.,* the Haedui.   [5]ūtor, ūtī, usus sum, enjoy.   [6]had been compelled to give up.   [7]succēdō, -ere, -cessī, -cessum, succeed.   [8]supply Haeduos after adaequare, that they had rivalled the Haedui in Caesar's favor.   [9]placed themselves under the protection of the Remi ; dīcō, I, assign.

XXXIX

Classes of people among the Gauls.   The Druids
(*B.* VI, 13).

In omni Galliā eorum hominum qui aliquo sunt numero[1] atque honore genera sunt duo. Nam plebes paene servorum habetur loco[2], quae nihil audet per se, nulli adhibetur[3] consilio. Plerique cum aut aere alieno[4] aut magnitudine tributorum[5] aut injuria potentiorum premuntur, sese in servitutem dicant[6] nobilibus ; quibus in hos eadem omnia sunt jura quae dominis in servos. Sed de his duobus generibus alterum est druidum[7], alterum equitum. Illi rebus divinis intersunt[8], sacrificia publica ac privata procurant[9], religiones interpretantur[10] ; ad eos magnus adolescentiae numerus disciplinae causā concurrit, magnoque hi sunt apud eos honore. Nam fere de omnibus controversiis[11] publicis privatisque constituunt ; et, si quod est admissum facinus, si caedes facta, si de finibus controversia est, iidem decernunt, praemia poenasque constituunt[12].

---

[1]estimation. [2]the common people are regarded almost as slaves. [3]adhibeō, -ēre, -hibuī, -hibitum, admit. [4]aes aliēnum, debt. [5]excessive taxes. [6]devote themselves. [7]druidēs, -um, M. pl. Druids. [8]have charge. [9]attend to. [10]expound everything connected with religion. [11]disputes. [12]determine.

XL

The Druids (*continued*).

Si qui aut privatus aut populus eorum decreto non stetit[1], sacrificiis interdicunt[2]. Haec poena apud eos est gravissima. Quibus ita est interdictum[3], hi numero[4] impiorum ac sceleratorum habentur[5], his omnes decedunt[6] ; aditum sermonemque defugiunt[7], ne quid ex contagione incommodi accipiant[8], neque his petentibus jus redditur neque bonos ullus communicatur[9].

His autem omnibus druidibus praeest[10] unus, qui summam
inter eos habet auctoritatem.   Hoc mortuo, aut, si qui ex
reliquis excellit[11] dignitate, succedit[12], aut, si sunt plures
pares, suffragio[13] druidum ; nonnunquam[14] etiam armis de
principatu contendunt.   Hi certo anni tempore in finibus
Carnutum, quae regio totius Galliae media habetur, considunt[15]
in loco consecrato.   Huc omnes undique qui controversias[16]
habent conveniunt eorumque decretis judiciisque parent.
Disciplina[17] in Britannia reperta atque inde in Galliam trans-
lata[18] esse existimatur ; et nunc qui diligentius eam rem[19]
cognoscere volunt plerumque illo discendi causā proficiscuntur.

---

[1]abide by their decision (dēcrētō is abl.).   [2]supply eōs: literally, they
exclude these from the sacrifices.   [3]those who are so excluded: [4]= in
numero.   [5]are accounted.   [6]supply dē viā, all make way for these.
[7]they avoid meeting them and conversing with them.   [8]lest they
receive any harm from coming in contact with these : incommodī Part.
Gen. after quid.   [9]neither to their petition is justice rendered, nor is
any public office shared with them.   [10]is over (with dat. H. L., 229, 4).
[11]excello, -ere, surpass.   [12]succēdō, -ere, -cessī, -cessum, succeed.
[13]suffragium, ī-, N., vote.   [14]sometimes.   [15]consīdo, -ere, sēdī,
-sessum, hold meeting.   [16]disputes.   [17]the system.   [18]from transferō, bring over.   [19] – disciplīnam.

XLI

The Druids (continued, B. VI, 14).

Druides a bello abesse consuerunt[1] neque tributa[2] unā[3] cum
reliquis pendunt[4]; militiae vacationem[5] omniumque rerum
habent immunitatem[6].   Tantis incitati praemiis et suā sponte[7]
multi in disciplinam conveniunt et a parentibus propinquisque
mittuntur.   Magnum ibi numerum versuum[8] ediscere[9] dicuntur.
Itaque annos nonnulli vicenōs[10] in disciplinā permanent.
Neque fas esse existimant ea litteris mandare[11], cum in reliquis
fere rebus, publicīs privatisque rationibus, Graecis litteris

utantur. Id mihi duabus de causis instituisse videntur; quod
neque in vulgum disciplinam efferri[12] velint neque eos qui
discunt litteris confisos[13] minus memoriae studere[14],—quod
fere plerisque accidit[15] ut praesidio[16] litterarum diligentiam
in perdiscendo ac memoriam remittant[17]. In primis hoc volun.
persuadere[18], non interire animas[19], sed ab aliis post mortem
transire ad alios; atque hoc maxime ad virtutem excitari
putant metu mortis neglecto. Multa praeterea de sideribus[20]
atque eorum motu[21], de mundi[22] ac terrarum magnitudine,
de rerum natura[23], de deorum immortalium vi ac potestate
disputant et juventuti tradunt.

---

[1] = consuēvērunt, [2]tribūtum, -ī, N., tax. [3]together. [4]pendō, -ere,
pependī, pensum, pay. [5]exemption. [6]freedom from public services.
[7]of their own accord, [8]versus, -us, M., verse. [9]ēdisco, -ere, learn by
heart. [10]twenty each. [11]commit. [12]spread abroad. [13]confīdo, -ere,
confisus sum, trust. [14]pay too little heed to memory. [15]happens.
[16]with the assistance of letters. [17]relax. [18]inculcate. [19]anima,
ae, F. soul. [20]sīdus, -eris, N., star. [21]mōtus, -us, M., motion. [22]mundus,
-ī, universe. [23]rerum natūra, the nature of things, science.

XLII

Religion of the Gauls (*B.* VI, 16).

Natio est omnis Gallorum admodum dedita religionibus[1];
atque ob eam causam qui sunt affecti gravioribus morbis[2],
quique in proeliis periculisque versantur[3], aut pro victimis
homines immolant[4] aut se immolaturos vovent, administrisque[5]
ad ea sacrificia druidibus utuntur, quod pro vita hominis nisi
hominis vita reddatur[6], non posse deorum immortalium numen
placari arbitrantur; publiceque ejusdem generis habent insti-
tuta sacrificia. Alii immani[7] magnitudine simulacra[8] habent,
quorum contexta[9] viminibus membra vivis hominibus com-
plent[10]; quibus succensis[11] circumventi[12] flammā exanimantur[13]
homines. Supplicia[14] eorum qui in furto[15] aut in latrocinio[16]

aut aliquā noxiā[17] sint comprehensi gratiora dis immortalibus
esse arbitrantur; sed, cum ejus generis copia deficit[18], etiam
ad innocentium supplicia descendunt[19].

---

[1]wholly given up to religious observances.   [2]those who are distressed
with incurable diseases.   [3]are engaged.   [4]sacrifice.   [5]administer, -trī,
M., assistant, attendant priest.   [6]reddō, -ere, -didī, -d'tum, give in
compensation.   [7]immense.   [8]simulācrum, -ī, N., images of men, sc.
hominum.   [9]contexō, -ere, -texuī, -textum, weave.   [10]compleō, -ēre,
-ēvī, -ētum, fill.   [11]succendō, -ere, -cendī, -censum, burn.   [12]surrounded.
[13]perish.   [14]punishment.   [15]furtum, -ī, N., theft.   [16]latrocinium, -ī, N.,
robbery.   [17]guilty act.   [18]fails.   [19]they resort to.

XLIII
The Gods of the Gauls (*B.* VI, 17).

Deum maxime Mercurium colunt; hujus sunt plurima
simulacra; hunc omnium inventorem[1] artium[2] ferunt[3]; hunc
viarum atque itinerum ducem; hunc ad quaestus[4] pecuniae
mercaturasque[5] habere vim maximam arbitrantur; post hunc
Apollinem et Martem et Jovem et Minervam. De his eandem
fere quam reliquae gentes habent opinionem[6]; Apollinem
morbos depellere[7], Minervam operum atque artificiorum initia
tradere[8], Jovem imperium caelestium[9] tenere, Martem bella
regere. Huic, cum proelio dimicare[10] constituerunt, ea quae
bello ceperint plerumque[11] devovent[12]; cum superaverunt
animalia capta immolant reliquasque res in unum locum con-
ferunt. Multis in civitatibus harum rerum exstructos[13] tumulos
locis consecratis conspicari[14] licet; neque saepe accidit ut
neglectā quispiam religione aut captā apud se occultare aut
positā tollere auderet gravissimumque ei rei supplicium cum
cruciatu[15] constitutum est.

---

[1]discoverer.   [2]handicraft.   [3]believe, regard.   [4]quaestus, -ūs, M.,
profit, gain.   [5]mercātūra, -ae, F., traffic.   [6]belief.   [7]ward off.   [8]in-
structs in the rudiments of works and arts, *i.e.*, mechanical arts.
[9]caelestēs, -ium, pl. heavenly gods, supply deōrum.   [10]fight a pitched
battle.   [11]generally.   [12]devote.   [13]piled up.   [14]see.   [15]torture.

XLIV
Marriages and funerals among the Gauls
(*B.* VI, 19).

Viri in uxores sicuti[1] in liberos vitae necisque[2] habent
potestatem; et cum pater familiae illustriore loco[3] natus
decessit[4], ejus propinqui conveniunt et de morte si res in
suspicionem venit[5] de uxoribus in servilem modum quaestionem[6]
habent et si compertum est[7], igni et omnibus tormentis ex-
cruciatas[8] interficiunt. Funera[9] sunt pro cultu[10] Gallorum
magnifica et sumptuosa[11]; omniaque quae vivis cordi fuisse[12]
arbitrantur in ignem inferunt etiam animalia ac paulo supra
hanc memoriam[13] servi et clientes quos ab iis dilectos esse
constabat, justis[14] funeribus confectis, una cremabantur.

---

[1]as also. [2]nex, necis, F., death. [3]somewhat distinguished family.
[4]dēcēdē, -ere, -cessī, -cessum, die. [5]if his death has been suspected.
[6]investigation. [7]comperio, -ire, comperī, compertum, find out. [8]after
being tortured. [9]funerals. [10]considering the civilization. [11]grand and
expensive. [12]cordī esse, be dear. [13]a little before our time. [14]regular.

XLV
Laws against Gossiping (*B.* VI, 20).

Quae civitates commodius[1] suam rem publicam administrare
existimantur, habent legibus sanctum[2] si quis quid de re publicā
a finitimis rumore aut fama acceperit uti ad magistrum deferat
neve[3] cum quo alio communicet quod[4] saepe homines teme-
rarios[5] atque imperitos falsis rumoribus terreri et ad facinus
impelli et de summis rebus consilium capere cognitum est.
Magistratus quae visa sunt[6] occultant quaeque esse ex usu
judicaverunt multitudini produnt. De re publica nisi per
concilium loqui non conceditur[7].

---

[1]well; literally, "*better than ordinary*" [2]sanciō, -īre, sanxī, sanctum, lay down by law. [3]= et ne. [4]because: join with cognitum est.
[5]rash. [6]seem good. [7]concēdō, -ere, concessī, concessum, allow.

XLVI
The Germans (*B.* VI, 21).

Germani multum ab hac consuetudine differunt. Nam neque druides habent qui rebus divinis praesint[1], neque. sacrificiis student[2]. Deorum numero[3] eos solos ducunt, quos cernunt et quorum aperte opibus juvantur Solem et Vulcanum et Lunam; reliquos ne famā quidem acceperunt[4]. Vita omnis in venationibus[5] atque in studiis rei militaris consistit[6]; ab parvulis[7] labori ac duritiae student[8]. Qui diutissime impuberes[9] permanserunt maximam inter suos ferunt laudem; hoc ali staturam, ali vires nervosque confirmari putant. In fluminibus perfluuntur[10] et pellibus ac parvis renonum tegmentis[11] utuntur, magna corporis parte nudā.

---

[1]H. L., 237, 1. [2]perform. [3]=in numerō. [4]not even by report have they heard of. [5]hunting. [6]consistō, -ere, -stitī, is spent. [7]from their earliest age : **parvulus**, diminutive of **parvus**. [8]they accustom themselves to toil and hardship. [9]impūbes, -eris, unmarried. [10]**perfluo, -ere, -fluxi, -fluxum**, bathe themselves. [11]skins of reindeer.

XLVII
Land Tenure among the Germans (*B.* VI, 22).

Agriculturae non student[1] majorque pars eorum victūs[2] in lacte, caseo[3], carne consistit. Neque quisquam agri modum certum[4] aut fines habet proprios[5] sed magistratus ac principes[6] in annos singulos gentibus[7] cognationibusque[8] hominum qui tum una coierunt[9] quantum et quo loco visum est agri[10] attribuunt[11] atque anno post alio transire cogunt. Ejus rei multas afferunt[12] causas; ne assidua consuetudine capti[13] studium belli gerendi agriculturāi[14] commutent[15]; ne latos fines parare studeant[16] potentioresque humiliores possessionibus expellant; ne accuratius ad frigora atque aestus vitandos aedificent; ne

qua oriatur pecuniae cup¡ditas qua ex re factiones dissension-
esque nascuntur ; ut animi aequitate[17] plebem contineant cum
suas quisque opes cum potentissimis aequari[18] videat.

[1]They pay no heed. [2]victus, -ūs, M., food. [3]caseus, -ī, M., cheese.
[4]fixed amount. [5]of his own. [6]join with attribuunt. [7]clans. [8]families.
[9]of the people who have met on the occasion. [10]Partitive Genitive
depending on quantum. [11]assign. [12]give. [13]charmed by habitual
custom. [14]abl. of Price : H.L., 293, 4. [15]exchange: i.e , abandon the
pursuit of war for agriculture. [16]aim at acquiring. [17]contentment.
[18]is on an equality with.

XLVIII
Warlike habits of the Germans (B. VI, 23).

Civitatibus maxima laus est[1] quam latissime[2] circum se
vastatis finibus sollitudines habere. Hoc proprium[3] virtutis
existimant, expulsos agris finitimos cedere[4] neque quemquam
prope audere consistere[5] ; simul hoc se fore tutiores arbitrantur
repentinae incursionis timore sublato[6]. Cum bellum civitas aut
illatum[7] defendit aut infert, magistratus qui ei bello praesint[7]
et vitae necisque[8] habeant potestatem deliguntur. In pace
nullus est communis magistratus sed principes regionum atque
pagorum[9] inter suos jus dicunt[10] controversiasque minuunt[11]
Latrocinia nullam habent[12] infamiam[13] quae extra fines cujusque civitatis fiunt atque ea juventutis exercendae ac desidiae[14]
minuendae causā fieri praedicant[15]. Hospitem[16] violare fas
non putant et qui quācumque de causā[17] ad eos venerunt ab
injuria prohibent, sanctos[18] habent, bisque omnium domus
patent[19] victusque communicatur[20].

[1]the greatest reputation that a state can have is. [2]as far and wide
as possible. [3]a characteristic. [4]that their neighbors being driven out
of their lands should retire before them. [5]settle. [6]from tollō : remove.
[7]bellum illatum, an aggressive war. [7]Final Rel. and Subj. : H. L.,
232, 2. [8]nex, necis, F., death. [9]pagus, -ī, M., canton. [10]administer
justice. [11]minuō, -ere, minuī, minūtum, settle. [12]regard. [13]disgrace.
[14]for the purpose of lessening indolence. [15]praedicō, -āre, -āvī, -ātum,
avow. [16]hospes, -itis, M., guest. [17]for any reason whatever. [18]sacred.
[19]pateō, -ēre, -uī, be open. [20]is shared.

XLIX

The Germans and the Gauls contrasted in bravery
(*B.*-VI, 24).

Ac fuit antea tempus cum Germanos Galli virtute super-
arent, ultro[1] bella inferrent, propter hominum[2] multitudinem
agrique inopiam trans Rhenum colonias mitterent. Itaque
ea[3] quae fertilissima Germaniae sunt loca circum Hercyniam
silvam quam Eratostheni et quibusdam Graecis fama notam
esse video, Volcae Tectosages[4] occupaverunt atque ibi conse-
derunt[5]; quae gens ad hoc tempus his sedibus sese continet
summamque habet justitiae et bellicae laudis opinionem.
Nunc quod in eadem inopia, egestate, patientia Germani permanent[6], eodem victu et cultu corporis utuntur; Gallis autem
provinciarum Romanarum propinquitas[7] et transmarinarum
rerum notitia[8] multa ad usus largitur[9], paulatim assuefacti
superari multisque victi proeliis, ne se quidem ipsi cum illis
virtute comparant.

---

[1] voluntarily. [2] population. [3] join with loca. [4] a Gallic tribe. [5] consīdō,
-ere, -sēdī, -sessum, settle. [6] as the Germans live in the same poverty,
want and endurance of hardships. [7] nearness. [8] knowledge of things
beyond the sea. [9] brings in many things they regard as essentials.

L

The Hercynian Forest (*B.* VI, 25).

Hujus Hercyniae silvae, quae supra demonstrata est, latitudo
novem dierum iter expedito patet[1]; non enim aliter finiri[2]
potest, neque mensuras[3] itinerum noverunt. Oritur[4] ab
Helvetiorum finibus rectaque fluminis Danuvii regione[5]
pertinet ad fines Dacorum[6]; multarumque gentium fines
propter magnitudinem attingit; neque quisquam est hujus
Germaniae qui se aut adisse ad initium ejus silvae dicat[7], cum[8]
dierum iter sexaginta processerit, aut quo ex loco oriatur

acceperit; multaque in ea genera ferarum nasci constat, quae
reliquis in locis visa non sint[7]; ex quibus quae maxime differant[7]
ab ceteris et memoriae prodenda videantur[7] haec sunt.

[1]extends over a journey of nine days, to a man lightly equipped.
[2]finio, -īre, īvī, -itum, define.ˉ [3]mensūra, -ae, F. measurement. [4]oricr,·
-īrī, ortus sum, starts, begins. [5]in a direct line with (i.e., parallel to).
[6]Dacı, orum, M. pl. the Dacians, a tribe on the Danube. [7]subj. in a
clause of Characteristic: H. L., 237, 1.

LI
One-horned cattle; the Elk (B. VI, 26, 27).

Est bos cervi figurā[1] cujus a media fronte[2] inter aures[3]
unum cornu exsistit[4] excelsius[5] magisque directum[6] his quae
nobis sunt nota, cornibus; ab ejus summo sicut palmae
ramique[7] late diffunduntur[8]. Eadem est feminae[9] marisque[10]
natura, eadem forma magnitudoque cornuum. Sunt item quae
appellantur alces[11]. Harum est consimilis capris[12] figura et
varietas pellium[13] sed magnitudine paulo antecedunt, mutil-
aeque sunt cornibus[14] et crura[15] sine nodis articulisque[16]
habent, neque quietis causā procumbunt[17] neque si quo
afflictae[18] casu[19] conciderunt erigere sese aut sublevare possunt.
His sunt arbores pro cubilibus; ad eas se applicant atque ita
paulum modo reclinatae quietem capiunt. Quarum ex vestigiis
cum est animadversum a venatoribus quo se recipere consuerint,
omnes eo loco aut ab radicibus subruunt aut accīdunt arbores,
tantum ut species earum stantium relinquatur. Huc cum se
reclinaverunt, infirmas arbores pondere affligunt atque unā
ipsae concidunt.

[1]of the shape of a deer: since the genitive has an adjectival force:
figurā is abl. of description; probably the reindeer is meant. [2]frons,
frontis, F., forehead. [3]auris, -is, F., ear. [4]exsisto, -ere, protrude.
[5]excelsus, -a, -um, high. [6]straight. [7]as it were branching hands
(hendiadys). [8]diffundō, -ere, fūdī, fūsum, spread. [9]fēmina, -ae, F.,
female. [10]mās, māris, adj., male. [11]alcēs, -ium, elks. [12]caper, -prī, M.,
goat. [13]piebald appearance. [14]literally: they are blunted in their
horns, i e., their horns are blunted. [15]crūs, crūris, N., leg. [16]without
knotted joints (hendiadys). [17]prōcumbō, -ere, -cubuī, -cubitum, lie
down. [18]afflīgō, -ere, flīxī, flīctūm, throw down. [19]cāsus, -ūs, M.,
accident.

LII

The primitive Ox (*B.* VI, 28).

Tertium est genus eorum[1] qui uri[2] appellantur. Hi sunt
magnitudine paulo infra[3] elephantos, specie[4] et colore et figura
tauri. Magna vis eorum est et magna velocitas. Neque homini
neque ferae quam conspexerunt parcunt. Hos studiose[5] foveis[6]
captos interficiunt[7]; hoc se labore durant[8] adolescentes atque
hoc genere venationis[9] exercent et qui plurimos ex his interfecerunt, relatis in publicum cornibus[10], magnam ferunt laudem.
Sed adsuescere[11] ad homines et mansuefieri[12] ne parvuli quidem[13]
possunt. Amplitudo cornuum et figura et species multum a
nostrorum boum cornibus differt[13]. Haec studiose conquisita[14]
ab labris[15] argento circumcludunt[16] atque in amplissimis epulis[17]
pro poculis[18] utuntur.

[1] literally, is of those; consists of those. [2] ūrus, -ī, M., wild ox or
bison. [3] a little less than. [4] of the appearance. [5] eagerly. [6] fovea, -ae,
F., pitfall, snare. [7] they eagerly capture in pitfalls and kill these.
[8] make themselves hardy. [9] vēnātiō, -ōnis, F., hunting. [10] when the
horns are brought into a public place: with publicum supply locum.
[11] adsuescō, -ere, -suevi, -suētum, become accustomed. [11] mansuēfaciō,
-ere, -fēcī, -factum, tame. [13] not even when caught young. [13] differō,
-ferre, distulī. dilātum, differ. [14] conquiro, -ere, -quīsīvī, -quīsītum, seek
out. [15] labrum, -ī, N. lip: translate, at the rim. [16] circumclūdō, -ere,
-clūsī, -clūsum, surround. [17] epulum, -i, N. (sing.): epulae, -ārum,
F. (pl.), banquet. [18] pōculum, -ī, N. cup: translate, as drinking cups.

LIII

A force left on the Rhine (*B.* VI, 29).

Caesar, postquam per Ubios exploratores comperit[1] Suebos
sese in silvas recepisse, inopiam frumenti veritus quod, ut supra
demonstravimus, minime omnes Germani agriculturae student
constituit non progredi longius; sed ne omnino metum reditus

sui barbaris[2] tolleret atque ut eorum auxilia tardaret[3], reducto exercitu, partem[4] ultimam pontis quae ripas Ubiorum contingebat[5] in longitudinem pedum ducentorum rescindit[6] atque in extremo ponte turrim constituit praesidiumque cohortium duodecim pontis tuendi causā ponit magnisque eum locum munitionibus firmat. Ei loco praesidioque Caium Volcatium Tullum adolescentem praefecit.

[1] comperiō, 4, comperī, compertum, find out. [2] dat. H. L., 285, 5, (b); translate : but that he might not altogether relieve the barbarians of all fear of his return. [3] tardō,, 1, keep back. [4] object of rescindit. [5] contingō, -ere, contigī, contactum, join. [6] rescindo, -ere, rescidī, rescissum, cut down.

LIV

A Roman Hero (B. VI, 38).

Erat aeger cum praesidio relictus Publius Sextus Baculus cujus mentionem superioribus proeliis fecimus ac diem jam quintum cibo[1] caruerat[2]. Hic diffisus[3] suae atque omnium saluti inermis[4] ex tabernaculo[5] prodit[6]; videt imminere[7] hostes atque in summo esse rem discrimine; capit arma a proximis atque in porta consistit. Consequuntur hunc centuriones ejus cohortis quae in statione erat; paulisper unā proelium sustinent. Relinquit animus Sextium[8] gravissimis acceptis vulneribus; aegre servatur. Hoc spatio interposito, reliqui sese confirmant tantum ut in munitionibus consistere audeant speciemque defensorum praebeant.

[1] cibus, -ī, M., food. [2] careō, ēre, caruī, caritum, be without (gov. abl.). [3] diffīdō, -ere, diffīsus sum, distrust (semi-deponent : H. L., 135, 5) fīdō and its compounds usually govern dat. of person and abl. of thing : fearing for his own safety and that of his comrades. [4] inermis, -e, adj., unarmed. [5] tābernāculum, -ī, N., tent. [6] prōdeo, -ire, -ii, -itum advance. [7] immineō, -ēre, be near. [8] Sextius faints, or becomes unconscious.

LV

Caesar returns in safety (*B.* VI, 41).

Germani desperatā expugnatione castrorum, quod nostros jam constitisse[1] in munitionibus videbant, cum eā praedā quam in silvis deposuerant trans Rhenum sese receperunt; ac tantus fuit etiam post discessum[2] hostium terror ut ea nocte, cum Caius Volusenus missus cum equitatu ad castra venisset, fidem non faceret[3] adesse cum incolumi Caesarem exercitu. Sic omnino[4] animos timor praeoccupaverat[5] ut paene alienatā mente,[6] deletis omnibus copiis, equitatum se ex fuga recepisse dicerent, neque incolumi exercitu Germanos castra oppugnaturos fuisse contenderent. Quem timorem Caesaris adventus sustulit[7].

---

[1]consistō, -ere, -stitī, stitum, take a position.   [2]discessus, -ūs, M., withdrawal.   [3]could not make them believe.   [4]completely.   [5]taken possession of.   [6]almost beside themselves.   [7]tollō, 3, sustulī, sublātum, remove.

VOCABULARY

ABBREVIATIONS

C stands for Caesar: the Roman numeral refers to Book of Caesar's Gallic war : the Arabic numeral to the chapter.

abl.	ablative.	intr.	intransitive.
acc.	accusative.	irreg.	irregular.
adj.	adjective.	M.	masculine.
adv.	adverb.	N.	neuter
cf.	compare.	num.	numeral.
comp.	comparative.	ord.	ordinal.
conj.	conjunction.	p.	page.
dat.	dative.	part.	participle.
defec.	defective.	pass.	passive.
dem.	demonstrative.	perf.	perfect.
dep.	deponent.	pl.	plural.
dim.	diminutive.	prep.	preposition.
distrib.	distributive.	pro.	pronoun.
F.	feminine.	rel.	relative.
gen.	genitive.	sc.	supply.
impers.	impersonal.	sing.	singular.
indecl.	indeclinable.	sup.	superlative.
indef.	indefinite.	tr.	transitive.
interrog.	interrogative.	v.	verb.

The quantity of vowels long or short by position and of diphthongs (which are all-long) and of short vowels is not given.

172

VOCABULARY

CAESAR : Bellum Gallicum, *Bk.* IV, 20—*Bk.* V, 23.

A

ā, ab, prep. with abl: (a only before consonants ; ab before vowels and consonants) ; ab millibus passuum octo, eight miles off (c. iv, 22); ab aperto latere, on the exposed flank (the right side) (c. iv, 26) : a Pirustis, on the side of the Pirustae (c. v, 1).

abdō, -ere, -didī, ditum, v. tr., hide.

abeō, -īre, -iī (-īvī), -itum, v. intr., go away.

abhinc, adv., ago ; abhinc decem annos or abhinc decem annis, ten years ago.

abjiciō, -jicere, -jēcī, -jectum, v. tr., throw away.

abiēs, -ietis, F., a fir-tree, spruce.

abluō, -ere, -luī, -lutum, wash off, purify (ab, luo, "wash ").

abnegō, -āre, -āvī, -ātum, refuse.

abscēdō, -ere, -cessī, -cessum, v. intr., go away, leave off.

absens, -tis (pres. part. of absum), adj., absent.

absistō, -ere, -stitī, v. intr., desist ; ab signis legionibusque non absistere, not to stop short of the standards of the legions (c. v, 17).

abstineō, -ēre, -uī, -tentum, v. tr., hold away ; refrain (abs=ab ; teneo, "hold ").

absum, -esse, -fuī, v. intr., be absent, distant from ; abesse decem millia passuum, to be ten miles off ; neque multum abesse quin, to be not far from (c. v, 2).

ac (used before consonants) ; another form of atque (used before vowels), which see.

Acamās, -ntis, M., *Acamas,* a Greek hero

accēdō, -ere, -cessī, cessum, v. intr., go towards, reach ; accessum est ad Britanniam omnibus navibus, all the ships reached Britain (c. v, 8); impers., accēdit, -cēdere, -cessit, it is added ; accessit etiam quod, there was also added the fact that (c. iv, 16) ; accedebat huc ut, to this was added the fact that (c. v, 16).

accidō, -ere, -cidī, happen : usually impers. ; accidit, accidere, accidit, it happens; opportune accidisse arbitratus, thinking that this had happened fortunately (c. iv, 22); accidit ut, it happened that (c. iv, 29).

accingō, -ere, -cinxī, -cinctum, gird on ; reflexive sē omitted

accipiō, -cipere, -cēpī, ceptum, v. tr., receive ; to hear.

accommodō, -āre, -āvī, -ātum, v. tr., fit to.

ācer, ācris, ācre, adj., keen, sharp, severe (comp., ācrior; sup., ācerrimus).

acernus, -a, -um, adj., *made of maple, maple.*

Achāicus, -a, -um, adj., *Achaian, Grecian.*

Achillēs, -is (or -ī, eī), M., *Achilles,* the chief Greek hero in the Trojan war; son of Peleus.

Achīvī, -ōrum, M. pl.: the Greeks.

aciēs, -ēī, F., edge ; acies ferri, the edge of the sword : line of battle ; aciem instruere, to draw up a line of battle ; acie certare, to fight in line of battle ; legiones in acie constituere, to draw up the legions in line (c. iv, 35).

ācriter, adv., fiercely, keenly (comp., ācrius ; sup., ācerrimē); acriter pugnatum est, a keen battle was fought.

actuārius, -a, -um, adj., impelled by oars, furnished with oars.

acūtus, -a, -um, adj., sharp, keen.

ad, prep. (with acc.), to, against, towards, near to, at, alongside (c. iv, 25) often used with gerund or gerundive, for the purpose of (c. iv, 23, 29, 31); ad pristinam fortunam, to complete his former good fortune (c. iv, 26); ad diem, on the right day, punctually (c. v, 1); ad Cantium, at Kent (c. v, 13); ad solis occasum, at sunset (c. v, 8); ad hunc modum, in this way.

adaequō, āre, āvī, ātum, v. tr., equal.

addō, -ere, -didī, -ditum, v. tr., add, join to.

addūcō, -ere, -duxī, -ductum, v. tr., lead to, bring to (of persons) (c. iv, 22, 36); induce (c. iv, 37).

adeō, -īre, -iī (-īvī), -itum, v. tr. and intr., approach, visit, reach.

adeō, adv., to this point, so, such, to that degree.

(adfor), -ārī, -ātus sum, speak to.

adfore, fut. Infin. of adsum; see adsum.

adhibeō, -ēre, -hibuī, hibitum, v. tr., summon, call in, admit; adhibitis principibus majoribusque natu, summoning the chiefs and elders (c. iv, 13).

adhortor, -hortārī, -hortātus sum, v. dep., encourage.

adhuc, adv., to this place, thus far, as yet.

adjiciō, -jicere, -jēcī, -jectum, v. tr, throw to, throw up; in litus telum adjici poterat, a dart could be thrown to the water's edge (c. iv, 23); aggerem ad munitiones adjicere, to throw up a mound against the fortifications (c. v, 9).

adimō, -ere, -ēmī, -emptum, v. tr., take away, deprive of.

aditus, -ūs, M., approach, landing-place (c. iv, 20); mercatoribus est aditus, merchants have access (c. iv, 2).

adjungō, -ere, -junxī, -junctum, v. tr., join to, add.

adjuvō, -āre, -jūvī, -jūtum, v. tr., aid, help, assist.

administrō, -āre, -āvī, -ātum, v. tr., do, manage; cum paulo tardius administratum esset, when this was done somewhat slowly (c. iv, 23); rempublicam administrare, to carry on the government.

admittō, -ere, -mīsī, -missum, v. tr., allow, permit; facinus admittere, to commit a crime; dedecus

admittere, to be guilty of a disgrace (c. iv, 25).

admodum, adv., very much, greatly; with numbers, fully, at least.

adolescens, -centis, M., a youth.

adorior, -orīrī, -ortus sum, v. tr. dep., rise up against; attack, assail.

adportō, -portāre, -portāvī, portātum, v. tr., convey to.

adsentiō, -sentire, -sensī, -sensum, v. intr., assent, approve.

adservō, -āre, -āvī, -ātum, v. tr., guard closely, closely cling to.

adspīrō, -spīrāre, -spīrāvī, -spīrātum (with dat.), breathe upon, am favorable to.

adstō, -stāre, -stitī, no sup., stand by, stand erect.

adsum, -esse, -fuī, v. intr., be present, near.

adventus, -ūs, M., arrival.

adversus, -a, -um, adj., turned to, opposed to, unfavorable: nocte adversa, in the teeth of night, or in a foul night (c. iv, 28); adversi venti, warring winds

adversus, prep. (with acc.), opposed to, over against.

advertō, -ere, -vertī, -versum, v. tr., turn to; animum advertere, to notice.

advolō, -āre, -āvī, -ātum, v. tr., fly to, hasten to.

aedēs, -is, F., a temple; in plural, a house or temples.

aedificium, -ī, N., dwelling, house.

aedificō, -āre, -āvī, -ātum, v. tr., build.

Aeduī, -ōrum, M. pl., the Aedui, a tribe of Gaul (France).

Aeduus, -a, -um, adj., Aeduan.

aeger, -gra, -grum, adj., sick (comp. aegrior; sup., aegerrimus).

aegrē, adv., with difficulty, scarcely, hardly.

Aeneas, -ae, M.; Aeneas, son of Anchises and Venus, and hero of the Aeneid.

aēneus, -a, -um, adj., made of bronze or copper.

aequinoctium, -ī, N., the equinox, either 21st March or 21st September; in Caesar, the latter.

aequō, -āre, -āvī, -ātum, v. tr., make equal.

aequor, -oris, N., sea.

aequus, -a, -um, adj., just.

aerātus, -a, -um, adj., of brass, brazen.

aes, aeris, N., bronze, copper (c. iv, 31) money; aes alienum, debt (literally, money belonging to another)

aestās, -ātis, F., summer; media aestate, in the middle of summer; extrema aestate, at the end of summer; prima aestate, at the beginning of summer; aestatem consumere, to spend the summer (c. v. 4).

aestimō, -āre, -āvī, -ātum, v. tr., value, think, reckon; litem aestimare, to assess the amount of damages (c. v, 1).

aestus, -ūs, M., tide.

aether, -eris, M., the bright upper air, sky

aetās, -ātis, F., period of life, age : per aetatem, on account of age (c. v. 3).

afferō, -ferre, attulī, allātum, v. tr., bring to, assign, report, announce.

affirmō, -āre, -āvī, -ātum, v. tr, assert, declare.

afflictō, -āre, -āvī, -ātum, v. tr., damage, wreck.

afflīgō, -ere, -flixī, -flictum, v. tr, damage ; navem affligere, to shatter a vessel (c. iv, 31); afflictus, downcast.

afflō, -āre, -āvī, -ātum, v. tr., breathe upon, blast.

affluō, -ere, -fluxī, -fluxum, v. tr., flow to ; throng, flock to.

Africus, -ī, M. (properly an adj., with ventus understood); the southwest wind, still called Africo by the Italians.

Agamemnon, -onis, M., Agamemnon, king of Mycenae in Greece, and commander of the Greek forces at Troy.

ager, agrī, M., a field, land ; pl., lands, territories.

agger, -eris, M., a mound.

agglomerō, -āre, -āvī, -ātum, v. intr. (with dat.), join themselves to.

aggredior, -gredī, -gressus sum, v. tr. dep., go against, assail, attack.

aggregō, -āre, -āvī, -ātum, join to ; se aggregare (military term), fall in (c. iv, 26).

agitō, -āre, -āvī, -ātum, v. tr., keep moving, pursue, ponder (freq. from agō).

agmen, -inis, N., an army on the march ; a column ; agmine certo: with unwavering course

agnoscō, -ere, -gnōvī, -gnitum, v. tr., recognize.

agō, agere, ēgī, actum, v. tr., move, go, do, drive ; clamoribus

actus, influenced by the shouts.

āiō, v. tr., defective, 3rd sing., ait.

Ajax, -ācis ; N. m.; Ajax, a Grecian hero, son of Oileus, king of the Locri in Greece. Sometimes called the lesser Ajax to distinguish him from the greater Ajax, son of Telamon, who, being defeated by Ulysses in the contest for the Arms of Achilles, went mad and slew himself.

alacritās, -ātis, F., dash, haste ; alacritate uti, to show dash (c. iv. 24).

albus, -a, -um, adj., white ; album plumbum, tin (c. v, 12).

aliēnus, -a, -um, adj., belonging to another ; another's ; strange, foreign, hostile ; aes alienum, debt (another's money)); alieno loco, on unfavorable ground ; alienum tempus, an unfavorable time (c. iv, 34).

aliō, adv., elsewhere.

aliquamdiū, adv., for some time ; for a while.

aliquantus, -a, -um, adj., considerable, some ; aliquantum itineris, some distance (c. v, 10).

aliquī, -quae, -quod, indef. pro., some one, any one.

aliquis, -qua, -quid. indep. pro., some one, any one ; aliquid temporis, some time.

aliter, adv., otherwise.

alius, -a, -ud (for declension see H. L., p. 48, 2), pro., another, other, different; alius...alius.one...another; alii...alii, some...others; alius alia ex navi, one from one ship, another from another (c. iv, 26).

allātus : see afferō.

almus, -a, -um, adj. nurturing; kindly (alo, "nourish ").

alō, alere, aluī, alitum or altum, v. tr., rear, nourish.

altāria, -ium, n, pl., altar (altus, " high ").

alter, -era, -erum, adj., one of two; alter...alter, the one...the other; alteri...alteri, the one party...the other party

altitūdō, -inis, F., height, depth.

altus, -a, -um, adj., high, deep ; in alto, on the deep ; also in pl. tranquilla per alta

alvus, -ī, F., belly.

ambiguus, -a, -um, adj., of doubtful meaning, dark.

ambo, -ae, -o, adj., both.

āmens, -tis, adj., out of one's mind, mad.

āmentia, -ae, F., madness, folly.

amīcē, adv., friendly.

amīcitia, -ae, F., friendship ; ab amicitia deficere, cast off an alliance.

amīcus, -a, -um, adj., friendly.

amīcus, -ī, M., a friend.

amittō, -ere, -mīsī, -missum, v. tr., lose.

amnis, -is, M., river.

amor, -ōris, love, desire.

amplē, adv., abundantly ; comp. amplius, more.

amplector, -plectī, -plexus sum, v. dep., embrace, encircle

amplius, neut. comp. of adj., amplus, more, further. Often used with numerals without any influence on the construction : amplius octingentae (naves), more than eight hundred ships.

amplus, -a, -um, adj., large, noble, distinguished ; amplissimo genere nātus, born of a most illustrious family.

an, interrogative participle, whether, or.

Ancalitēs, -um, pl. M., the Ancalites, a British tribe in Berkshire and Oxfordshire.

Anchīsēs, -ae, M., Anchises, father of Aeneas.

ancora, -ae, F., an anchor; navem tenere in ancoris, to keep a ship at anchor ; ancoram tollere, to weigh anchor (c. iv, 23); in ancoris exspectare, to wait at anchor (c. iv, 23) : ancoram jacere, to cast anchor (c. iv, 28); ad ancoras naves deligare, to ride at anchor (c. v, 9).

ancilla, -ae, F., a hand-maid, servant.

Androgeōs, -ī, M., Androgeos, a Greek hero

Andromachē, -ēs, F., Andromache, wife of Hector

anguis, -is, M. and F., snake, serpent.

angulus, -ī, M., a corner.

angustē, adv., narrowly, closely ; angustius milites collocare, to stow the soldiers in somewhat narrower space than usual.

angustiae, -ārum, pl. F., defile, strait (of sea).

angustus, -a, -um, adj., narrow, contracted ; angusta viarum = angusta loca viarum, the narrow places of the streets

anima, -ae, F., life, soul ; animam deponere, to relinquish his life.

animadvertō, -ere, -vertī, -versum, v. tr., notice.

animal, -ālis, N., animal.

animus, -ī, M., mind, soul, spirit, courage ; magni animi, of great courage (c. v, 6); animis impeditis, when the attention of all was engaged (c. v, 7); animi voluptatisque causā, for sentiment and amusement (c. v, 12); fidens animi, confident in soul ; conversi (sunt) animi, our feelings were altered.

annon, interrog. particle, or not (in the second member of a direct question.

annōtinus, -a, -um, adj., of the year before.

annus, -ī, a year ; primis ab annis, from my early years.

anser, -eris, M., a goose.

ante, (1) adv., previously, before ; paucis ante diebus, a few days before ; (2) prep. with acc. only ; before, in front of, in advance of. For ante quam see antequam

anteā, adv., previously, before.

antepōnō, -ere, -posuī, -positum, v. tr., prefer.

antequam, conj., before.

antīquus, -a, -um, adj., old, ancient.

Ap. = Appius, a Roman praenomen (see cognomen).

aperiō, -īre, uī, -tum, v. tr., open.

apertus, -a, -um, adj., open, exposed ; aperto litore, on an open shore (c. iv, 23); ad latus apertum (c. iv, 25) ; ab latere aperto, on the exposed flank (on the right side) (c. iv,26).

Apollo, -inis, M., Apollo

appāreō, -ēre, -pāruī, -pāritum, v. intr., attend, appear

apparō, -āre, -āvī, -ātum, v. tr., prepare, make preparations for, provide for.

appellō, -āre, -āvī -ātum, v. tr., call.

appellō, -ere, -pulī, -pulsum, v. tr., bring to land (of ships); in passive, call at, touch at (c. v, 13).

Appius, -ī, Appius, a Roman praenomen (see nomen).

apportō, -āre, -āvī, -ātum, v. tr., bring, carry to (a place).

appropinquō, -āre, -āvī, -ātum (with dat.), v. intr., approach, come near (c. iv, 25, 28).

aptō, -āre, -āvī, -ātum, v. tr., fit, fit on.

aptus, -a, -um, adj., fit, suitable.

apud, prep. (with accusative); near, at, beside; apud urbem, near the city; apud eum, in his command (c. v, 11).

aqua, -ae, F., water.

aquātiō, -ōnis, F., fetching water, watering; aquationis causā, to obtain water (c. iv, 11).

aquila, -ae, F., an eagle, standard of the legion as opposed to signa, standards of the cohorts (c. iv, 25).

aquilifer, -ferī, M., the eagle-bearer, the standard-bearer.

āra, -ae, F., an altar.

Arar, -aris, M., the Arar (now the Saone), a tributary of the Rhodanus (Rhone).

arātrum, -ī, N., a plough.

arbiter, -trī, M., judge; dare arbitros, to appoint arbitrators (c. v, 1).

arbitrium, -ī, N., a judgment, decision.

arbitror, -ārī, -ātus sum, v. tr. dep., think, suppose, consider.

arbor, -oris, F., a tree.

arceō, -ēre, -uī, no sup., confine, restrain.

arcessō, -ere, -īvī, -ītum, v. tr., send for, summon (c. iv, 27).

ardens, -ntis, adj., on fire, eager; blazing (ardeo).

ardeō, -ēre, arsī, arsum, be on fire; be eager.

Arduenna, -ae, F., the Ardennes, a forest of north-eastern Gaul, which extended through the territories of the Treveri to those of the Remi (c. v, 3).

arduus, -a, -um, adj., lofty, towering.

argentum, -ī, N., silver, money.

Argī, -ōrum, pl. M., Argos, a city of Argolis, in the eastern part of the Peloponnesus.

Argīvī, -ōrum, M. pl., the Argives, the Greeks.

Argīvus, -a, -um, adj., Argive, Grecian.

Argolicus, -a, -um, adj., Argolic (belonging to Argos).

Argos (only used in nom. and acc. sing.), N., see Argi.

āridus, -a, -um, adj., dry. As a substantive, aridum, dry land; ex arido, on the shore (c. iv; 24); in arido (c. iv, 26).

ariēs, -etis, M., a battering ram.

arma, -ōrum, pl. N., arms; in armis esse, to bear arms (c. v. 3); ab armis discedere, to lay down arms.

armāmentum, -ī, N., tackle (of a vessel).

armātūra, -ae, F., armor; levis armaturae milites, light-armed soldiers.

armātus, -a, -um, adj., armed.

armentum, -ī, N., herd (aro, to plough).

armiger, -gera, -gerum, adj., armor-bearer.

armipotens, -ntis, adj., powerful in arms.

armō, -āre, -āvī, -ātum, v. tr., arm; copiae armatae, forces in arms (c. iv, 23); armato milite, with armed soldiery; ad armandas naves, for the equipment of the vessels (c. v, 1).

arō, -āre, -āvī, -ātum, v. tr., plough.

arrectus, -a, -um, adj., raised: luminibus arrectis, with eyes distended; pectora arrecta, uplifted breasts; arrectis auribus, with eager ears.

arrigō, -ere, -rexī, -rectum, v. tr., lift, raise.

ars, -tis, F., cunning.

artifex, -icis, M., contriver, plotter.

artus, -ūs, M., limb.

artus, -a, -um, adj., confining, tight.

arvum, -ī, N., a field.

arx, -cis, F., citadel; summa ab arce, from the top of the citadel.

Ascānius, -ī, M., Ascanius or Iulus, son of Aeneas.

ascendō, -ere, -scendī, -scensum, v. tr., ascend, mount; navem ascendere, to embark; vestram ascendere in urbem, to go into your city.

ascensus, -ūs, M., ascent.

Asia, -ae, F., Asia.

aspectus, -ūs, M., appearance.

asper, -era, -erum, adj., rough. aspris=asperis.

aspiciō, -ere, -spexī, -spectum, v. tr., behold.

ast = at, conj., but.

astans (see asto), used as an adj., standing by.

astō, astāre, astitī, astitum, v. intr., stand by.

astrum, -ī, N., star (ἄστρον).

Astyanax, -actis, M., Astyanax, son of Hector.

asȳlum, -ī, N., place of refuge, sanctuary (ἄσυλον).

at, conj., but, yet.

āter, ātra, ātrum, adj., black, gloomy.

atque (contracted ac ; atque, before vowels, ac, before consonants), conj., and also, and even, and (stronger than et); par atque, the same as; aliter atque, different than ; contra atque, otherwise than.

Atrebas, -atis, adj., *Atrebatian.*

Atrebatēs, -um, M., *the Atrebates,* a people of Belgic Gaul in the modern Artois or Arras *(Flemish Atrecht).*

atrium, -ī, N., court.

Atrīdae, -ārum, M. pl., *the sons of Atreus, i.e.,* Agamemnon and Menelaus.

Atrius, -ī, M., *Quintus Atrius,* an officer in Caesar's army, who was left on the south coast of Britain to look after the fleet while Caesar marched inland on his second expedition, 54 B.C.

attingō. -ere, -tigī, -tactum, v. tr., touch, reach ; terram attingere, reach land (c. v, 23).

attollō, -tollere, v. tr., raise.

attrectō, -āre, -āvī, -ātum, handle, (ad, tracto).

auctor, -ōris, M.; me auctore, at my suggestion.

auctōritās, -ātis, F., authority, influence, power, prestige.

auctumnus (or autumnus), -ī, M., autumn.

audācia, -ae, F., boldness, daring.

audāciter, adv., boldly.

audacter, same as audaciter.

audax, -ācis, adj., bold, daring.

audeō, -ēre, ausus sum, semidep. v. tr. and intr., dare, be bold ; audēre in proelio, to be bold for battle

audiō, -īre, -īvī, -ītum, v. tr., hear.

augurium, ī, N., omen by the utterance of birds ; omen (avis ; root GAR, "to call").

aula, -ae, F., a hall.

aura, -ae, F., air.

aurātus, -a, -um, adj., gilded.

aureus, -a, -um, adj., golden, of gold.

aurīga, -ae, M., a charioteer, driver.

auris, -is, F., an ear.

aurum, -ī, N., gold.

Aurunculeius, -ī, M., *Lucius Aurunculeius Cotta,* one of the lieutenants of Caesar in Gaul. He fell in an ambuscade planned by Ambiorix, 54 B.C.

Auster, -trī, M., south wind.

ausum, -ī, N., daring deed (audeo).

aut, conj., or; aut...aut, either .. or.

autem, conj., but, moreover, yet, also, now. (Never put first in a clause).

Automedon, -ontis, M., *Automedon,* charioteer of Achilles

autumnus, see auctumnus.

auxilior, -ārī, ātus sum, v. intr. dep. (with dat.), give help.

auxilium, -ī, N., aid, support ; in plural, auxilia, -orum, auxiliary troops.

āvehō, -ere, -vexī, -vectum, v. tr. carry away.

āvellō, -ere, -vellī, or -vulsī, -vulsum, v. tr., tear away.

āversus, -a, -um, (perf. part. pass. of averto used as an) adj., turned away.

āvertō, -ere, -tī, -sum, turn away.

avidus, -a, -um, adj., eager, covetous.

āvius, -a, -um, adj. (a, "away from," via), pathless ; N. avium, as subst., bypath.

avus, -ī, M., a grandfather.

axis, -is, M., axle, axis ; the axis of heaven, heaven.

B

barbarī, -ōrum, M. pl., barbarians, a name first applied by the Greeks, then by the Romans, to the people of other nations.

barbarus, -a, -um, adj., savage, barbarous.

Belgae, -ārum, pl. M., *the Belgae,* a general name applied to a warlike people of north-eastern Gaul, from the Mosa *(Meuse)* to the Sequana *(Seine),* partly Celtic, partly Teutonic. The chief tribes were the Remi, Morini, Nervii, Suessiones.

Belgium, -ī, N., *Belgium,* the part of Gallia Belgica inhabited by the Bellovaci, Atrebates and the Ambiani.

bellicōsus, -a, -um, adj., warlike.

Bēlīdēs, -dae, M., *(patronymic), son of Belus;* see Palamēdēs.

bellum, -ī, N., war; bellum populo Romano facere, to make war against the Roman people (c. iv, 22).

bene, adv., well, prosperously ; comp., melius ; sup., optimē.

Bibrocī, -ōrum, M. pl., *the Bibroci*, a tribe of Britain which occupied *Berks, Sussex, Surrey* and adjoining district.

biduum, -ī, N., a space of two days.

bigae, -ārum (=bī-jugae; bis, jugum, a yoke), F. (pl), a car or chariot drawn by two horses.

bipatens, -entis, adj., opening in two ways, swinging.

bipennis, -is, F., double axe.

bis, num. adv., twice.

bonus, -a, -um, adj., good ; comp., melior; sup., optimus.

bōs, bovis, M. or F., an ox, cow ; pl., boves, cattle.

. brāchium, -ī, N., arm.

brevis, -e, adj., short, brief ; brevī (tempore), in a short time, soon (c. iv, 33).

breviter, adv., shortly, briefly.

Britannī, -ōrum, pl. M., *Britons*.

Britannia, -ae, F., *Britain*.

Britannicus, -a, -um, adj., British.

brūma, -ae, F. (= brevima = brevissima (dies) the shortest day), the winter solstice ; Dec. 21st.

C

C., an abbreviation for Caius, a Roman praenomen (see cognomen) as in Caius Julius Caesar, Caius Volusenus, Cains Trebonius.

cadō, cadere, cecidī, cāsum, v. intr., fall : set ; cadentia sidera, setting stars.

caecus, -a, -um, adj., blind (Verg. 244), caeco Marte resistunt, they resist in aimless war

caedēs, -is, F., slaughter, murder.

caedō, caedere, cecidī, caesum, v. tr., cut, slay.

caelicola, -ae, M. and F., one who dwells in heaven ; heavenly being ; (caelum, colo).

caelum, -ī, N., sky, heavens.

caerimōnia, -ae, F., rite, reverence, veneration, awe.

caeruleus, -a, -um, adj., deep blue, sky-blue.

Caesar, -aris, M.

Calchás, -ntis, M., *Calchas*, a Greek soothsayer.

cālīgō, -inis, F., thick darkness.

campus, -ī, M., plain, field.

canō, canere, cecinī, cantum, v. tr. and intr., sing, prophesy (because oracles were expressed in verse).

Cantium, -ī, N., *Kent*, a county in south-eastern England.

capillus, -ī, M., hair; esse promisso capillo, to wear long hair (c. v, 14).

capiō, capere, cēpī, captum, v. tr., take ; portum capere, to make the harbor (c. iv, 36); so. insulam capere (c. iv, 26, v. 8); capere consilium, to form a plan (c. v, 8).

captivus, -ī M., a captive, prisoner.

captus, -a, -um (perf. part. pass. of capio), taken, captured, charmed, influenced.

capulus, -ī, M., the handle, hilt (capio: hence, "the thing grasped").

caput, -itis, N., head.

Capys, -yos, M., *Capys*, a Trojan.

cardō, -inis, M., hinge.

careō, -ēre, -uī. -itum. or cassum, be without (with abl.)

carina, -ae, F., hull of a vessel, keel.

carmen, -inis, N., song.

carō, -nis, F., flesh ; carne vivere, to live on flesh (c. v, 14).

cārus, -a, -um, adj., dear, beloved, agreeable to.

Carvilius, -ī, M., *Carvilius*, a petty king of Kent (c. v, 22).

Cassandra, -ae, F., *Cassandra*, daughter of Priam, inspired by Apollo with the gift of prophecy, but doomed by him never to be believed.

Cassī, -ōrum, pl. M., the *Cassi*, a British tribe that inhabited Herefordshire.

Cassius, -ī, M., *Caius Cassius Longus*, one of the assassins of Caesar. He died 42 B.C., at Philippi.

Cassivellaunus, -ī, M., *Cassivellaunus*, or *Caswallon*, the able commander-in-chief of the British army opposed to Caesar. His chief town was Verulamium, (now *St. Albans*).

cassus, -a, -um, perf. part. pass. of careo, deprived of (with abl.); (see careo).

castellum, -ī, N , a fortress.

Casticns, -ī, M., *Casticus*, a chief of the Sequani, whom Orgetorix induced to seize the supreme power in his state.

castrum, -ī, N., a hut, fort ; in pl., castra, -ōrum, a camp; castra ponere. to pitch a camp; **castra munire**; to fortify a camp, to pitch a camp; **castra movere**, to advance; **castra navalia**, an encampment on the shore for protecting the fleet and the troops while landing; sometimes connected with the ships drawn up on land (c. v, 22).

cāsū, (abl. of **cāsus,** used as an) adv., by chance.

cāsus, -ūs, M., chance, misfortune, emergency.

caterva, -ae, F., band.

catulus, -ī, M., whelp, cub.

causa, -ae, F., cause; **sine causā,** without reason (c. iv, 27 ; c. v, 6).

causā, adv. (really abl. of **causa,** with the noun depending on it in the gen.), for the sake of, on account of ; **mea causa,** for my sake; often with gerundives, **frigoris depellendi causa,** for the purpose of warding off the cold (c. iv, 22).

cavō, -āre, -āvī, -ātum, v. tr., make hollow, pierce.

cavus, -a, -um, adj., hollow.

cēdō, cēdere, cessī, cessum, v. intr., go, yield; fall back, retire; **insequi cedentes,** to overtake the retreating foe (c. v, 16).

celeritās, -ātis, F., swiftness, speed.

celeriter, adv., quickly; comp., **celerius;** sup., **celerrimē.**

celsus, -a, -um, adj., high, lofty.

Cenimagnī, -ōrum, M., pl., *the Cenimagni.* The word Cenimagni is said to be a corruption for **Iceni magni.** They inhabited Norfolk and Suffolk, north of the Trinobantes.

centum, num. adj., indecl., hundred.

Cerēs, -eris, F., *Ceres,* goddess of agriculture.

cernō, cernere, crēvī, crētum, v. tr., see perceive.

certāmen, -inis, N., conflict, battle, struggle.

certē, adv., at least, certainly.

certātim, adv. with emulation, earnestly (**certo**).

certō, -āre, -āvī, -ātum, v. intr., strive, contend.

certus, -a, -um, adj., certain, fixed, true; **aliquem certiorem facere,** inform ; **certior fieri,** to be informed ; **certus locus,** a definite place ; **certa dies,** a fixed day (c. v, 1).

cervix, -icis, F., neck.

cessō, -āre, -āvī, -ātum, v. intr., cease.

(cēterus), -a, -um (nom. sing. not found; usually in plural), the rest, others.

ceu, adv., as, just as, as if.

ciō, -ēre, -cīvi, -cītum, v. tr., stir up.

Cingetorix, -igis, M., *Cingetorix;* (1) a Gaul attached to Caesar, and rival of Indutiomarus for the chieftainship of the Treveri (c. v, 3). (2) a British chief of Kent (c. v, 22).

cingō, cingere, cinxī, cinctum, v. tr., surround.

cinis, -eris, M., ashes.

circā, adv. and prep. (with acc.); about, around, in the neighborhood of (see **circum**).

circiter, adv. (with numeral adjectives) ; about, nearly.

circneō, see **circumeō.**

circuitus, -ūs, M., circumference.

circum, prep. (with acc.), around.

circumdō, -dare, -dedī, -datum, v. tr., place around, surround ; **urbem muro** (abl.) **circumdare,** or **urbi** (dat.) **murum circumdare,** to surround the city with a wall.

circumeō, īre, -iī (-īvī), -itum or **circuitum,** v. tr., go around, visit ; **hiberna circumire,** to inspect the winter quarters (c. v, 2).

circumerrō, -āre, -āvī, -ātum wander round.

circumfundō, -fundere, -fūdī, -fūsum, v. tr., pour around ; in passive, surround, crowd around.

circumsistō, sistere, -stetī, no sup., v. tr. and intr., surround

circumspiciō, -spicere, -spexī, -spectum, v. tr., be around

circumstō, -stāre, -stetī, no sup., v. tr. and intr., stand around, surround.

circumvolō, -āre, -āvī, -ātum, v. intr., surround

citerior, -ōris, adj. (p. 59, 2), on this side, hither; **Gallia citerior,** Gaul on this (*i.e.,* the Roman) side of the Alps (*Northern Italy*), opposed to **Gallia ulterior,** Gaul beyond the Alps (*France*).

citō, adv., rapidly, swiftly ; comp., **citius;** sup. **citissimē.**

cīvis, -is, M. or F., citizen.

cīvitās, -ātis, F., state, commonwealth ; **civitati consulere,** to take measures for the benefit of the state (c. v, 3).

clādēs, -is, F., slaughter, disaster.

clam, adv., secretly.

clāmor, -ōris, M., shout.

clangor, -ōris, M., braying (of trumpets).

clārescō, -ere, clāruī, no sup., grow clear.

clārus, -a, -um, adj., bright, clear, distinguished.

classis, -is, F., fleet.

Claudius, -ī, M., *Claudius*. Appius Claudius, consul with Lucius Domitius, B.C. 54. He was brother of the infamous Clodius whom Milo murdered, and was a well known lawyer and politician of Rome.

claustrum, -ī, N., bar.

clipeus, -ī, M., a shield.

Cn. = Cneius, see Pompeius, Servilius.

Cneius, -ī, M., see Cn.

coactus, -a, -um, (perf. part. pass. of cogo used as an adj.), forced; coactis lacrimis, by his forced tears.

coepī, -isse, v. defec., begin, began.

coeptus, -a, -um, perf. part. pass. of coepī, begun.

coerceō, -ēre, -ercuī, -ercitum, v. tr., check, restrain.

cognōmen, -inis, N., a family name, a name. Each Roman had regularly three names, the praenomen, indicating the individual like our Christian name; the nomen indicating the gens, or clan, or tribe to which he belonged; the cognomen or family name. Caius (praenomen), Julius (nomen), Caesar (cognomen); an agnomen was often added for honor or character, as Africanus to Scipio.

cognōscō, cognoscere, cognōvī, cognitum, v. tr., know, learn, ascertain (c. v, 11).

cōgō, cōgere, coēgī, coactum, v. tr., collect, compel, oblige; equitatum cogere, to collect cavalry (c. v, 3; iv, 22, 34).

cohors, -tis, F., a cohort, the tenth part of a legion (see legio).

cohortor, -ārī, -ātus sum, v. tr. dep., exhort, encourage, animate, urge; cohortati inter se, urging each other (c. iv, 25).

collaudō, -āre, -āvī, -ātum, v. tr., praise, extol.

colligō, -ligere, -lēgī, -lectum, v. tr., collect, assemble.

collis, -is, M., a hill.

collocō, -āre, -āvī, -ātum, v. tr., station; curru collocare, station themselves with their chariots; in statione collocati, stationed on guard (c. v, 15).

colloquor, -loquī, -locūtus sum, v. dep., talk together, confer; inter se collocuti, holding a conference among themselves (c. iv, 30).

collum, -ī, N., neck.

colō, colere, coluī, cultum, v. tr., till, cultivate:

color, -ōris, M., color.

coluber, -brī, M., serpent.

columba, -ae, F., dove.

coma, -ae, F., hair.

comans, -tis, adj., crested, hairy.

comes, -itis, M., companion.

comitor, -ārī, -ātus sum, v. tr. dep., attend, be a companion to.

commeātus, -ūs, M., a coming and a going; supplies; duobus commeatibus, by two relays (c. v, 23).

commendō, -āre, -āvī, -ātum, v. tr., commit to protection, entrust.

commīlitō, -ōnis, M., fellow-soldier, comrade.

committō, -ere, -mīsī, -missum, v. tr., engage; committere proelium cum hostibus, to engage in battle with the enemy; nihil his committere, to trust nothing to these (c. iv, 5).

Commius, -ī, M., *Commius*, a Gaul, chief of the Atrebates.

commodē, adv., conveniently, profitably.

commodum, -ī, N., convenience, profit; quas suī quisque commodī fecerat, which each had made for his own convenience (c. v, 8).

commodus, -a, -um, adj., convenient, favorable, fit, easy.

commoror, -morārī, -morātus sum, v. dep. intr., delay, stay, remain.

commoveō, -movēre, -mōvī, -mōtum, v. tr., disturb, agitate, alarm.

commūniō, -īre, -īvī, -ītum, v. tr., fortify strongly.

commūnis, -e, adj., common, general, affable, courteous: communi consilio, after joint deliberation (c. v, 11; communēs, in common (c. v, 14).

commūtātiō, -ōnis, F., change.

compāges, -is, F., joint, fastening.

comparō, -āre, -āvī, -ātum, v. tr., make ready, prepare; copias comparare, to collect forces; re frumentaria comparata, after collecting a supply of corn (c. iv, 7).

compellō, -ere, -pulī, -pulsum, v. tr., drive in a body.

compellō, -āre, -āvī, -ātum, v. tr., address.

comperiō, -perīre, -perī, -pertum, v. tr., find out, discover.

complector, -plectī, -plexus sum, v. dep., embrace.

compleō, -ēre, -plēvī, -plētum, v. tr., fill completely; naves militibus complere, to man ships with soldiers (c. iv, 26).

complūrēs, -plūra, adj. pl., very many, several.

comportō, -āre, -āvī, -ātum, v. tr., bring together, collect.

compositō, adv., by agreement.

comprehendō, -ere, -prehendī, -prehensum, v. tr., seize, arrest.

compressus, -a -um, perf. part. pass. of comprimo.

comprimō, -ere, -pressī, -pressum, v. tr., suppress.

comprendō, -ere, -dī, -sum, grasp; grasp (with the mind), comprehend.

concēdō, -cēdere, -cessī, cessum, v. tr., leave; superis concessit ab oris, he left the realms above.

concidō, -ere, -dī, no sup., fall down (cado).

conciliō, -āre, -āvī, -ātum, v. tr., win over, reconcile.

concilium, -ī, N., a meeting, assembly; habere concilium, to hold a meeting (c. iv, 19).

conclāmō, -āre, -āvī, -ātum, v. intr., shout, or cry out together.

concrescō, -crēvī, -crētum, v. intr., grow together.

concrētus, -a, -um, perf. part. pass. of concresco, used as an adj., matted.

concurrō, -currere, -currī, -cursum, v. intr., run together, rush.

concursus, -ūs, M., attack; ex eo concursu, from that collision (c. v, 10).

concutiō, -ere, -cussī, -cussum, shake vigorously (cum quatio).

condensus, a, um, adj., very thick.

condiciō, -ōnis, F., terms.

condō, -ere, -didī, -ditum, v. tr., found, establish, build.

condōnō, -āre, -āvī, -ātum, v. tr., forgive, pardon.

Condrūsī, -ōrum, pl., M., the Condrusi, a people of north-eastern Gaul, on the right bank of the Mosa (Meuse) in the district of the modern Namur and Liège.

condūcō, -ere, duxī, ductum, v. tr., bring together, hire.

confercio, -ire -fersī -fertum, v. tr., pack together; to cause to take close order; legione conferta, owing to the legion being in close order (c. iv, 32).

conferō, -ferre, -tulī, collātum, v. tr., bring together, gather, collect; se conferre, to betake oneself.

confertus, -a, -um, perf. part. pass. of confercio, used as an adj. in close array.

confestim, adv., immediately after the battle.

conficiō, -ficere, -fēcī, -fectum, v. tr., do thoroughly; bello confecto, when the war was over (c. iv, 16); rem conficere, to complete a matter (c. iv, 11); itinere confecto, after the march was made (c. iv, 14).

confīdō, -fīdere, -fīsus sum, semi-dep., v. intr., trust thoroughly.

configō, fīgere, -fixī, -fixum, v. tr., pierce.

confirmō, -āre, -āvī, -ātum, v. tr., establish: pace confirmata, when peace was made (c. iv, 28).

confiteor, -ērī, -fessus sum, confess, acknowledge (fateor).

confligō, -ere, -flixī, -flictum, v. tr., strike; proelio confligere, to engage in battle (c. v, 15).

confundō, -ere, -fūdī, -fūsum, pour together, confuse.

congemō, -ere, -uī, no sup., groan, deeply (con, intensive).

congerō, -ere, -gessī, -gestum, heap together.

congredior, -gredī, -gressus sum, v. tr., meet, charge; inter se congredi, to charge each other.

conjiciō, -jicere, -jēcī, -jectum, v. tr., throw together (at a point); in fugam conjicere, to put to flight; se in fugam conjicere, to betake oneself to flight (c. iv, 12); culpam in aliquem conjicere, to cast the blame on some one (c. v, 27); in vincula conjicere, to throw into prison (c. iv, 27).

conjugium, -ī, N., wedlock; husband (jungo, root jug).

conjungō, -ere, -junxī, junctum, v. tr., unite, join.

conjunx, -ugis, M. and F., one joined; husband, wife, spouse (cum, jungo).

conjūrātiō, -ōnis, F., league; facere conjurationem, to form a league (c. iv, 30).

cōnor, -ārī, -ātus sum, endeavor, attempt.

consanguinitās, -ātis, F., blood-relationship, kin.

conscendō, -ere, -scendī, -scensum, v. tr., embark in, mount; in navem conscendere, to embark on a vessel (c. iv, 23; v. 7); in equum conscendere, to mount a horse.

conscius, -a, -um, adj., conscious, knowing my purpose, agmina conscia, confederate bands.

consequor, -sequī, -secūtus (or sequūtus) sum, v. tr. dep., follow, follow up.

conserō, -ere, seruī, -sertum, v. tr., join together, unite, bring together; proelium or pugnam or manum conserere, to engage in battle

consīdo, -ere, -sēdī, -sessum, v. intr., settle, halt; copiae considunt, the forces encamp (c. v, 9).

consilium, -ī, N., plan, design; wisdom, prudence; capere consilium, to form a plan (c. v, 8) inire consilium, to adopt a plan (c. iv, 32); communi consilio, after joint deliberation (c. v, 6); publico consilio, by a public plan (c. v, 1); consilio instituto, from carrying out his appointed plan (c. v, 4).

consimilis, -e, adj., very like, like in every particular.

consistō, -ere, -stitī, -stitum, v. intr., stand, halt; consist of; consistit in carne, it consists of flesh; in fluctibus est consistendum, they had to keep their footing among the waves (c. iv, 24), stand still

consōlor, -ārī, -ātus sum, v. tr. dep., console, comfort, cheer (c. v, 4).

conspectus, -ūs, M., sight appearance; conspectu in medio, amid the gazing throng

conspiciō, -spicere, -spexī, -spectum, v. tr., observe, see.

conspicor, -ārī, -ātus sum, v. tr. dep., see, get a sight of, espy.

constat, -stāre, -stitit, impers. v., it is agreed, well known.

constituō, -ere, -stituī, -stitūtum, v. tr., draw up; aciem constituere, to draw up a line of battle (c. iv, 35); hiberna constituere, to appoint the winter quarters (c. iv, 38); classem, navem constituere, to moor a fleet, a ship: die constituta, on a set day; his rebus constitutis, when this was arranged (c. v, 5).

cōnstō, -stāre, -stitī, -statum, v. intr., be formed; impers. constat, it is admitted, it is certain.

consuescō, -suescere, -suēvī, -suētum, v. intr., become accustomed (c. v, 7, 21).

consuētūdō, -inis, F., custom, habit; ex consuetudine, according to custom (c. iv, 32).

consul, -ulis, M., a consul, one of the two chief magistrates chosen annually at Rome.

consulō, -ere, -uī, ultum, v. tr., deliberate, plan; alicui consulere, to consult for one's benefit; aliquem consulere, to ask one's advice; in aliquem consulere, to take measures against one; consulere sibi, to look after himself; civitati consulere, to take measures for the interest of the state (c. v, 3).

consultō, adv., on purpose, designedly; often de consulto; consulto cedere, to purposely retreat (c. v, 16).

consultum, -ī, N., decree, resolution, decision.

consūmō, -ere, -sumpsī, -sumptum, v. tr., spend, waste; tempus consumere, to waste time; aestatem consumere, to spend the summer (c. v, 4); magna parte diei consumpta, after a great part of the day had been spent (c. v, 9).

contemnō, -ere, -tempsī, -temptum, v. tr., despise, hold in contempt.

contendō, -ere, -tendī, -tentum, v. intr., hasten to, push forward; in fines Sugambrorum contendit, he marches into the territories of the Sugambri (c. iv, 18; iv, 37; v, 9); remis contendere, to strive at the oars (c. v, 8); dispari proelio contendere, to fight an unequal battle (c. v, 16).

contentiō, -ōnis, F., struggling; gaining a battle.

contentus, -a, -um, adj. (with abl.), content with.

contestor, -ārī, -ātus sum, v. dep., invoke.

contexō, -ere, -texuī, -textum, v. tr., weave, bind together.

contextus, -a, -um, perf. part. pass. of contexo, used as an adj., interwoven.

conticescō, ere, -ticuī, no sup., v. intr., be silent.

continens, -ntis (properly pres. part. of contineo, used as an) adj., with terra understood; literally, the uninterrupted land, the continent, i.e., Gaul. bella continentia, uninterrupted wars (c. v, 11).

contineō, -ēre, -tinuī, -tentum, v. tr., hold together, bound, restrain, hem in ; se continere, to keep themselves together (c. iv, 3ŋ); civitatem in officio continere, to keep the state loyal (c. v, 3) ; in officio continere, to keep him loyal (c. v, 7).

contingō, -ere, -tigī, -tactum, v. tr., touch, extend to, reach.

continuus, -a, -um, adj., continuous.

contorqueō, -ēre, -torsī, -tortum, v. tr., hurl vigorously

contrā, prep. (with acc. only), against, opposite to ; contra Gallias, facing the divisions of Gaul (c. iv, 20) ; contra Galliam, facing Gaul, i.e., France (c. v, 13).

contrā, adv., contrary to ; contrā atque esset dictum, contrary to what had been said (c. iv, 13).

contrahō, -ere, -traxī, tractum, v. tr., draw together, collect.

contrārius, -a, -um, adj., opposite, contrary.

convellō, -ere, -vellī, -vulsum, v. tr., rend, tear away.

conveniō, īre, -vēnī, -ventum, v. tr. and intr., come together, assemble ; with acc., interview, meet.

conventus, -ūs, M., an assembly, assize ; conventum peragere, to hold an assize (c. v, 1).

convertō, -ere, -vertī, -versum, v. tr., turn, turn about ; in fugam convertere, to turn in flight ; animi conversi, our feelings were changed.

convocō, -āre, -āvi, -ātum, v. tr., summon, assemble.

convolvō, -ere, volvī, -volūtum, v. tr., roll together.

coorior, -oriri, -ortus sum, v. intr. dep., of a storm ; arise, spring up.

cōpia, -ae, F., abundance, plenty, pl.; copiae, forces, supplies ; summis copiis, with all his forces (c. v, 17); copias instruere, to draw up troops (c. v, 18).

cor, cordis, N., heart.

cōram, prep. (with abl.), face to face with, in presence of ; coram populo, in presence of the people ; coram perspicit, he sees in person (c. v, 11)

Coroebus, -ī, M., Coroebus, son of Mygdon, a suitor of Cassandra

corpus -oris, N., body.

corripiō, -ripere, -ripuī, -reptum, v. tr., seize violently, carry off.

corrumpō, -ere, -rūpī, -ruptum, v. tr., break in pieces, destroy, ruin, bribe.

Cōrus (or Caurus), i, .M., the N.-W. wind.

coruscus, -a, -um, adj., gleaning.

cotīdiānus -a, -um, adj., daily.

cotīdiē, adj., daily.

costa, -ae, F., rib.

Cotta, -ae, M., see Arunculeius.

Crassus, -ī, M., Marcus Licinius Crassus, surnamed Dives (the Rich), was a member of the First Triumvirate along with Caesar and Pompey (60 B.C.). He fell at Carrhae, 53 B.C. in a war against the Parthians.

crātēr,-ēris, M., mixing-bowl (κρατήρ, κεράννυμι).

crēber, -bra, -brum,adj., numerous. frequent.

crēdō, -ere, -didi, -ditum, v. tr. and intr., trust, believe.

crescō, crescere, crēvī, crētum, v. intr., increase, grow, grow up.

crētus, -a -um, pref. part. pass. of cresco, sprung from

Crēūsa, -ae, E., Creüsa, wife of Æneas.

crimen, -inis, N., charge (Verg. 65).

crīnis, -is, F., hair ; passis crinibus, with hair all loose

cruciātus, -ūs, M., torture.

crūdēlis, -e, adj., cruel, hardhearted.

cruentus, -a, -um, adj., bloody.

culmen, -inis, N., roof.

culpa, -ae, F., blame; culpam conjicere, to throw the blame(c. iv, 27).

culpō, -āre. -āvī, -ātum, blame, hold guilty (culpa).

cum, prep. (with abl.), with. along with ; enclitic with me, te, se, nobis, vobis, quibus, as mecum, tecum, secum, nobiscum, vobiscum, quibuscum.

cum (also written quum), conj., when, after, since, although ; cum... tum, both...and, cum (or quum) primum, as soon as.

cumulus, -ī, M., heap.

cunctor, -ārī, -ātus sum, v. dep., delay, hesitate, doubt.

cunctus, -a, -um, adj., all together, in a body

cupidē, adv., eagerly.

cupidō, -inis, F., desire.

cupĭdus, -a, -um, adj., desirous of (with genitive); cupĭdus rerum novarum, anxious for a change of government (c. v, 6).

cupĭō, -ere, -ivi (-ii), -itum, v. tr., long for, wish, desire.

cupressus, -ī, F., cypress (κυπά-ρισσος).

cūr, adv., why? for what purpose?

cūra, -ae, F., care, anxiety.

cūrō, -āre, -āvī, -ātum, v. tr., care for; in Caesar always with acc. of object and gerundive part.; exercitum transportandum curare, to cause the army to be transported (c. iv, 29); naves aedificandas curare, to have ships built (c. v, 1).

currō, -ere, cucurrī, cursum, v. intr., run; curritur, they run.

currus, -ūs, M., chariot.

cursus, -ūs, M., a running (c. iv, 35); voyage; tenere cursum, to hold on their course (c. iv, 28); passage (c. v, 13).

curvus, -a, -um, adj., bent, winding.

cuspis, -idis, F., spear.

custōs, -ōdis, M., guard, watch.

Cybelē, -ēs, F., Cybele, a Phrygian goddess.

D

● Danaī, -ōrum, M., pl., the Greeks.

Dardania, -ae, F., Troy.

Dardanidae, -ārum, M., the descendants of Dardanus, i.e., the Trojans.

datus, perf. part. of do.

dē, prep. (with abl.), of, from, concerning; his de rebus certior factus, being informed of these events; de tertia vigilia, after the third watch was set (c. v, 9); multis de causis, for many reasons; qua de causa, and for this reason; de oppidis demigrare, to remove from the towns; de improviso, unexpectedly (c. v, 22).

dea, -ae, F., goddess.

dēbeō, -ēre, -uī, -itum, owe, ought, (de, habeo).

dēcēdō, -ere, -cessi, -cessum, v. intr., retire, leave, depart from; e vita decessit, he died.

decem, indecl. card. num., ten.

dēcernō, -ere, -crēvī, -crētum, v. tr., decree.

decimus, -a, -um, ord. num. adj., tenth.

dēclīvis, -e, adj., sloping.

decōrus, -a, -um, adj., graceful.

dēcrétum, -ī, N., decree, decision; stare decreto, to abide by a decision.

dēcurrō, -ere, -curri, or -cucurrī, cursum, run down.

decus, -oris, N., ornament, honor.

dēdecus, -oris, N., disgrace; dedecus admittere, to commit a disgraceful act (c. iv, 25).

dēditiō, -ōnis, F., surrender; in deditionem accipere (or recipere), to receive on surrender; in deditionem venire, to surrender.

dēdō, -ere, -didi, -ditum, v. tr., give up, surrender.

dēdūcō, -dūcere, -duxi, -ductum, v. tr., lead away, bring down, withdraw; navem deducere, to launch a vessel; suos deducere, to withdraw their men (c. iv, 30). ●

dēfatīgātus, -a, -um, adj., wearied, exhausted.

dēfectiō, -ōnis, F., revolt, rebellion.

dēfendō, -ere, -fendi, fensum, v. tr., defend, repel, guard.

dēfensor, -ōris, M., defender.

dēferō, -ferre, -tuli, -lātum, v. tr., carry down or away; report, announce; paulo infra deferri, to be carried a little farther down (c. iv, 36); Caesaris mandata deferre, to bear the orders of Caesar (c. iv, 27); offer (c. v, 6); report (c. v, 6).

dēfessus, -a, -um, adj., weary, exhausted.

dēficiō, -ficere, -fēcī, -fectum, v. tr., fail, be insufficient, run short; si tempus anni deficeret, if the time of the year was insufficient (c. iv, 20); ab amicitia populi Romani deficere, to cast off the alliance of the Roman people (c. v, 3); deficit ignis, the fire fails.

dēfīgō, -fīgere, -fixī, -fixum, v. tr., fix, fasten, drive down (c. v, 18).

dēfixus, -a, -um, perf. part. pass. of defigo (c. v, 18).

dēflagrō, -āre, -āvī, ātum, v. intr., be burned down.

dēfugiō, -fugere, -fūgī, -fugitum, v. intr. and tr., flee from, avoid.

dējiciō, -jicere, -jēci, -jectum, v. tr., throw down, cast down; de spe dejectus, disappointed in hope; magno sui cum periculo dejici, to be driven down with great danger to themselves (c. iv, 28).

dēgener, -eris, aaj., unworthy of the race, degenerate (de,"fron";genus, "race").

deinceps, adv., one after the other, in succession, in turn

deinde, adv., thereafter, afterwards, then, next.

Dēiphobus, -ī, M., *Deiphobus*, son of Prian.

dēlătus, see dēfero.

dēlābor, lābi, lapsus sum, v. dep., slip.

dēlectus, -a, -um, adj., chosen.

delecta corpora virum = delectos viros

dēligō, -āre, āvī, ātum, v. tr., fasten; navem ad ancoram deligare, to anchor.

dēligō, -ere, -lēgī, -lectum, v. tr., choose, select, levy.

dēlitescō, -litescere, -litui, no sup., v. intr., lie hid, lie in a n bush.

dēlubrum, -ī, N., shrine.

dēmens, -ntis, M., foolish

dēmetō, -ere, -messuī, -messum, v. tr., cut down, reap.

dēmigrō, -āre, -āvī, -ātum, v. intr., n ove fron, depart fron, e nigrate.

dēminuō, -ere, -minui, -minūtum, v. tr., lessen, in pair.

dēmittō, -ere, -misi, missum, v. tr., send down; se animo demittere, to lose heart; demissum lapsi per funem, gliding down by a hanging rope

dēmō, -ere, dempsī, demptum, take away (de-emo).

dēmonstrō, -āre, -āvī, -ātum, v. tr., point out, show, state, n ention ; explain.

dēmoror, -ārī, -ātus sum, keep waiting, delay.

dēni, ae, -a, dietrib. nun. adj., co n panies of ten (c. v, 14).

dēnique, adv., at last, finally ; in a word, in short.

densus, -a, -um, adj., thick, closely packed, crowded.

dēnuntiō, -āre, -āvī, -ātum, v. tr., announce, declare, threaten, order.

dēpascor, -pasci, -pastus sum, v. dep., feed upon

dēpereō, -perire, -perii (perivi), no sup., v. intr., be lost, perish.

dēpēnō, -pōnere, -posni, -positum, v. tr., lay aside, cast away; animam deponere, to relinquish his life;

spem deponere, to give up hope (c. v, 19).

dēprecor, -ārī, -ātus sum, v, tr. dep., beg for n ercy ; re usandi aut deprecandi causa, for the purpose of denying the fact or of begging hin for n ercy (c. v. 6).

descendō, -ere, -dī, -sum, go down, descend (scando, "climb").

dēserō, -serere, -serui, -sertum, v. tr., desert, leave.

dēsertus, -a, -um, adj., deserted.

dēsīderō, -āre, -āvī, -ātum, v. tr., wish for, long for, want ; neque ulla omnino navis desideratur, not a single ship is lost at all (c. v, 23).

dēsiliō, -ire, -siluī, -sultum, v. intr., leap down, dis n ount.

dēsinō, -sinere, -sivī, -(-sii), -situm, v. intr., leave off, cease, stop.

dēsistō, -ere, -stiti, -stitum, v. intr., leave off, give over, cease fron ; proelio desistere, to give up the battle ; sententia desistere, to give up the notion.

dēstinō, -āre, -āvī, -ātum, v. tr., appoint.

dēsuescō, -ere, -suēvi, -suētum, render unaccusto n ed ; desuetus, unaccusto n ed.

dēsum, -esse, -fuī, v. intr., be wanting, fail, be lacking.

dēsuper, adv., fron above.

dēterreō, -ēre, -terruī, -territum, v. tr., frighten, frighten off.

dētineō, -ēre, -ui, -tentum, hold or keep back ; detain (de, teneo).

dētrīmentum, -ī, N., loss, damage.

deus, -1, M., a god.

devolvō, volvere, -volvī, -volūtum, v. tr., roll down.

dexter, -tra, -trum, adj., right, on the right hand.

dextera or dextra (with manus understood), adj., the right hand.

dicō, dicere, dixi, dictum, v. tr., say, speak, tell, appoint; causam dicere, to plead a cause; de quo ante ab nobis dictum est, of who n we have n ade n ention before (c. v, 6); mirabile dictu, wonderful to relate

dictum, -ī, N., word, order, com-n and.

diēs, -ēī, M. or F. (in sing.), M. (in pl.), day.

differō, differre, distuli, dilātum, v. tr., spread, scatter ; put off, delay; inter se differre, to differ fron each other: multum differunt, they differ greatly (c. v, 14).

difficultās, -ātis, F., difficulty, trouble.

diffugiō, -fugere, -fūgi, -fugitum, v. intr., flee in different directions.

dīgerō, -ere, -gessi, -gestum, v. tr., expound.

dignitās, -ātis, F., splendor; tribuere dignitatem, to treat with respect (c. v. 7).

dignus, -a, -um, adj., worthy of deserving.

dīgredior, -ī, -gressus sum, depart (dis, gradior).

dījūdicō, -āre, -āvī, -ātum, v. tr., decide, deternine.

dīlectus, -ūs, M., levy.

dīlectus, -a, -um, adj., chosen.

dīligō, -ere, -lexī, -lectum. v. tr., value, esteen, love.

dīmicō, -āre, -āvī, -ātum, v. tr., fight; cum dimicaretur, since the battle was fought (c. v, 16).

dīmidium, -ī, N., niddle, half; dimidio minor, half the size (c. v, 13).

dīmittō, -ere, -misi, -missum, v. tr., send in different directions.

Diomēdēs, -is, M., Diomede, a fanous Greek hero, son of Tydeus.

diripiō, -ere, -ui, -reptum, tear asunder; plunder (rapio).

dīrus, -a, -um, adj., fearful, terrible, dread.

dis, (abbreviated) di-), inseparable prefix, apart, asunder, in pieces.

dis, dītis, adj.. rieh ; comp., dītior ; sup., dītissimus.

discēdō, -ere, -cessi, -cessum, v. intr., depart, withdraw; ab armis discedere, lay down arns; ab signis dis edere, to desert their standards (c. v, 16).

discessus, -ūs, M., departure.

discō, discere, didici, no sup., v. tr. and intr., learn.

discors, -cordis, adj., different.

disjiciō, -ere, -jēci, -jectum, dash apart, destroy (jacio, throw).

dispār, -paris, adj., unequal, unlike ; dispari proelio, in an unequal contest (c. v, 16).

dispergō, -ere, -spersi, -spersum, v. tr., scatter, disperse.

dispersus, -a, -um (perf. part. pass. of dispergo, used as an) adj., scattered.

dispōnō, -ere, -posui, -positum, v. tr., set in order, draw up (of forces). -

dispositus, -a, -um, perf. part. pass., arranged.

distribuō, -ere, -tribuī, -tribūtum, v. tr., assign, distribute.

districtus, -a, -um, (perf. part. pass. of distringo, used as an) adj., occupied with, busy.

diū, adv., long, for a long time ; comp., diūtius ; sup., diūtissimē.

diurnus, -a, -um, adj., by day.

dīva, -ae, F., goddess.

divellō, -ere, -vellī, -vulsum, v. tr., separate.

dīversus, a, -um, (perf. part. pass. of diverto used as an) adj., in different directions; some one way, some another way.

dīves, -itis, adj., rich; comp., dīvitior ; sup., dīvitissimus.

Diviçcō, -ōnis, M., Divico, chief of the Helvetii, who led an army against Cassius, B.C. 107, and headed an embassy to Caesar, B.C. 58.

dīvidō, -ere, dīvīsī, dīvīsum, v. tr., divide, separate.

dīvīnus, -a, -um, adj., divine.

dīvus, -ī, M., =deus, god.

dō, dare, dedī, datum, v. tr., give ; in fugam dare, to put to flight (c. iv, 26); dare operam, to take pains (c. v, 7); dare arbitros, to appoint judges (c. v, 1); vela dare, set sail ; vitam dare, to grant him his life ; ruinam dare, to fall in ruins ; dare poenas, to be punished.

doceō, docēre, docuī, doctum, v. tr., teach, inform, point out.

doctor, -ōris, M., a teacher.

doctrīna, -īnae, F., teaching, learning, knowledge.

doctus, -a, -um. (perf. part. pass. of doceo used as an) adj., learned, experienced.

doleō, dolēre, doluī, dolitum, v. intr. and tr., grieve, be grieved.

Dolopēs, -um, M., pl., Dolopes, a tribe of southern Thessaly.

dolor, -ōris, M., grief, pain; hoc dolore exardescere, to be aroused through grief of this (c. v, 4).

dolus, -ī, M., craft, fraud ;- per dolum, by deceit (c. iv, 13).

domesticus, -a, -um, adj., domestic; bellum domesticum, civil war (c. v, 9).

dominātus, -ūs, M., tyranny.

dominor, -ārī, -ātus sum, hold sway.

Domitius, -ī, M., *Lucius Domitius Ahenobarbus,* consul with Appius Claudius, B.C. 54. He was a staunch aristocrat, and brother-in-law of Marcus Cato. He fell at Pharsalia, B.C. 48, by the hand of Antony.

domō, -āre, -uī, -itum, v. tr., tame, subdue.

domus, -ūs, F., a house, home; **domī,** at home; **domum,** home; **domo,** from home.

dōnec, conj., till, until.

dōnō, -āre, -āvī, -ātum, v. tr., give, present.

dōnum, -ī, N., gift, present.

Dōricus, -a, -um, adj., *Doric=Grecian.*

dormiō, -īre, -īvī, -ītum, v. intr., sleep, rest.

dracō, ōnis, M., serpent.

dubius, -a, -um, adj., doubtful, uncertain.

ducentī, -ae, -a, card. num. adj., two hundred.

dūcō, dūcere, duxī, ductum, v. tr., lead, draw; **ductus,** chosen; **gemitus ducere,** utter groans.

ductor, -ōris, M., leader.

dūdum, adv., a while ago, lately.

dulcis, -e, adj., sweet.

dum, conj., until

Dumnorix, -igis, M., *Dumnorix,* chief of the Aedui, and brother of Divitiacus. He was always hostile to the Romans, and was killed while trying to escape from Caesar (c. v, 7).

duo, -ae, -o, num. adj. pl., two.

duodecim, indecl. num. adj., twelve.

duodēnī, -ae, -a, distrib. num. adj., twelve at a time, companies of twelve (c. v, 14).

duplicō, -āre, -āvī, -ātum, v. tr., double; **numerum obsidum duplicavit;** he demanded double the number of hostages (c. iv, 36).

dūrō, -āre, -āvī, -ātum, v. tr., harden, make hard.

Dūrus, see **Laberius.**

dūrus, -a, -um, adj., hard, severe, difficult.

dux, ducis, M., leader, general, guide.

Dymās, -antis, M., *Dymas,* a Trojan.

E

ē (ō before consonants; **ex,** generally before vowels, sometimes before consonants); prep. (with abl.); from, out of, in accordance with, in consequence of, on; **una ex parte,** on one side, **ex equo,** on horseback, **ex itinere,** on the march; **ex litteris,** in accordance with the despatch (c. iv, 38); **ex usu,** of advantage (c. v, 6); **ex hac fuga protinus,** immediately after this defeat (c. v, 17); **duabus ex partibus,** on two sides (c. v, 21).

Eburōnēs, -um, pl. M., *the Eburones,* a Belgic tribe, living between the Meuse and the Rhine, dependents of the Treveri.

edax, -ācis, adj., consuming, devouring (edo).

ecce, interj., lo! behold!

ēdisserō, -ere, -uī, -tum, v. trans., tell.

ēdūcō, -ere, -duxī, -ductum, v. tr., lead out, lead forth; raise aloft.

efferō, efferre, extulī, ēlātum, v. tr., bring forth.

efficiō, -ficere, -fēcī, -fectum, v. tr., effect, make; **opus efficere,** to complete a work; with **ut** and subjunctive, cause that; **reliquis ut navigari commode posset, effecit,** he caused that it might be suitably sailed with the rest, *i.e.,* he had the rest put in sailing trim (c. iv, 31).

effor, -ārī, -ātus sum, speak out, utter.

effigiēs, -ēī, F., image.

effugiō, -fugere, -fūgī, -fugitum, v. tr. and intr., escape.

effugium, -ī, N., escape.

effulgeō, -ēre, -fulsī, no sup., shine forth.

effundō, -ere, -fūdī, -fūsum, v. tr., pour out; **se effundere,** to spread out, scatter.

egens, -tis, adj., needy.

egēnus, -a, -um, adj., needy, in want, destitute.

egeō, -ēre, -uī, no sup., am needy; with abl., am in need of.

ego, meī, pers. pron. I; pl. **nōs,** we.

ēgredior, -gredī, -gressus sum, v. intr. dep., go out; disembark; **navi egredi,** to disembark (c. iv, 21; 23).

ēgregiē, adv., admirably, splendidly.

ēgregius, -a, -um, adj., eminent, marked, remarkable.

ēgressus, -ūs, M., landing (c. v, 8).

ējiciō, -jicere, -jēcī, -jectum, v. tr., cast out, throw out ; in litore ejicere, to cast up on shore (c. v, 10) ; ex silvis ejicere, to rush out of the woods (c. v, 15) ; se in agros ejicere, to spread themselves over the territory (c. v, 10).

ējusmodī (=ejus modi), of such a kind, of such a sort.

ēlābor, -lābī, -lapsus sum, v. dep., escape from.

ēmicō, -āre, -uī, -ātum, v. intr., leap

ēmittō, -ere, -mīsī, -missum, v. tr., send out, hurl.

ēmoveō, -ēre, ēmōvī, ēmōtum, v. intr., move out.

enim (placed after the first emphatic word in its clause), conj., for, in fact.

ensis, -is, M., sword.

eō, adv., thither, to that place, to such a degree ; correlative of quo before comparatives ; eo magis, so much the more (c. v, 1).

eō, īre, īvī (iī), itum, v. intr., go, march.

eōdem, adv., to the same place, in the same direction, to the same purpose.

Ēōus, -a, -um, adj., Eastern.

Ēpēos, -ī, M., Epeos, a Greek who built the wooden horse.

Ēpytus, -ī, M., Epytus, a Trojan.

ēques, -itis, M , a horseman, cavalry soldier ; pl. equites, cavalry.

equester, -tris, -tre, adj., belonging to horsemen, cavalry.

equidem, adv., truly, indeed.

equitātus, -ūs, M. cavalry.

equus, -ī, M., horse.

ēreptus, -a, -um, perf. part. pass., snatched.

Erīnys, -os, F., Erinys, one of the Furies.

ergō, conj., therefore, accordingly.

ēripiō, ripere, ripuī, -reptum, v. trans., snatch.

errō, -āre, -āvī, -ātum, v. intr., wander, err, be wrong.

error, -ōris, M., mistake.

ērubescō, -ere, -uī, no sup., v. incept. (ex, rubesco, "become red at"), feel shame about.

ēruō, -ere, -uī, -ūtum, tear or dig out ; overthrow.

ēruptiō, -ōnis, F., attack, sortie.

essēda, -ae, F., a war chariot of the Britons.

essedārius, -ī, M., a charioteer.

essedum, -ī, N., same as esseda.

et, conj., and ; et...et, both...and, = etiam

etiam, adv., even.

etsī, conj., even if, although.

Eurus, -ī, M., Eurus, the east wind.

Eurypylus, -ī, M., Eurypylus, a Trojan.

ēvādō, -vādere, -vāsī, -vāsum v. intr., go forth, ascend.

ēveniō, -venire, -vēnī, -ventum, v. intr., come to pass, happen.

ēvenit, it happens.

ēventus, -ūs, M.., result ; ex eventu, from the mishap (c. iv, 3).

ēvertō, -vertere, -vertī, -versum, v. tr., overthrow, drive out, destroy.

ēvincō, -ere, -vicī, -victum, conquer utterly.

ēvocō, -āre, -āvī, -ātum, v, tr., call out, summon.

ex : see ō.

examinō, -āre, -āvī, -ātum, v. tr., test ; ad certum pondus examinatus, of a fixed standard weight, literally, weighed to a fixed weight (c. v, 12).

exardescō, -ere, -arsī, -arsum, v. intr., be kindled, burst forth ; hoc dolore exarsit, he was roused through grief at this (c. v, 4).

excēdō, -ere, -cessī, -cessum, v. intr., leave, depart.

excellō, -ere, -celluī, -celsum, v. intr., excel, surpass.

excelsus, -a, -um, adj., high.

excidium, -ī, N., destruction.

excīdō, -ere, -cīdī, -cīsum, v. tr., cut away

excipiō, -cipere, -cēpī, -ceptum, v. tr., take the place of (c. v, 17).

excitō, -āre, -āvī, -ātum, v. tr., arouse.

exclāmō, -āre, -āvī, -ātum, v. intr., cry out, shout.

exclūdō, -clūdere, -clūsī, -clūsum, v. tr., shut out, prevent ; a navigatione excludere, to prevent from sailing (c. v, 23).

excutiō, -cutere, -cussī, cussum, v. tr., shake off, arouse.

excūsō, -āre, -āvī, -ātum, v. tr., justify (of a charge).

exemplum, -ī, N., an exanple, sanple, pattern.

exeō, -īre, -iī (īvī), -itum, v. intr., go out.

exerceō, -ēre, -ercuī, -ercitum, v. tr., exercise, trai.n.

exercitātiō, -ōnis, F., training, practise, exercise.

exercitus. -ūs, M., a trained band ; an arny ; **exponere exercitum,** to land an arny (c. v, 2);.

exhālō, -āre, -āvī, -ātum, v. tr., breaihe out.

exigō, -ere, -ēgī, -actum, v. tr., drive out, pass the lime ; **exacta hieme,** when winter had passed, at the end of winter.

exiguitās, -ātis, F., shortness.

exiguus, -a, um. adj., snall, scanty.

exilium, -ī, N., exile.

existimātiō, -ōnis, F., reputation.

existimō, -āre, -āvī, -ātum, v. tr., suppose, think, consider.

exitium, -ī, N., destruction.

exitiālis, -e, adj., ruinous.

exitus, -ūs, M., issue, end.

exoptātus, -a, -um, perf. part. pass. of **exopto,** used as an adj., longed for

exoptō, -āre, -āvī, -ātum, v. tr., wish, lesire.

exorior, -oriri, -ortus sum, v. dep., arise.

expediō, -īre, -īvī(iī), -itum, v..tr., extricate.

expeditus, -a, -um, adj., lightly equipped, free, unencunbered, without baggage ; **ad usum expeditior,** nore efficient for service (c. iv, 25) ; **expeditus receptus,** a quick retreat (c. iv, 33); **legiones expeditae,** legions without baggage (c. v, 2).

expellō, -ere, -puli, -pulsum, v. tr., drive out, expel.

expendō, -ere, -pendi, -pensum, v. tr., pay.

experior, -iri, -pertus sum, v. dep., try, test.

expleō, -ēre, -plēvī, -plētum, v. tr., fill up.

explicō, -āre, -āvī, (plicuī), -plicātum (-plicitum), v. tr., set forth, tell

explōrātor, -ōris, M., scout, spy.

explōrō, -āre, -āvī, -ātum, v. tr., investigate, reconnoitre.

expōnō, -ere, -posui, -positum, v. tr., place .out, deploy ; disenbark ; **expositae hostium copiae,** the forces of the enemy deployed (c. iv, 23) ; **cum essent expositi milites,** when the forces had landed (c. iv, 37) ; **exposito exercitu,** when the arny had landed (c. v, 9).

exprōmō, -ere, -prompsī, -promptum, v. tr., utter

expugnō, -āre, -āvī, -ātum, v. tr., take by storn, capture.

exsanguis, -sangue, adj., pale.

exscindō, -ere, -scidi, -scissum, v. tr., destroy

exspectō, -āre, -āvī, -ātum, v. tr., wait lo-, await : in ancoris exspectare, to wait at anchor (c. iv, 23) ; wait for ; long expected.

exstinguō, -ere, -nxī, -nctum, v. tr., extinguish, kill.

exstō, stāre, no perf., no sup., v. intr., be out ; **capite solo ex aqua exstare,** to have their heads alone out of the water (c. v, 18).

exsuperō, -āre, -āvī, -ātum, v.tr., tower above, conquer.

exsultans, -tis, adj., rejoicing.

exsultō, -āre, -āvī, -ātum, v. intr., leap forth.

exterus, -a, -um, adj. (rarely used in positive), outside, foreign, strange ; conp., **exterior ;** sup., **extrēmus.**

extemplō, adv., innediately.

extrā, prep. (with acc.), outside of, beyond.

extrahō, -trahere, -traxī, -tractum, v. tr., drawout, withdraw; **id facile extrahere,** to waste this easily (c. v, 22).

extrēmus, -a, -um, adj. (sup. of **exterus)** of place or tine, last ; **hieme extrema,** at the end of winter ; **extremi,** rear-guard (c. v, 10); **flamma extrema,** expiring flane ; **audere extrema,** to dare the greatest dangers ; **extrema in morte,** in death's extrenity.

exuō, -ere, -ui, -ūtum, v. tr., strip off, deprive ; **exutas vinclis palmas,** her hands freed fron chains.

exuviae, -ārum, F. pl., spoils:

ēvincō, -vincere, -vīci, -victum, v. tr., overcone

F

faber, -brī, M., a worknan, wright.

fabricātor, -oris, M., contriver

fabricō, -āre, -āvī, -ātum, v. tr., nake contrive.

faciēs, -ēī, F., appearance.

facile, adv., easily, readily; conp., facilius; sup., facillimē.

facilis, -e, adj., easy.

faciō, facere, fēci, factum, v. tr., do, nake; magni facere, to value highly; pluris facere, to value nore highly; castra facere, to pitch a canp; iter facere, to nake a narch; vim facere, to do violence; imperata facere, to obey connands; facere periculum, to nake an attenpt (c. iv, 21); iter facere, to nake a narch (c. iv, 32); bellum populo Romano facere, to nake war against the Ronan people (c. iv, 22); proelio facto, after the battle was fought (c. iv, 27); rebellionem facere, to renew the war (c. iv, 30); vim facere, offer violence (c. v, 7); pro sano facere, to act as a sane nan (c. v, 7). (For passive see flo.

factum, -ī, N., action, deed.

facultās, -ātis, F., opportunity.

fāgus, -ī, F., beech tree.

fallō, -ere, fefellī, falsum, v. tr., deceive.

falsus, -a, -um, adj., false.

fāma, -ae, F., renown.

famulus, -ī, M., attendant.

fandō, abl. of gerund of for, speak.

fās (indecl. noun), N., right; lawful.

fastigium, i, N., roof.

fātālis, -e, adj., deadly.

fateor, fatērī, fassus sum, v. dep., confess.

fātum, i, N., destiny, fate.

fātur, 3rd sing. pres. indic. of (for) fari, fatus sum, speak.

faucēs, -ium, F. pl., jaws.

fax, facis, F., torch.

fēliciter, adv., luckily, prosperously.

fēmineus, -a, -um, adj., pertaining to a wonan.

fenestra, -ae, F., window.

fere, adv., alnost, nearly.

feriō, -īre, no perf., no sup., v. tr., strike.

ferō, ferre, tuli, lātum, v. tr., bring, bear, carry, endure; fertur, it is said; auxilium ferre, to bring aid; injurias ferre, to inflict wrongs; legem ferre, to propose a law; consuetudo fert, the custon adnits of

(c. iv, 32); impetum ferre, to nake an attack (c. iv, 35); graviter ferre, to be annoyed (c. y, 6); ut fert illorum opinio, according to their ideas (c. v, 13).

ferreus, -a, -um, adj., of iron, iron.

ferrum, -ī, N., iron; acies ferri, the edge of the sword

ferus, -a, -um, adj., fierce, bold.

fessus, -a, -um, adj., weary.

festinō, -āre, -āvī, -ātum, v. intr., hasten.

festus, -a, -um, adj., festal.

fētus, -a, um, adj., pregnant, filled with.

fīctus, -a, -um (perf. part. pass. of fingo used as an) adj., idle, feigned, false.

fidēlis, -e, adj., faithful, trusty.

fidens, -ntis, adj., confident.

fidēs, -ēī, F., faith, loyalty; in fidem recipere, to receive under one's protection (c. iv, 22); fidem sequi, to be loyal to (c. v, 20); eos in fidem recipere, to adnit then to his protection (c. iv, 22); fidem interponere, to pledge his word (c. v, 6); promise.

fido, fidere, fisus sum, v. seni-dep., trust, confide.

fidūcia, -ae, F., trust, confidence.

fīdus, -a, -um, adj., trustworthy

fīgō, -ere, fīxī, fīxum, v. tr., fasten in press

figūra, -ae, F., forn, shape.

filia, -ae, F., daughter.

filius, -ī, M., son.

fingō, fingere, finxī, fictum, v. tr., form, shape, nake.

finis, -is, M. and F., end, linit; pl., fīnes, M., boundaries, territories.

fīnitimus, -a, -um, adj., bordering upon, adjoining; in pl., finitimi, -orum, neighbors.

fīō, fieri, factus sum (pass. of faciō), becone, take place; fit, it happens; certior fieri, to be inforned; non sine causa fieri, to be not without a reason (c. v, 6).

firmiter, adv., firnly; firmiter insistere, to stand firnly, to get a good footing (c. iv, 26).

firmus, -a, -um, adj., strong.

fixus, -a, -um, adj., fixed, resolute.

flagitō, -āre, -āvi, -ātum, v. tr., denand, ask earnestly.

flāgrō, -āre, -āvī, -ātum, v. intr., blaze.

flamma, -ae, F., flame.

flectō, -ere, flexuī, flexum, v. tr., bend, turn.

fleō, flēre, flēvī, flētum, v. intr. weep.

flētus, -ūs, M., tears, weeping.

flō, flāre, flāvī, flātum, v.intr.,blow.

fluctus, -ūs, M., flood, wave.

flūmen, -inis, N., river.

fluō, fluere, fluxī, fluxum, v. intr., flow, ebb.

fluvius, -ī, M., river.

fodiō, fodere, fōdī, fossum, v. tr., dig.

foedō, -āre, -āvī, -ātum,v. tr., mar, defile.

fons, fontis, M., fountain.

for, fārī, fātus sum, v. tr. dep., speak, say.

fore=futurum esse (fut. inf. of sum).

forem=essem.

foris, -is, F., door, gate.

forma, -ae, F., form, shape.

formīdō, -inis, F., dread; formidine capti, overcome with fear.

formō, -āre, -āvī, -ātum, v. tr., shape.

fors, -tis, F., chance, luck; used adverbially = forte.

fortasse, adv., perhaps, by chance.

forte, adv., perhaps, by chance.

fortis, -e, adj., strong, brave.

fortiter, adv., courageously, bravely.

fortūna, -ae, F., success, good fortune (Verg. 385).

Fortūna, -ae, F., Fortuné, goddess of Fortune

fossa, -ae, F., ditch, trench.

fractus, -a, -um, perf. part. pass. of frango, broken.

fragor, -ōris, M., breaking, crash.

frangō, frangere, frēgī, fractum, v. tr., break.

frāter, -tris, M., a brother.

fraus, fraudis, F., deceit, deception.

fremitus, -ūs, M., noise, din (of battle,

fretum, -ī, N., strait, sea.

frigidus, -a, -um, adj., cold.

frīgus, -oris, N., cold.

frons, frondis, F., bough.

frūgēs, -um, pl. F., meal; salsae fruges, salted cake, used in sacrifice.

frūmentārius, -a, um, adj., pertaining to corn; res frumentaria, a supply of corn.; inopia frumentaria, want of corn.

frūmentor, -ārī, -ātus sum, v. dep., fetch corn, forage.

frūmentum, -ī, N., corn.

frustrā, adv., without effect, in vain.

fuga, -ae, F., flight; in fugam dare, to put to flight (c. iv, 26); ex fuga recipere, to recover from panic (c. iv, 27).

fugiō, fugere, fūgī, fugitum, v. tr. and intr., flee, flee from, run away.

fugitīvus, -a, -um, adj., fleeing; as a noun, fugitīvus, -ī, M., a runaway slave.

fulgeō, ēre or ere, fulsī, no sup., v. intr., gleam, shine.

fulmen, -inis, N., thunderbolt.

fulvus, -a, -um, adj., tawny.

fūmō, -āre, no perf., no sup., v. intr., smoke.

fūmus, -ī, M., smoke.

funda, -ae, F., a sling.

fundāmentum, -ī, N., foundation.

funditor, -ōris, M., a slinger.

fundō, fundere, fūdī, fūsum, v. tr., pour forth; exercitum fundere, to rout an army.

fundus, -ī, M., bottom.

fūnis, -is, M., rope, cable.

fūnus, -eris, N., death.

furens, -tis, adj., raving; furentibus Austris, when the south winds rage; sponsa furens, his prophetic betrothed.

furiātus, -a, -um, adj., frenzied.

furō, -ere, -uī, no sup., rave.

furor, -ōris, M., rage, madness, fury.

furtim, adv., by stealth.

futūrus, -a, -um, fut. part. of sum; res futurae or futura (neut. pl.), the future.

G

Galba, -ae, M., Galba; Servius Galba, great-grandfather of the Emperor Galba. He served under Caesar in Gaul, and was praetor 54 B.C. After Caesar's death he served against Antony in the war of Mutina, 43 B.C.

galea, -ae, F., helmet.

Gallī, -ōrum, pl. M., *the Gauls*; the people who inhabited Gallia Transalpina (or Ulterior), Further Gaul (*France*), and Gall:a Cisalpina (or Citerior), Hither Gaul (*Northern Italy*).

Gallia, -ae, F., Gaul; in pl. Galliae, divisions of Gaul.

Gallicus, -a, -um, adj., *Gallic*.

gallīna, -ae, F., hen.

Gallus, -ī, M., *a Gaul*, an inhabitant of Gallia.

gaudeō, gaudēre, gavīsus sum, v. intr., semi-dep., rejoice.

gaudium, -ī, N., joy, gladness, delight.

gāza, -ae, F., treasure.

gelidus, -a, -um, adj., cold, icy.

geminus, -ī, adj. twin-born; pl. geminī = duo

gemitus, -ūs, M., a groan, sigh.

gener, -erī, M., a son-in-law.

genitor, -ōris, M., father.

gens, gentis, F., nation, race, tribe, clan.

genus, -eris, N., birth, kind; amplissimo genere natus, descended from a most illustrious family; toto hoc in genere pugnae, in all this kind of battle (c. v, 16).

Germānī, -ōrum, M. pl., *the Germans*.

Germānia, -ae, F., *Germany*.

Germānicus, -a, -um, adj., *German*.

Germānus, -a, -um, adj., *German*.

gerō, gerere, gessī, gestum, v. tr., carry, bear, carry on; bellum gerere, to wage war.

gladius, -ī, M., sword.

glomerō, -āre, -āvī, -ātum, v. tr., gather together.

glōria, -ae, F., glory, fame.

Gorgō, or ōn, -ōnis, F., a Gorgon.

gradus, -ūs, M., step.

Grāiī, -ōrum, M. pl., *Greeks*.

Grāius, -a, -um, adj., *Grecian*

grāmen, -inis, N., grass.

grātēs, only in nom. and acc. pl., F., thanks (grātus).

grātia, -ae, F., favor, influence (c. v, 4); pl. gratiae, thanks; agere gratiās, to give thanks; gratiam facere, to pardon; gratiam habere, to feel thankful; gratiam referre, to return thanks; gratiā (abl. with genitive), for the sake of.

grātus, -a, um, adj., pleasing.

gravis, -e, adj., heavy.

gravitās, -ātis, F., weight, importance.

graviter, adv., heavily; graviter ferre, feel pained at (c. v, 4).

gravō, -āre, -āvī, -ātum, v. tr., make heavy, burden.

gressus, -ūs, M., step.

gūbernātor, -ōris, M., pilot, steersman.

gurges, -itis, M., whirlpool.

gustō, -āre, -āvī, -ātum, v. tr., taste.

H

habeō, -ēre, -uī, -itum, v. tr., have, hold, possess; regard, consider; magnī habere, to value highly (c. iv, 21).

haereō, haerēre, haesī, haesum, v. intr., hold fast, stick to (with abl. or dat.).

hasta, -ae, F., spear.

haud, adv., not at all (negativing single words, especially adjectives and adverbs); with verbs chiefly in the phrase haud scio an, I don't know whether.

hauriō, -īre, hausī, haustum, v. tr., drink up.

hebetō, -āre, -āvī, -ātum, v. tr., make dull (hebes, hebetis, "blunt").

Hector, -oris, M.: *Hector*, son of Priam and bravest of the Trojans, slain by Achilles after the latter had pursued him thrice round Troy. His body was dragged to the Grecian fleet at the wheels of Achilles' chariot, and was afterwards ransomed by the aged Priam, who, securing a twelve days' truce, performed the funeral obsequies. The story is to be found in Hom. Iliad, xxii and xxiv. See vv. 270 and 540-543.

heī, interj. with dat., alas!

Hecuba, -ae, F., *Hecuba*, wife of Priam and mother of Hector.

Helena, -ae, F., *Helen*, wife of Menelaus, king of Sparta. Eloped with Paris to Troy in fulfilment of Venus' promise to give Paris the most beautiful woman in the world for wife, in return for his awarding to her (Venus) the apple of Discord. Upon this fateful event hinged the Trojan war. At the close of the war she returned home with Menelaus, and in the Odyssey, Bk. IV, we find her discharging the duties of hostess-wife as peacefully as if nothing had happened. See, however, note on v. 567. In v. 569

she is called *Tyndaris*, i.e., *daughter of Tyndarus*.

hērēditās, -ātis, F., heirship, inheritance.

hērī, adv., yesterday

heu, interj., alas !

Hesperius, -a, -um, adj., Western.

hīberna, -ōrum, pl. N. (properly neut. pl. of the adj., **hībernus** agreeing with **castra** understood), winter quarters; **hīberna constituere,** to appoint the position of the winter quarters (c. iv, 38; **hīberna circumire,** to inspect the winter quarters (c. v, 2).

Hibernia, -ae, F., *Ireland.*

hīc, haec, hōc ; dem. pron. this, he, she, it ; **hīc . . . ille,** the latter . . . the former.

hīc, adv., here ; then, hereupon.

hiemo, -are, -āvī, -ātum, v. intr., winter, pass the winter.

hiems, -is, F., winter, storm.

hinc, adv., hence from this time.

Hispānia, -ae, F., *Spain.*

hodiē, adv., to-day (= **hoc diē**).

homō, -inis, M. or F., a human being; man ; pl. **hominēs,** inhabitants.

hōra, -ae, F., hour. The Romans divided the period between sunrise and sunset into twelve equal parts, each of which was called **hōra** ; so also with the night. The length of each **hōra** would depend on the season of the year.

horrendus, -a, -um, adj., dreadful.

horreō, -ēre, -uī, no sup., v. tr. and intr., dread, shudder at.

horrescō, -ere, horruī, no sup., begin to shudder.

horribilis, -e, adj., dreadful, frightful

horridus, -a, -um, adj., dreadful.

horror, -ōris, M., dread.

hortor, -ārī, -ātus sum, v. tr., dep., urge, cheer, encourage, incite.

hospes, -pitis, M., visitor, guest, friend, host.

hostia, -ae, F., a victim offered in sacrifice

hostis, -is, M., an enemy.

hūc, adv., hither, here, to this place.

hūjusmodī, of this kind, of this sort.

hūmānus, -ā, -um, adj., civilized.

humerus, -ī, M., shoulder.

humī (locative), on the ground.

humilis, -e, adj., low, poor, humble.

humilitās, -ātis, F., lowness, lowness in the water (c. v, 1).

humus, -ī, F., ground.

Hypanis, -is, M., *Hypanis,* a Trojan.

I

ibi, adv., in that place, there.

ictus, -ūs, M., stroke.

Īda, -ae, F., *Mt. Ida,* near Troy.

Īdaeus, -a, -um, adj., belonging to Mt. Ida, *Idaean.*

idcircō, adv., on this account, for this reason, therefore.

idem, eadem, idem, dem. pro., the same.

idōneus, -a, -um, adj., fit, suitable, convenient.

igitur, conj., therefore, accordingly, then.

ignārus, -a, um, adj., ignorant.

ignis, -is, M., fire.

ignōrō, -āre, -āvī, -ātum, v. tr., to be ignorant of.

ignoscō, -ere, ignōvī, ignōtum, v. intr. (with dat.), pardon.

Īliacus, -a, -um, adj., of or belonging to Ilium, *i.e.,* Troy.

ilicet, adv., straightway.

Īlium, -i ; N. n.: *Ilium,* another name for *Troja, i.e., Troy,* though Troja and Ilium seen to have been names applied to different districts of the same city. In recent years wonderful discoveries have been made through the excavations of Dr. Schliemann in the Troad. Remains of a prehistoric city of great wealth and grandeur have been unearthed beneath the ruins of the historical city, Ilium, on the site of the present town of Hissarlik. The destruction of the Homeric Ilium is usually assigned to 1184 B.C. The historic Ilium was founded about 700 B.C.

ignōtus, -a, -um, adj., not known, unknown.

illābor, -lābī, -lapsus sum, v. dep., glide into.

ille, illa, illud, dem. pro., that, that well known ; he, she, it ; **ille . . . hic,** the former . . . the latter.

illō, adv., to that place, thither ; **eodem illo,** to that same place.

illūdō, -lūdere, -lūsi, -lūsum, v. tr., mock, jeer at

Illyricum, -ī, N., *Illyricum,* a district comprising the modern *Dalmatia, Bosnia and Herzegovina.*

imāgō, -inis, F., form.

imbellis, -e, adj., unwarlike, useless.

imber, -bris, M., a shower.

immānis, -e, adj., vast, huge, enormous, in nense.

Immanuentius. -ī, M., *Immanuentius*, father of Mandubracius (c. v, 20).

immisceō, -ēre, -miscuī, mixtum, v. intr., mingle with.

immensus, -a, -um, adj., in nense.

immemor, -oris, adj., unnindful.

immittō, -ere, -misī, -missum, v. tr., send or drive into (the enenys line); se immittere, rush into.

immixtus, -a, -um, perf. part. pass. of immisceō, ningled with.

immo, adv., on the contrary, no indeed, yes indeed ; used in answers to correct or nodify either by contradicting or by strengthening.

immolō, -āre, -āvī, -ātum, v. tr., sacrifice.

impedimentum, -ī, N., hindrance ; pl. baggage (of an arny); sarcinae, the kit of the individual soldiers.

impediō, -īre, -ivi, -itum, v. tr., hanper, hinder; religionibus impediri, to be hanpered by religious scruples (c. v, 6); navigationem impedire, to prevent sailing (c. v, 7); animis impeditis, when their attention was distracted (c. v, 7).

impeditus, -a, -um, perf. part. pass. of impedio used as an) adj., hanpered, inpassable; loca impedita, inaccessible places (c. v, 19).

impellō, -ere, -pulī, -pulsum, v. tr., hurl forward.

imperātor, -ōris, M., connander-in-chief, general.

imperātum, -ī, N., connand, order.

imperitus, -a, -um, adj., unskilled in, inexperienced in (with genitive, c. iv, 22).

imperium, -ī, N., connand, authority, governnent ; authority (c. iv, 21); power (c. v, 6); enpire

imperō, -āre, -āvī, -ātum, v. intr. (with dat.), connand, order; magnum eis numerum obsidum imperat, he levies a large nunber of hostages fron them (c. iv, 22 ; iv, 27).

impetrō, -āre, -āvi, -ātum, v. tr., obtain by request, obtain.

impetus, -ūs, M., attack, assault ; impetum sustinere, to withstand an attack (c. iv, 37); facere impetum, to nake an attack (c. v, 15).

impius, -a, -um, adj., wicked.

impleō, -ēre, -plēvi, -plētum, v. tr., till up, fill.

implicō, āre, -plicāvī (or -plicui), -plicātum (or plicitum), v. tr., entwine around

importō, -āre, -āvi, -ātum, v. tr., bring or carry to ; inport.

improbus, -a, -um, adj., bad, fierce.

imprōvīsus, -a, -um, adj., unforeseen ; de improviso, unexpectedly, suddenly.

imprōvidus, -a, -um, adj., nnsuspecting.

imprūdens, -tis, adj., not foreseeing, unwise ; imprudentibus nostris, while our men were off their guard (c. v, 15).

imprūdentia, -ae, F., indiscretion, thoughtlessness.

imus, -a, um, sup. of inferus.

in, prep. with (1) acc. (after words signifying notion), to, into, upon, against ; (2) abl. (after words signifying rest), in, at, during, anong ; in hiemem, for the winter (c. iv, 29); in primis, especially (c. v, 6); in itinere, while on the narch (c. iv, 11); in ancoris, at anchor.

inānis, -e, adj., enpty, vain, useless.

incendium, -ī, N., fire.

incendō, -ere, -cendī, -censum, v. tr., set on fire, burn, inflane.

inceptum, -i, N., beginning ; design (incipio).

incensus, -a, -um, perf. part. pass. of incendō, used as an adj., burning.

incertus, -a, -um, adj., uncertain ; incertis ordinibus, when their ranks were broken (c. iv, 32) ; erring (Verg. 224).

incidō, -ere, -cidī, no sup., fall upon.

incipiō, -ere, -cēpi, -ceptum, v. tr., begin, connence.

incitō, -āre, -āvī, -ātum, v. tr., urge, arouse, encourage ; equis incltatis, with their horses at full gallop (c. iv, 26, 33); remis incitare, tō row hard (c. iv, 25).

inclēmentia, -ae, F., lack of pity, cruelty (clemens).

inclūdō, -ere, -clūsi, -clūsum, v. tr., shut in.

inclutus, -a, um, adj., renowned.

incognitus, -a, -um, adj., unknown.

incola, -ae, M., an inhabitant.

incolō, -colere, -colui, -cultum, v. tr., live in, inhabit.

incolumis, -e, adj. safe, in safety.

incomitātus, -a, -um, adj., unaccompanied.

incommodum, -ī, N., loss, disaster.

incrēdibilis, -e, adj., incredible.

incumbō, -ere, -cubuī, -cubitum (dat.), lean upon, press down

incursiō, -ōnis, F., inroad, invasion.

incurrō, -ere, currī (or cucurrī), cursum, run into or against.

incūsō, -āre, -āvi, -ātum, v. tr., accuse, blane.

inde, adv., fron that place, thence; after that, then.

indicium, -ī, N., sign, infornation.

indignor, ārī, -ātus sum, v. dep., to be wrathful

indignus, -a, -um, adj., unworthy.

indomitus, -a, -um, adj., stubborn.

indulgeō, -ēre, -sī, -tum, with dat., yield to.

indutiae, -ārum, F. pl., a truce, arnistice.

induō, -ere, -duī, -dūtum, v. tr., put on.

Indutiomārus, -ī, M., *Indutioma-rus*, a leading man anong the Treveri, and rival of Cingetorix, who sided with the Ronans (c. v, 2).

inēluctābilis, -e, adj., inevitable.

ineō, -īre, -ii (īvī), -itum, v. tr. and intr., enter, enter upon; inire consilium, to forn a plan (c. iv, 32; v, 23); secunda inita vigilia, at the beginning of the second watch (c. v, 23).

inermis, -e, adj., unarned, defenceless.

iners, -ertis, adj., lifeless.

infāmia, -ae, F., ill report, infany.

infandus, -a, -um, adj., unspeakable.

infēlix, -fēlīcis, adj., unhappy, unfortunate.

infensus, -a, -um, adj., hostile.

inferō, -ferre, -tulī, illātum, v. tr., carry in, bring in; bellum hostibus inferre, to nake war on the eneny; signa inferre, to advance; bello illato, when the war was over (c. v, 12); periculum inferebat, bring danger (c. v, 16).

inferus, -a, -um, adj., below, lower; conp., inferior; sup., infimus or imus.

infestus, -a, -um, adj., hostile.

inficiō, -ficere, -fēcī, -fectum, v. tr., stain.

infimus : see inferus.

infīnitus, -a, um, adj., boundless, immense.

infirmus, -a, -um, adj., weak, feeble.

infrā, (1) adv., below; (2) prep. (with acc.), below, beneath.

infula, -ae, F., fillet, a white and red band of woolen stuff worn upon the forehead as a sign of consecration.

ingeminō, -āre, -āvī, -ātum, v. tr., redouble.

ingens, -tis, adj., huge, great, vast.

ingrātus, -a, -um, adj., unthankful, thankless, ungrateful.

ingredior, -gredī, -gressus sum, v. tr., dep., enter upon.

ingruō, -ere, ingruī, no sup.; rush on.

inhibeō, -hibēre, -hibuī, -hibitum, v. tr., check, restrain.

injiciō, -jicere, -jēci, -jectum, v. tr., throw or cast into.

inimīcus, -a, -um, adj., unfriendly, hostile; as a noun, a private eneny.

inīquus, -a, -um, adj., uneven; disadvantageous, unjust.

initium, -ī, N., beginning, connencenent; in initio, in the beginning.

injūria, -ae, F., wrong, outrage, injustice.

innoxius, -a, -um, adj., harnless.

innuptus, -a, -um, adj., unwed.

inopia, -ae, F., want, scarcity, poverty.

inquit, (verb defective), says he.

insānus, -a, -um, adj., mad.

insānia, -ae, F., nadness.

insciens, -tis, adj., not knowing, unaware, ignorant; Caesare insciente, without the knowledge of Caesar (c. v, 7).

inscius, -a, -um, adj., not knowing, ignorant of a thing.

insequor, -sequī, -secūtus (or sequūtus) sum, v. tr. dep., overtake, attack; insequi cedentes, to overtake the retreating eneny (c. v, 16).

insērtō, -āre, -āvi, -ātum, v. tr., put into.

insideō, -ēre, -sēdī, -sessum, v. tr., am seated in, occupy.

insidiae, -ārum, F. pl., anbush; hence, wiles

insigne, -signis, N., badge, decoration.

insignis, -e, adj., noted, renarkable.

insinuō, -āre, -āvī, -ātum, v. tr., nake a way into ; se insinuare, to nake their way anong (c. iv, 33).

insistō, -sistere, -stiti, no sup., v. intr., stand, take one's position ; firmiter insistere, to get a firn foothold (c. iv, 26, 33).

insolenter, adv., haughtily, arrogantly.

insonō, -āre, -sonuī, -sonitum, v. intr., re-echo.

insons, -sontis, adj., guiltless.

inspiciō, -ere, -spexi, -spectum, v. tr., look into.

instabilis, -e, adj., unsteady.

instar, N., indeed., inage ; instar montis, as high as a nountain.

instaurō, -āre, -āvī -ātum, v. tr., renew

insternō, -ere, -strāvī, -strātum, v. tr., lay upon, cover over.

*instituō, -ere, -stituī, -stitūtum, v. tr., draw up troops; decide upon ; bellum parare instituit, he decided to prepare for war (c. v, 3) ; ab instituto consilio, fron his appointed plan (c. v, 4) ; naves instituere, build ships

institūtum, -ī, N., custon, usage, law.

institūtus, -a, -um, perf. part. pass. of instituo.

instō, -stāre, -stitī, no sup., v. intr., press on

instruo,. -ere, -struxī, -structum, v. tr., build, draw up ; navem instruere, to build a ship (c. v, 2) ; omnibus rebus instrui, to be fully equipped (c. v, 5) ; copias instruere, to draw up forces (c. v, 18).

insuēfactus, -a, -um, adj., unaccustoned.

insuētus, -a, -um, adj., unused, unaccustoned ; navigandi insuetus, unused to sailing (c. v, 6).

insula, -ae, F., island.

insultans, -tis, adj., insulting, scoffing.

insuper, adv., noreover, besides, above.

integer, -gra, -grum, adj., uninpaired, fresh.

intellegō, -ere, -lexi, -lectum, v. tr., understand, know ; intellectum est, it was observed (c. v. 16).

intemerātus, -a, -um, adj., unsullied.

intendō, -ere, -dī, intensum or intentum, v. tr., stretch

intentus. -a, -um, perf. part. pass. used as an adj., eager.

inter, prep. (with acc.), between, anong.

intercōdō, -ere, -cessi, -cessum, v. tr., intervene, cone to pass.

interclūdō, -ere, -clūsi, -clūsum, v. tr., hem in

intedicō, -ere, -dixi, -dictum, v. tr., forbid.

intereā, adv., in the neantine, neanwhile.

interest, interesso, interfuit, intr., inpersonal ; it is of inportance ; mea interest, it is of inportance to ne ; viri interest, it is of inportance to the man ; magni interesse, it is of great inportance (c. v, 4).

interficiō, -ficere, -fēci, -fectum, v. tr., kill, destroy, slay.

interim, adv., neanwhile, in the neantine.

interior, conparative adj., fron obsolete interus), inner ; interiores, those of the inland parts (c. v, 14); pars interior, the inland part (c. v, 12).

intermittō, -ere, -mīsi, -missum, v. tr., discontinue ; brevi tempore intermisso, after the lapse of a short interval (c. iv, 34); intermissa profectione, postponing his departure (c. v, 7); non intermisso remigandi labore, without relaxing the exertion of rowing (c. v, 8) ; vento intermisso, after the wind had died down (c. v, 8) ; ne nocturnis quidem temporibus ad laborem militum intermissis, not even the night tine interrupting the exertions of the soldiers (c. v, 11), intermisso spatio, after a tine (c. v, 15).

interpōnō, -ere, -posuī, -positum, v. tr., allege ; fidem interponere, to pledge his word (c. v, 6).

interpretor, -āri, -ātus sum, v. tr. dep., expound.

interrogō, -āre, -āvī, -ātum, v. tr., ask, inquire.

interrumpō, -ere, -rūpī, -ruptum, v. tr., break down, break up.

intersum, -esse, -fuī, v. intr., be present, take part in (with dative).

intervallum, -ī, N., an interval of space or tine.

interveniō, -īre, -vēnī, -ventum, v. int., cone between, cone upon.

intexō. -ere, -uī, -tum, v. tr., in-weave, interlace.

intono, -are, -uī, -itum, v. intr., thunder.

intorqueō, -ēre, -torsi, -tortum, v. tr., hurl against (see note.

intrā prep. (with acc.), between, within.

intrŏitus, -ūs, M.ˈ an entrance.

intueor, -tuéri, -tuitus sum, v. tr. dep., behold, consider, regard.

intus, adv., within.

inultus, -a, -um, adj., unavenged

inūsitātus, -a, -um, adj., unusual; inusitatior, somewhat novel (c. iv, 25).

inūtilis, -e, adj., useless, unservice-ahle; inutilis ad navigandum, un-seaworthy (c. iv, 29).

invādō, -ere, -sī, -sum, v. tr., go against, attack.

inveniō, -īre, -vēni, -ventum, v. tr., come upon, find out, discover.

inventor, -ōris, m., discoverer.

invicem, adv., by turns, alternately.

invidia, -ae, F., envy, ill-will. .

invisus, -a, -um, adj., hateful.

invītus, -a, -um, adj., unwilling; se invito, against his will.

involvō, -ere, -vī, -ūtum, enroll, enwrap.

ipse, ipsa, ipsum, dem. pro.; self, himself, herself, itself, themselves; ipso terrore equorum, by mere terror caused by the horses (c. iv, 33).

ïra, -ae, F., anger.

irritus, -a, -um, aˈj., useless, un-availing.

irruō, 3, -ruī. -rutum, v. intr., rush against.

is, ea, id, dem. pro. this, that, he, she, it, they; before ut, is=talis, such; with comparatives eo (abl.) the: eo magis, all the more.

iste, ista, istud, dem. pro., that, that of yours.

ita, adv., in this way, so, thus : in the following manner, therefore ; non ita magnus, not very large (c. iv, 37).

Ītalia, -ae, F., Italy.

itaque, conj., and so, therefore, ac-cordingly.

item, adv., just, so, also, in like manner.

iter, itineris, N., journey, march; iter magnum, a forced march; ex itinere oppugnare, to storm by direct assault; ex itinere, on the march;

iter facere, to nake a narch (c. iv, 32); iter cōnficere, to complete a narch.

iterum, adv., again, a second time.

Ithacus, -a, -um, adj., Ithacan in Verg. 104.

Itius, -ī, M., Itius, a port on the northern coast of Gaul, opposite Britain. From it Caesar sailed to Britain. It is said to be Boulogne, or Wissant.

Iūlus, -ī, M., Iulus, son of Aeneas, also called Ascanius

J

jaceō, -ēre, -uī, no sup., v. intr., lie, lie dead.

jaciō, ere, jēci, jactum, v. tr., throw, cast; ancoram jacere, cast anchor (c. iv, 28).

jactō, -āre, -āvī, -ātum, v. tr. (freq. from jaciō), keep throwing, utter wildly.

jaculor, -ārī, -ātus sum, v. dep., fling, hurl.

jam, adv., now, already.

jamdudum, adv., at once.

jānua, -ae, F., door.

jampridem, adv., now for a long time.

juba, -ae, F., crest.

jubeō, -ēre, -jussi, -jussum, v. tr., order.

jūdicō, -āre, -āvī, -ātum, v. tr., decide.

jugum, -ī, N., yoke.

Jūlius, -i, M., see Caesar.

jūmentum, -ī, N., baggage animal.

junctūra, -ae, F., joint.

jungō, -ere, junxi, junctum, v. tr., join.

Jūno, -ōnis, F., Juno, wife of Jupiter and queen of heaven.

Jūpiter, Jovis, Jovī, Jovem, Jove, M., Jupiter.

jūs, jūris, N., right.

jūsjūrandum, jūris jūrandi, N., an oath.

jussum, -ī, N., command.

jussus, -ūs, M., command.

justus, a, -um, adj., just.

juvenilis, -e (also juvenālis), adj., youthful.

juvenis, -is, M., a young man.

juventa, -ae, F., youth (period of).

juventūs, -ūtis, F., youth (collective noun).

juvō, -āre, jūvi, jūtum, v. tr., delight; nos juvat, it delights us.

juxtā, adv., and prep., next, close to.

K

Kalendae, -ārum, F., pl., the Kalends, the first day of each nonth.

Karthāgō, -inis, F., Carthage, a city of Northern Africa.

Karthāginiensis, -is, adj., a Carthaginian.

L .

L. = Lucius, a Ronan praenomen.

Laberius, -ī, M., Laberius; Quintus Laberius Durus, a tribune in Caesar's arny in Gaul.

lābes, -is, F., slipping, downfall.

Labiēnus, -ī, M., Titus Labienus, one of Caesar's lieutenants in the Gallic wars. On the outbreak of the civil war he went over to Ponpey and fell at Munda in Spain, 45 B.C.

labō, -āre, -āvī, -ātum, v. tr., totter.

labor, -ōris, M., toil, suffering, exertion.

lābor, lābi, lapsus sum, v. intr. dep., slip, go astray; propter imprudentiam labi, to fall away fron allegiance on account of thoughtlessness (c. v, 3).

labōrō, āre, -āvī, -ātum, v. intr., toil, labor, be in trouble.

labrum, -ī, N., lip.

lāc, lactis, N., nilk; lacte et carne vivere, to live on nilk and flesh (c. v, 14).

Lacaena, -ae, F., Spartan wonan.

lacessō, -essere, -essīvī, -essitum, v. tr., provoke, assail, assault.

lacrima, -ae, F., a tear.

lacrimō, -āre, -āvī, -ātum, v. intr., weep.

lacus, -ūs, M., lake.

laedō, laedere, laesi, laesum, v. tr., harn, hurt, offend, injure; pro numine laeso, for the offended deity

laetus, -a, -um, adj., joyful, glad, pleasant.

laeva, sc. manus, left hand.

laevus, -a, um, adj., left, left hand; hence (1) unpropitious.

lambō, -ere, lambi, no sup., v. tr., lick.

lāmentābilis, e, adj., to be lamented.

Lāocoōn, -ontis, M., Laocoon, priest of Apollo, though we find him sacrificing to Neptune.

lapsō, -āre, no perf., no sup. (lābor), slip.

lapsus, perf. part. of dep. v., lābor.

lapsus, -ūs, M., gliding.

Larissaeus, -a, -um, adj., belonging to Larissa, a town of Thessaly: an epithet of Achilles, who came from Larissa.

largus, -a, -um, adj., bounteous.

lassus, -a, -um, adj., faint, weary.

latē, adv., widely, broadly; longe lateque, far and wide (c. iv, 35); quam latissime, as widely as possible (c. iv, 3).

latebra, -aé (rare in sing.), F., lurking place.

lateō, latēre, latuī, no supine, v. tr., lie hid, be concealed.

latus, -eris, N., side, flank: ab latere aperto, on the exposed flank, i.e., the right (c. 25, 26).

lātus, -a, -um, adj., broad, wide.

laudō, -āre, -āvī, -ātum, v. tr., praise.

laurus, -ūs, F., laurel, bay-tree.

laus, -dis, F., praise.

laxō, -āre, -āvī, -ātum, v. tr., loose.

lēgātiō, -ōnis, F., an embassy.

lēgātus, -ī, M., (1) an ambassador; (2) lieutenant-general in the army, an officer of senatorial rank in command of different divisions in the field, under the imperator. They were appointed by the Senate and were usually three in number, but Caesar had ten in Gaul.

legiō, -ōnis, F., a legion; a division of the Roman army consisting, when complete, of 6,000 infantry and 300 cavalry. The infantry was divided into ten cohorts, each cohort into three maniples, and each maniple into two centuries. The cavalry consisted of tén squadrons (turmae).— legione conferta, owing to the legion being in close order (c. iv, 32); legioni aliquem praeficere, to appoint one over a legion (c. v, 1); legiones expeditae, legions without baggage, or in light marching order (c. v, 2).

legiōnārius, -a, -um, adj., of or belonging to a legion; milites legionarii, common soldiers.

lēgitimus, -a, -um, adj., lawful poena legitima, the legal penalty.

legō, legere, lēgī, lectum, v. tr., choose, select ; read ; skim over.

lēnis, -e, mild, gentle.

leō, ōnis, M., lion.

lepus, -oris, M., a hare.

lētum, -ī, N., death.

levis, -e, adj., light ; milites levis armaturae, light-armed soldiers.

lēvis, e, adj., smooth.

levō, -āre, -āvī, -ātum, v. tr., relieve, lighten.

lex, lēgis, F., law, terms, conditions.

liberāliter, adv., courteously, generously.

līberō, adv., freely, without restraint.

līberī, -ōrum, pl. M., children (the singular is not found except in late writers).; unus ex liberis, one child.

līberō, -āre, -āvī, -ātum, v. tr., free, acquit ; poena līberare, to relieve from punishment.

lignum, -ī, N., wood.

ligō, -āre, -āvī, -ātum, v. tr., bind.

limbus, -ī, M., border, belt, band, girdle.

līmen, -inis, N., threshold.

līmōsus, -a, -um, adj., muddy, miry.

lingua, -ae, F., tongue, language.

linquō, -ere, līquī, no sup., v. tr., leave.

lis, lītis, F., a dispute, law suit ; litem aestimare, to estimate the amount of damages (c. v, 1).

litō, -āre, -āvī, -ātum, v. intr., propitiate.

littera (or litera), -ae, F., a letter of the alphabet ; pl. litterae, -arum, literature, or a despatch, letter ; ex litteris, in accordance with the despatch (c. iv, 38).

litus, -oris, N., water's edge, coast.

locō, -āre, -āvī, -ātum, v. tr., place, station ; castra locare, to pitch a camp.

locus, -ī, M., a place ; pl., loca or loci ; obsidum loco, as hostages (c. v, 5) ; in loca superiora, up the country (c. v, 8 ; loca temperatiora, more temperate climate (c. v, 12).

locūtus, -a, -um, perf. part. of loquor : which see.

longaevus, -a, -um, adj., of great age, aged (longus, aevum).

longē, adv., far ; with comparatives and superlatives, far, by far ; longe melior, far better ; longe optimus,

by far the best ; longius, too far (c. v, 7) ; longe lateque, far and wide (c. iv, 35).

longinquus, -a, -um, adj., remote, distant.

longitūdō, -inis, F., length, extent.

longus, -a, -um, adj., long.

loquor, loquī, locūtus (or loquūtus) sum, v. tr. dep., speak.

lōrum, -ī, N., thong.

lūbricus, -a, -um, adj., slippery.

Lūcifer, -ī, M., Lucifer, the morning star (lux, ferō).

Lūcius, -ī, M., Lucius.

lūcrum, -ī, N., profit, gain, advantage.

luctus, -ūs, M. grief.

lūgeō, ēre, luxī, no sup., v. tr. and intr., lament, mourn for.

Lugotorix, -igis, M., Lugotorix, a British chief who was captured in an attack on Caesar's camp.

lūmen, -inis, N., light ; eyes.

lūna, -ae, F., moon ; moonlight.

lūpus, -ī, M., a wolf.

lustrō, -āre, -āvī, -ātum, v. tr., traverse ; survey, scan.

lūsus, -ūs, M., sport play.

lux, lūcis, F., light ; primā luce, at daybreak ; ortā luce, at daybreak (c. v, 8).

Lydius, -a, -um, adj., belonging to Lydia.

M

M. = Marcus, a Roman praenomen.

Machāōn, -onis, M., Machaon, a Greek surgeon, son of Aesculapius.

māchina, -ae, F., engine of war.

mactō, -āre, -āvī, -ātum, v. tr., sacrifice.

maestus, -a, -um, adj., sad.

magis (comp. of adv., magnopere), more, rather (sup. maximē).

māgnitūdō, -inis, F., size.

magnopere, adv. (often written magno opere), greatly ; comp., magis ; sup., maximē, especially.

magnus, -a, -um, adj., large, great (comp. major ; sup. maximus) ; magni, at a high price ; pluris, at a greater price ; maximi, at a very high price ; majores natu, elders ; majores, ancestors ; res major, matter of more than usual importance ; **maximam partem**, for the most part ; **magni habere**, to value highly ; **magni interesse**, to be of great importance (c. v, 4).

major: see **magnus**.

mājōrēs, -um, M., ancestors.

male, adv., badly (comp., **pējus** ; sup., **pessimē**).

ma¡us, -a, -um, adj., bad, evil, wicked (comp., **pējor**; sup., **pessimus**).

mandātum, -ī, N., order, command, charge.

mandō, -āre, -āvī, -ātum, v. intr. (with dative), entrust, bid ; **se fugae mandare**, to consign themselves to flight (c. v, 18).

Mandubrācius, ī-, M., Mandubracius, a chief of the Trinobantes, a British tribe.

manē, adv., in the morning, early.

maneō, -ēre, -mansī, -mansum, v. tr. and intr., remain, await, stay ; **in officio manere**, to remain in allegiance, to remain loyal (c. v, 4); await; be steadfast.

manica, ae, F., handcuff, fetter.

manifestus, -a, -um, adj., clear, plain, evident.

manus, -ūs, F., hand ; band of men ; **manum conserere**, to engage in battle; **delecta manus**, a picked band.

Marcus, -ī, M., *Marcus;* a Roman praenomen.

mare, -is, N., the sea ; **et mari et terra**, both by sea and land.

maritimus, -a, -um, adj., of or belonging to the sea; maritime ; **ora maritima**, the sea coast (c. iv, 20); **aestus maritimi**, tides (c. iv, 29), **regiones maritimae**, the districts lying on the sea; **res maritimae**, naval movements.

Mars, -tis, M., *Mars*, the Roman god of war.

māter, -tris, F., mother.

māteria, -ae, F., timber.

mātūrus, -a, -um, adj., early.

maximē, adv., superlative of **magnopere**, which see.

maximus, -a, -um, adj., superlative of **magnus**, which see.

mēcum ; with me.

mediterrāneus, -a, -um, adj., inland, central.

medius, -a, -um, adj., middle ; **medius mons**, the middle of the

mountain ; **media de nocte**, after midnight; **ad mediam noctem**, about midnight.

Meldī, -ōrum, or Meldae, -ārum, pl. M., the *Meldi* or *Meldae*, a people of Gallia Belgica, on the coast east of the Parisii, near the modern town of *Meaux*, which still preserves the name.

melior, melius, adj., comp. of **bonus**, better.

membrum, -ī, N., limb.

meminī, -isse, v. defec., remember.

memor, -oris, adj., mindful.

memorābilis, -e, adj., memorable, deserving to be related.

memoria, -ae, F., memory, recollection; **memoria tenere**, to recollect ; **nostra memoria**, in our day ; **memoria proditum**, handed down by tradition (c. v, 12); **post hominum memoriam**, within the memory of man.

memorō, -āre, -āvī, -ātum, v. tr., relate.

Menāpiī, -ōrum, pl. M., the *Menapii*, a people of Gallia Belgica, between the Mosa (*Meuse*), and the Scaldis (*Schelat*) ; their chief town was Menapiorum Castellum (now *Kessel*).

mendācium, -ī, N., falsehood.

mendax, -ācis, adj., lying, false.

Menelāus, -ī, M., *Menelaus*, son of Atreus, brother of Agamemnon, husband of Helen and king of Sparta.

mens, mentis, F., mind.

mensa, -ae, F., table.

mensūra, -ae, F., measure; **certae ex aqua mensurae**, accurate measurements by the water clock (c. v, 13).

mentior, -īrī, mentitus sum, v. dep., tr., lie, speak falsely.

mercātor, -tōris, M., trader.

mercēs, -cēdis, F., price.

mercor, -ārī, ātus sum, v. tr., dep., buy.

mereō, -ēre, -uī, -itum, v. tr., gain, deserve.

merīdiānus, -a, -um, adj., midday; **meridiano fere tempore** at about noon (c. v, 8).

merīdjēs, -ēī, M., mid-day ; **ad meridiem spectat**, it faces the South (*i.e.*, the sun at noon) (c. v, 13).

meritum, -ī, N., service, kindness, benefit ; **pro meritis**, for his kindness; **merito ejus a se fieri**, to be done by him according to the deserts of the latter (c. v, 4).

mētior, -īrī, mensus sum, v. tr., dep., measure, measure out.

meto. metere, messuī, messum, v. tr., reap.

metuō, -ere -ī, metūtum, v. tr., fear.

metus, -ūs, M., fear.

meus, -a, -um, poss. adj. pro.; my, mine.

micō, -āre, -uī, no sup; flash.

mīles, -itis, M., a soldier.

mīlitāris, -e, adj., of or belonging to a soldier, military; res militaris, military science.

mīlitia, -ae, F., military service.

mille, adj. or noun, indecl., a thousand; pl. millia or milia.

millia passuum, miles: mille passus, a Roman mile, or 1,616 yards (see passus).

Minerva, -ae, F., Minerva, a Roman goddess who presided over wisdom and war.

minister, -trī, M., servant.

minor, -ārī, -ātus sum, v. tr., threaten; aliquem morte or alicui mortem minari, to threaten anyone with death.

minor, -us, adj. (comp. of parvus; sup., minimus, less; as a noun, minores (with or without natu), descendants; dimidio minor, half the size (c. v, 13).

minuō, -ere, -uī, -minūtum, v. tr., lesson, diminish.

minus, comp. adv. of parum (which see), less; sup., minimē.

mīrābilis, -e, adj., wonderful.

mīror, -ārī, -ātus sum, v. tr. dep., admire, wonder at.

mīrus, -a, -um, adj., wonderful, strange, marvellous.

misceō, -ēre, -uī, mistum or mixtum, v. tr., mingle, filled with confusion

miser, -era, -erum, adj., wretched, unfortunate.

miserābilis, -e, adj., wretched.

misereor, -ērī, -itus sum, v. intr., dep. (with genitive), feel pity for.

miserescō, -escere, no perf., no sup., v. intr. (with genitive), feel pity for.

mittō, -ere, mīsī, missum, v. tr., send.

mōbilitās, -ātis, F., activity, speed.

mōbilis, -e, adj., easily moved.

moderor, -ārī, -ātus sum, v. tr. and intr., manage, check.

modo, adv., only, merely, at all; modo...modo, now...now, at one moment...at another; non modo...sed etiam, not only...but also; paulum modo, only a little.

modō; see modus.

modus, -ī, M., a measure, amount, manner, method; modo fluminis, like a river; nullo modo, by no means; modo oratoris, in the capacity of an ambassador (c. iv, 27).

moenia, -ium, pl., N., walls of a city, fortifications.

mōles, -is, F., mass

molestō, adv., with trouble, with annoyance; res multas moleste ferre, to be annoyed at many things.

mōlior, -iri, -itus sum, v. dep., perform with toil, undertake.

mollis, -e, adj., smooth, soft.

Mona, ae, F., Mona, the Isle of Man. Anglesey, was also called Mona, but its position does not answer Caesar's description (c. v, 13).

moneō, -ēre, -uī, -itum, v. tr., advise, warn, remind.

mons, montis, M., mountain; summus mons, the top of the mountain.

monstrō, āre, -āvī, -ātum, v. tr., point out, show.

monstrum, -ī, N., prodigy, monster

montānus, -a, -um, adj., mountain.

mora, -ae, F., delay.

morātus, -a, -um, perf. part. dep., moror; see moror.

Morini, -ōrum, pl. M., the Morini, a people of Gallia Belgica, on the northeastern coast in the neighborhood of Calais. Their chief town was Gesoriacum, afterwards Bononia (now Boulogne).

morior, mori, mortuus sum, v. dep., die.

moror, -ārī, -ātus sum, v. intr. and tr. dep., delay.

mors, -tis, F., death.

morsus, -ūs, M., bite.

mortālis, -e, adj., mortal, human.

mōtus, -ūs, M., motion, evolution; Galliae motus, an uprising in Gaul (c. v, 5).

moveō, movēre, mōvī, mōtum, v. tr., move, set in motion; arma movere, to take up arms; bellum movere, to undertake a war; castra movere, to break up camp: odia movere, to stir up hatred

mox, adv., presently, soon; then, afterwards.

mucrō, -ōnis, M., edge, point.

mūgītus, -ūs, M., bellowing.

multitudō, -inis, F., crowd, multitude.

multō, adv. (used before comparatives), adv., much, by much, greatly; multo melior, much better (conp., plūs; sup., plūrimum).

multum, adv. (not used before comparative, otherwise same as multo).

multus, -a, -um, adj., much, many; conp., plus; sup., plurimus.

mūnīmentum, -ī, N., defence, fortification.

mūniō, -īre, -īvī, itum, v. tr., protect, fortify; iter munire, to build a road.

mūnītiō, -ōnis, F., defence.

mūrus, -ī, M., wall.

mūtō, -āre, -āvī, -ātum, v. tr., change, exchange.

Mycēnae, -ārum, F. pl., *Mycenae*, a city of Argolis, of which Aganennon was king.

Mygdonidēs, -ae, M., patronymic, *son of Mygdon*, epithet of Coroebus.

Myrmidonēs, -um, M., pl., *Myrmidons*, a people of Thessaly, followers of Achilles.

N

nactus, -a, -um, perf. part. dep. nanciscor, having obtained.

nam, conj., for; stands first in a sentence and explains some previous statement.

namque, conj., for indeed, for truly, a little more emphatic than nam.

nanciscor, nancisci, nactus (or nanctus) sum, v. tr., dep., obtain, get.

narrō, -āre, -āvī, -ātum, v. tr., tell.

nascor, -cī, nātus sum, v. intr., dep., be born (c. v, 12); be born from.

nātiō, -tiōnis, F., tribe, people, nation.

nātūra, -ae, F., form; natura, by nature, naturally; natura triquetra, triangular in form (c. v, 13).

nātus, -a, -um, (perf. part. dep., used as an), adj., descended from, born from.

nātus, -ūs, M., used only in the abl., by birth; majores natu, ancestors; minores natu, descendants.

nauta, -tae, M., a sailor.

nāvālis, -e, adj., naval; pugna navalis, a sea-fight.

nāvigātiō, -ōnis, F., sailing (c. iv, 36).

nāvigium, -ī, N., a vessel, ship.

nāvigō, -āre, -āvī, -ātum, v. intr., sail.

nāvis, -is, F., a ship; navis longa, a ship of war; navis oneraria, a ship of burden; navem tenere in ancoris, to keep a ship at anchor; navem conscendere, to embark (c. iv, 23) (elsewhere in Caesar we find conscendere in navem); navem constituere, to moor a ship (c. iv, 24); naves solvere, set sail (c. v, 8); navem subducere, to draw a vessel on shore, to beach a vessel (c. v, 11).

nē, conj., (in final clauses) that not, lest; (after verbs of fearing) that; (after verbs of beseeching, ordering, commanding) not to.

nē, adv., not; ne...quidem, not... even (the emphatic word between ne and quidem, as ne unus quidem, not a single one); also used in negative imperative sentences, ne hoc feceris, don't do this.

-ne, interrog. enclitic particle. In single direct questions; -ne is not to be translated except by laying stress on the word to which it is joined, in double questions, -ne...an, whether...or.

nebula, -ae, F., mist.

nec: see neque.

necessāriō, adv., necessarily, unavoidably.

necesse, indecl. adj. (used with est (+acc. and inf.), necessary, unavoidable, inevitable, needful.

necessitās, -ātis, F., need, necessity.

necne, adv., used in alternative indirect questions; or not; annon, is used in direct questions.

necō, -āre, -āvī, -ātum, v. tr., put to death, kill, destroy.

nefandus, -a, -um, adj., horrid.

nefārius, -a, -um, adj., wicked, atrocious.

nefās, indecl. N., a crime (against divine law), impious deed; nefas est dictu, it is wrong to say.

neglegō, -ere, -lexi, -lectum, v. tr., slight, neglect, be indifferent to, despise.

negō, -āre, -āvī, -ātum, v. tr., say no or not; deny, refuse; often=dicit non: negat se esse aegrum, he says that he is not sick.

negōtium, -ī, N., business n atter.

nēmō, -inis (only used in the sing. ; the dat. and abl. are supplied by nullus ; Caesar uses only nemo, neminem), indef. pro., no one ; non nemo, sonebody ; nemo non, everybody.

Neoptolemus, -ī, M., Neoptolenus, also called Pyrrhus, son of Achilles.

Neptūnius, -a, -um, adj., founded by Neptune.

Neptūnus, -ī, M., Neptune, god of the sea.

nepōs, -ōtis, M., grandson ; nephew; pl., nepótes, descendants.

nequāquam, adv., not at all, by no n eans.

neque, or nec (in Caesar nec is not found before vowels), conj., nor, and not ; neque...neque or nec...nec, neither...nor ; nec quisquam, and no one ;' neque quidquam, and nothing (c. iv, 20).

nēquidquam (nēquīquam), adv., in vain, to no purpose.

Nēreus (dissyllable), Nērēī, and Nēreos, M., Nereus, a sea deity.

nesciō -scire, -scīvī (or scii), -scitum, v. tr., not to know.

neu ; see neve.

neuter, -tra, -trum (gen. neutrius, dat. neutrī, adj., neither (of two).

nēve, or neu, conj., nor ; and...not; neve...neve, or neu...neu, neither ...nor.

nex, necis, F., death; generally a violent death.

ni = nisi, conj., unless.

nihil, indecl. N., nothing.

nihilō (abl. of difference fron nihilum) by nothing : nihilo tamen sēcius, nevertheless (c. y, 7).

nihilo minus, or nihilominus, adv., none the less, nevertheless.

nihilo sēcius, adv. (literally, otherwise by nothing ; sēcius, conp. of secus, differently, otherwise) ; sane n eaning as nihilominus.

nihilum, -ī, N., nothing ; nihili aestimare, to value at nothing.

nimbus, -ī, M., rain-cloud.

nimiō, adv., too n uch, exceedingly.

nisi, conj., if not, unless.

nitidus, -a, -um, adj., shining, bright.

nītor, niti, nisus (or nixus) sum, v. intr., dep.

nōbilis, -e, adj., noble, noted, fa n ous.

nōbilitās, -ātis, F., nobility.

noceō, -ēre, nocuī, nocitum, v. intr. (with dative, hurt, harn, injure.

noctū, (an old abl. of obsolete noctus, -ūs ; used as an) adv., by night, at night.

nocturnus, -a, -um, adj., of or belonging to night, nocturnal.

nōdus, -i, M., knot.

nōlō, nōlle, nōluī, no sup.; v. irreg., be unwilling, not to wish.

nōmen, -inis, N., nane ; reputation (see cognomen for praenomen, nomen).

nōminātim, adv., by nane ; nominatim evocare, to sun non expressly (c. v, 4).

nōn, adv., not ; usually preceding the word with which it should be construed. Before a negative word an indefinite affirmative is produced as, non nemo, sonebody ; non nunquam, sonetines; non nihil, sonething ; after a negative, a general affirnative is forned, as nemo non, everybody; nunquam non, every tine ; nihil non, everything.

nōnāgintā, num., adj., ninety.

nōndum, adv., not yet.

nonnullus, -a, -um, adj., sone ; generally in pl., nonnulli, -ae, -a, several.

nonnunquam, adv., sonetines.

nōnus, -a, -um, num. ord. adj., ninth.

nōs, pl. of ego.

noscō, noscere, nōvī, nōtum, v. tr., becone acquainted with, learn ; pf. novi, I know.

noster, -tra, -trum, poss. adj. pro., our, ours, our own ; pl., nostri, our troops, our men (milites understood).

nostrum or nostri, gen. pl. of ego.

Notus, -ī, M., the South Wind = Auster (see Auster).

notus, -a, -um, (perf. part. pass. of nosco used as an) adj., known, well known.

novem, num. adj., nine.

nōvi, -isse, v. defect., know.

novitās, -ātis, F., novelty, strangeness.

novus, -a, um, adj., new, fresh, recent, strange (no conp. ; sup. novissimus) ; agmen novissimum, the rear ; agmen primum, the van ; res novae, a change in affairs, a revolution.

nox, noctis, F., night, darkness ; prima nocte, at nightfall ; media nocte, at nidnight; multa de nocte, late at night; adversa nocte, in the face of night (c. iv, 28).

nūbēs, -is, F., a cloud.

nubō, -ere, nupsī, nuptum, v. intr. (with dative), properly to veil oneself for a husband, hence said of a wonan, to narry; a man was said uxorem ducere or uxorem in matrimonium ducere.

nūdus, -a, -um, adj., naked.

nūllus, a, -um, adj. (for declension), none, no one.

num, interrog. particle.

nūmen, -inis, N., will, power, divinity.

numerus, -ī, M., number.

nummus, -ī, M., noney; pro nummo uti, to use as noney (c. v, 12).

nunc, adv., now.

numquam, adv., never.

nuntiō, -āre, -āvī, -ātum, v. tr., announce, tell, narrate; nuntiatur, word is brought: nuntiatum est, word was brought.

nuntius, -ī, M., nessenger, tidings.

nūper, adv., lately, recently.

nūrus, -ūs, F., daughter-in-law.

nusquam, adv., nowhere, in no place.

nūtō, -āre, -āvī, -ātum, v. int., nod, sway to and fro.

nūt-us, -ūs, M., nod, connand; ad nutum, at a nod or signal (c. iv, 23).

O

Ō, interj., o! oh!

ob, prep. (with acc.), on account of, for; ob eam rem, for this reason; quam ob rem, wherefore, accordingly.

obdūcō, -ere, -duxi, -ductum, v. tr., draw over, cloud.

objiciō, -jicere, -jēci, -jectum, v. tr., thrust or put in the way of, place in front of; to present

objectus, -a, -um (perf. part. pass. of objicio used as an) adj., opposite (c. v, 13).

obliviscor, -liviscī, -litus sum, v. dep. (with genitive); forget.

obruō, -ere, -ruī, -rutum, v. tr., overwhelm.

obscūrus, -a, -um, adj., dark.

observō, -āre, -āvī, -ātum, v. tr., watch, observe.

obses, -sidis, M. or F. a hostage; obsidum loco, as hostages (c. v, 5).

obsideō, -sidēre, -sēdī, -sessum, v. tr., besiege, blockade.

obsidiō, -ōnis, F., siege, blockade.

obstinātē, adv., firmly, stubbornly.

obstupescō, -ere, -stupni, no sup., become anazed

obtegō, -ere, -texi, -tectum, v. tr., hide, conceal.

obtemperō, -āre, -āvī, -ātum, v. intr. (with dat.), comply with, obey, conforn to.

obtestor, -ārī, -ātus sum, v. dep., inplore, adjure.

obtineō, -tinēre, -tinui, -tentum, v. tr., hold, posses (c. v, 20).

obtruncō, -āre, -āvī, -ātum, v. tr., cut to pieces.

occāsus, -ūs, M., setting : occasus solis, sunset, west (c. iv, 28; v, 8); fall, destruction

occidō, -cidere, -cidi, -cāsum, v. intr., fall, be killed; occidens sol, sunset, west (c. v, 13).

occidō, -ere, -cidi, -cīsum, v. tr., kill.

occultō, -āre, -āvī, -ātum, v. tr., cover, hide, conceal.

occultus, -a, -um, adj., hidden, concealed.

occumbō, -ere, -cubui, -cubitum, v. intr., yield to; occumbere morti, to neet death

occupātus, -a, -um (perf. part. pass. of occupo used as an) adj., busied with; nostris omnibus occupatis, while all our men were busy (c. iv, 34); occupatos in munitione castrorum, busied with the fortifying of the canp (c. v, 15).

occupātiō, -ōnis, F., being busied with, business affairs; occupationes reipublicae, state affairs (c. iv, 16); has tantularum rerum occupationes, business consisting of such trifles (c. iv, 22).

occupō, -āre, -āvī, -ātum, v. tr., take, seize.

occurrō, -ere, -curri, -cursum, v. tr. (with dat.), neet.

Ōceanus, -ī, M., the ocean.

octāvus, -a, -um, ord. num. adj., eighth.

octingenti, -ae, -a, card. num. adj., eight hundred.

octō, card. num. adj., eight.

octodecim, card. num. adj., eighteen.

octogintā, card. num. adj., eighty.

oculus, -ī, M., eye.

ódī, ·isse, v. tr. defect., hate.

ōdium, -ī, N., hatred.

offerō, -ferre, obtulī, oblātum, v. tr., bring before, present, offer ; se obtulit hostibus, he faced the eneny ; oblati per lunam, neeting us in the noonlight ; se...offert, presents himself.

officium, -ī, N., duty, allegiance ; officium praestare, to do one's duty ; in officio esse, to be loyal (c. v, 3) ; in officio manere, to renain loyal (c. v,4); in officio continere, to keep him loyal, or in service (c. v, 7).

Olympus, -ī, M., Olynpus, a nountain in Thessaly, the fabled abode of the gods.

ōmen, -inis, N., onen, sign.

omnīnō, adv., in all, altogether, in all; after negatives, at all; nihil omnino, nothing at all; with nunerals, in all; decem omnino, ten in all.

omnipotens, -tis, adj., alnighty, onnipotent.

omnis, -e, adj., all, the whole; omnes ad unum, all to a nan; maritima omnis, wholly naritine, or on the sea (c. v, 14).

onerārius, -a, -um, adj., of burden, navis oneraria, a transport (c. iv, 22, 25).

onerō, -āre, -āvī, -ātum, v. tr., load.

onus, -eris, N., load, burden.

opācus, -a, -um, shady.

opera, -ae, F., toil, aid; dare operam, to take pains (c. v, 7) ; multae operae, of great trouble (c, v, 11).

opīmus, -a, -um, adj., rich.

opinió, ōnis, F., belief, notion ; opinio timoris, the inpression of fear, praeter opinionem, contrary to expectation ; celerius omni opinione, sooner than anyone expected ; ut fert opinio illorum, according to their ideas (c. v, 13).

oportet, -ēre, -uit, v. int., inpers.; it is necessary, it behoves (c. iv, 29).

oppōnō, -ere, -posui, -positum, v. tr., place against, oppose, withstand; oppositi (perf. part. pass. and as an), adj., opposing.

opportūnē, adv., favorably, suitably.

opportūnus, -a, -um, adj., fit, suitable, advantageous.

opprimō, -ere, pressi, pressum, v. tr., burden, crush, destroy.

oppugnātiō, -ōnis, F., assault, attack.

oppugnō, -āre, -āvī, -ātum, v. tr., storn, attack.

(ops), nom. wanting : gen., opis, F., might, power, help; pl., opes, wealth, resources.

optimē : see bene.

optimus : see bonus.

optō, -āre, -āvī, -ātum, v. tr., wish for, desire.

opus, -eris, N., work, labor, magno opere or magnopere, greatly; quanto opere, how greatly ; tanto opere or tantopere, so nuch, so greatly.

opus, indecl. neut., found only in the expression opus est, erat, etc., there is or was, etc., need, it is or was necessary.

ōra, -ae, F., coast ; ora maritima, sea coast (c. iv, 20).

ōrāculum, -ī, N., oracle.

ōrātiō, -ōnis, F., a speech ; orationem percipere, to hear a speech (c. v. 1).

orātor, -ōris, M., speaker; modo oratoris, as an anbassador (c. iv, 27).

orbis, -is, M., a circle ; orbis terrarum, the circle of lands, i.e., around the Mediterranean, the whole world to the early Ronans ; orbe facto, forning a circle ; corresponding to our forning square to resist an attack (c. iv, 37) ; circuit, coil.

orbus, -a, -um, adj., bereft, deprived of.

Orcus, -ī, M., Orcus, the lower world, the shades ; death

ordior, -iri, orsus sum, begin.

ordō, -inis, M., an arrangenent; rank, line ; ordines servare, to keep the ranks (c. iv, 26).

Orgetorix, -igis, M., Orgetorix, a Helvetian noblenan.

oriens, -tis, (pres. part. of orior used as an) adj., rising ; sol oriens, the rising sun, hence, the east (c. v, 13).

orior, -iri, -tus sum, v. intr. dep., rise, spring fron ; orta luce, at daybreak (c. v, 8); quibus orti ex civitatibus, and sprung fron these states (c. v, 12).

ornus, -ī, F., nountain ash.

ōrō, -āre, -āvī, -ātum, v. tr., pray for, beseech ; magnopere orant, they earnestly ask.

os, oris, N., nouth, face.

os, ossis, N., bone.

osculum, -ī, N., kiss.

ostendō, -ere, -tendī, -tensum (or tum), v. tr., tell, show, declare.

Othryadēs, -ae, M., *son of Othrys = Panthus.*

P

Palamēdēs, -is, M., *Palamedes,* king of Euboea, a Greek who lost his life through the wiles of Ulysses

Palladium, -ī, N., *the Palladium,* an image of Pallas (Minerva), supposed to have fallen from Heaven. On its preservation depended the safety of Troy. It was carried off by Diomede and Ulysses.

Pallas, -adis, F., *Pallas* or *Minerva,* the goddess of war, wisdom, and art.

pābulātiō, -ōnis, F., foraging, getting fodder.

pābulātor, -ōris, M., a forager.

pābulor, -āri, -ātus sum, v. dep., forage, seek forage.

pābulum, -ī, N., fodder, forage.

pācātus, -ta, -tum (perf. part. pass. of paco used as an) adj., peaceful, quiet.

pācō, -āre, -āvī, -ātum, v. tr., subdue, pacify.

pāgus, -ī, M., district, canton; the word still exists in the French *pays,* as *Pays de Calais.*

pallidus, -a, -um, adj., pale.

palma, -ae, F., palm (of the hand), hand

palūs, -ūdis, F., marsh.

pandō, -ere, pandī, pansum or passum, v. tr., stretch, spread out, open.

Panthūs, -ī (voc., Panthū), M., *Panthus,* priest of Apollo in the Trojan citadel.

pār, paris, adj., equal; par est, it is fit, it is proper; par proelium, a drawn battle; pari spatio, of the same extent (c. v, 13).

parātus, -a, -um (perf. part. pass. of paro used as a) adj., prepared, ready.

parcō, -ere, -pepercī (or parsī), parcitum (or parsum), v. intr. (with dat.), spare.

parens, -tis, M. or F., a parent.

pārens, -tis, (pres. part. of pareo used as an) adj., obedient.

pāreō, -ēre, -uī, -itum, v. intr. (with dat.), obey.

pariēs, -etis, M., a partition wall of a house.

pariter, adv., equally, evenly.

Paris, -idis ; N. m. : *Paris,* also called *Alexander,* son of Priam and Hecuba. When born he was exposed on Mount Ida, because his mother dreamed that she was delivered of a blazing torch, which was interpreted by the seer to signify that the child would be the destruction of Troy. Paris was brought up by shepherds, and so signalized himself in protecting the people that he obtained the name of "man defender" (Ἀλέξανδρος). He married the nymph Oenone. Afterwards he was chosen a judge in the dispute about the golden apple. Having awarded the prize to Venus, against Juno and Minerva, he incurred the hatred of the two latter goddesses. He went to Sparta, carried off Helen, wife of Menelaus, king of Sparta, and hence arose the Trojan war.

parma, -ae, F., small round shield.

parō, -āre, -āvī, -ātum, v. tr., prepare, get ready, equip, procure; bellum parare, prepare for war (c. v, 3).

pars, -tis, F., part, district, region; in ea parte, in that direction (c. iv, 32); per omnes partes, in every direction (c. iv, 33); omnibus partibus, in every quarter

partim, adv., partly; partim... partim, partly...partly (c. v, 6).

parum, adv., too little, little; (comp. minus; sup., minimē).

parvulus, -a, um, adj., very little, young; ab parvulo, from boyhood.

parvus, -a, -um, adj., small, trifling; (comp. minor; sup., minimus.

pascō, -ere, pāvī, pastum, v. tr., feed upon

pascor, -ci, -pastus, v. dep., feed upon.

passim, adv., in every direction.

passus, -ūs, M., a step, pace. As a measure of distance, two paces, reckoned from the heel to the same heel, like our two military steps, or=five Roman pedes (see pes), about 4 ft. 10¼ in. English measure; mille passus = 1616 yards, or 144 yards short of the English mile.

passus, -a, -um, perf. part. pass. of pando (see pando); passis crinibus, with hair all loose

pastor, -ōris, M., shepherd.

patefaciō, -facere, -fēcī, -factum, v. tr., open; pass., patefīō, fierī, factus sum.

patens, -tis, adj., open.

pateō, -ēre, -uī, no sup., v. intr., be open, stand open, extend.

pater, -tris, M., father.

patescō, -ere, patuī, v. intr., begin to be open or obvious.

patior, patī, passus sum, v. tr. dep., allow, suffer, bear.

patria, -ae, F., fatherland, native land; patriā pellere, to banish.

patrius, -a, -um, adj., paternal.

paucitās, -ātis, F., fewness, small number (c. iv, 30, 31).

paucus, -a, -um, adj., some, few (generally in pl.); paucis diebus, within a few days (c. iv, 27 ; v, 2).

paulātim, adv., gradually.

paulisper, adv., for a short time.

paulō, adv., (abl. of paulus), by a little, just a little ; with comparative adjectives or adverbs, a little ; paulo longius, a little further (c. iv, 32); paulo tardius, a little too slowly (c. iv, 23).

paululum, adv., a little, gradually.

paulum, adv., a little.

pauper, -ĕris, adj., poor (comp. pauperior, sup. pauperrimus).

pavitō, -āre, -āvī, -ātum, v. intr., be in dread ; pavitans, used as an adjective, trembling

pavor, -ōris, M., fear.

pax, pācis, F., peace.

peccō, -āre, -āvī, -ātum, v. intr., do wrong, sin.

pectus, -oris, N., breast.

pecus, -oris, N., cattle (collectively).

pedes, -itis, M., a foot-soldier ; pl., pedites, infantry.

pedester, -tris, -tre, adj., on foot, on land ; copiae pedestres, land forces ; copiae navales, naval forces ; in pedestribus proeliis, in battles on land (c. iv, 24).

peditātus, -ūs, M., infantry (collectively).

pējor, -us, adj. (comp. of malus ; sup., pessimus), worse.

pelagus, -ī, N., sea.

Pelasgī, -ōrum, M. pl., Pelasgi or Greeks.

Pelasgus, -a, -um, adj., Pelasgic, Grecian.

Peliās, -ae, M., Pelias, a Trojan.

Pēlīdēs, -ae, M., a descendant of Peleus = Neoptolemus or Pyrrhus, son of Achilles

pellax, -ācis, adj., deceitful, false.

pellis, -is, F., skin, hide; pellibus vestiri, to clothe themselves with skins (c. v, 14).

pellō, -ere, pepulī, pulsum, v. tr., expel, drive out ; patria pellere, to exile (N. A. 1).

Pelopēus, -a, -um, adj., belonging to Pelops, an ancient King of Elis, after whom all Southern Greece was called Peloponnesus, or "island of Pelops." Hence Grecian

Peloponnēsus, -ī, F., the Peloponnesus (now the Morea), the part of Greece south of the isthmus of Corinth.

penātēs, -ium, pl. M., the Penates, or household gods, presiding over the house and all that it contained

pendeō, -ēre, pependī, no sup., v. intr., hang, be suspended.

pendō, -ere, pependī, pensum, v. tr., weigh out (in early times payments were made by weighing out metal, hence), pay.

Pēneleus, -ī, M., Peneleus, a leader of the Boeotians in the Trojan war.

penetrāle, -is, N., inner part, shrine.

penitus, adv., within.

per, prep. (with acc.), through, by means of, by ; per omnes partes, in every direction (c. iv, 33).

peragō, -ere, -ēgī, -actum, v. tr., accomplish, bring to an end ; conventus peragere, to hold assizes (c. v, 2).

percipiō, -cipere, -cēpī, -ceptum, v. tr., take in, learn, perceive ; percipere orationem, to hear a speech (c. v, 1).

percontātiō, -ōnis, F., enquiry.

percurrō, -ere, -currī (or -cucurrī), -cursum, v. intr., run along.

perdūcō, -ere, -duxī, -ductum, v. tr., complete, bring to a destination ; naves perduxit, he brought the ships to their destination (c. v, 23).

pereō, -īre, -iī or (-īvī), -itum, v. intr., perish, die.

perequitō, -āre, -āvī, -ātum, v. tr., ride, ride through.

pererrō, -āre, -āvī, -ātum, v. tr., wander over.

perferō, -ferre, -tulī, -lātum, v. tr., carry, bring, report ; endure ; consilio perlato, after their plan was reported (c. iv, 21).

perfidia, -ae, F., faithlessness, treachery.

perfuga, -ae, M., a deserter, runaway.

perfundō, -ere, -fūdī, -fūsum, v. tr., sprinkle, steep.

perfugium, -ī, N., refuge.

Pergama, -ōrum, N. pl., *Pergama*, the citadel of 'Iroy : hence *Troy*.

perīculum, -ī, N., danger ; facere perīculum, to run the risk (c. iv, 21).

Periphras, -antis, M., *Periphras*, one of the companions of Pyrrhus at the back of 'Iroy.

perītus, -a, -um, adj., with gen., acquainted with ; rei mīlitaris perītus, skilled in military affairs.

perjūrus, -a, um, adj., foresworn.

perlātus, -a, um, perf. part. pass. of perferō (see perferō).

permaneō, -ēre, -mansī, -mansum, v. intr., stay, remain, continue ; in ea sententiā permanere, to adhere to that policy (c. iv, 21).

permittō, -ere, -mīsī, -missum, v. intr., entrust ; fortunas ejus fidei permittere, to entrust their fortunes to his protection (c. v, 3).

permōtus, -a, -um, perf. part. pass., influenced.

permoveō, -ēre, -mōvī, -mōtum, v. tr., rouse, disturb, alarm, induce.

perpaucī, -ae, -a, adj. pl., very few.

perpetuus, -a, -um, adj., constant, unbroken ; in perpetuum, for ever (c. iv, 34).

perrumpō, -ere, -rūpī, -ruptum, v. tr., break through.

persaepe, adv., very often.

persequor, -sequī, -secūtus sum, v. tr. dep., follow up, pursue, overtake (c. v, 10).

persolvō, -ere, -solvī, -solūtum, v. tr., pay to the full.

perspiciō, -spicere, -spexī, -spectum, v. tr., see, observe, reconnoitre ; coram perspicit, he sees in person (c. v, 11).

perstō, āre, -stitī, -stātum, v. intr., persist, continue.

petō, -ere, petīvī, petītum, v. tr., ask.

perterreō, -ēre, -uī, -itum, v. tr., greatly alarm, frighten, terrify.

perterritus, -a, -um, perf. part. pass., used as an adj., frightened.

pertineō, -ēre, -tinuī no sup., v. intr., tend, extend ; hoc pertinet, this side extends (c. v, 13).

perturbātiō, -ōnis, F., confusion, consternation.

perturbō, -āre, -āvī, -ātum, v. tr., disturb greatly, agitate.

perveniō, -īre, -vēnī, -ventum, v. intr., reach, arrive at.

pervius, -a, -um, adj., with a way through.

pēs, pedis, M., foot; pedem referre, to retreat (c. iv, 25) ; pedibus proeliari, to fight on foot (c. iv, 23); pedibus, on foot (c. v, 18) ; as a measure of length=11.64 in. ; 5 Roman pedes= passus. (See passus.)

phalanx, -gis, F., a band of soldiers in solid column, a host

Phoebus, -ī, M., *Phoebus*, a poetical name of Apollo.

Phoenix, -icis, M., *Phoenix*, a friend of Achilles.

Phrygēs, -um, M., pl., inhabitants of Phrygia, a name given to the North-west part of Asia Minor in which 'Iroy was situated, hence *Phrygians, Trojans*.

Phrygius, -a, -um, adj., *Phrygian*, Trojan.

Phthia, -ae, F., *Phthia*, a town in 'Ihessaly and birthplace of Achilles.

pietās, -ātis, F., duty to the gods, to one's country, or to one's parents ; hence, piety, patriotism or filial affection.

pineus, -a, -um, adj., of pine.

piō, -āre, -āvī, -ātum, v. tr., expiate

Pirustae, -ārum, M. pl., the *Pirustae*, a tribe of Macedonia, on the southern border of Illyricum, in what is now the modern *Herzegovina*.

Pisō, -ōnis, M., *Piso*, an Aquitanian noble (c. v, 12).

piscis, -is, F., fish.

placeō, -ēre, -uī, -itum, v. intr. (with dat.), please ; placet, impers., it pleases.

plācō, -āre, -āvī, -ātum, v. tr., appease.

plangor, -ōris, M., beating of the breasts, mourning.

plānus, -a, -um, adj, flat, level.

plebs, plēbis, (plēbēī or plēbī), F., the common people, the commons.

plēnē, adv., fully, completely.

plēnus, -a, -um, adj., full (with genitive).

plērīque, plēraeque, plēraque, pl. adj., most, several ; interiores plerique, most of the inland people (c. v, 14).

plērumque, adv., mostly, generally, usually.

plērusque, plēraque, plērumque, adj., most; generally plerique.

plumbum, -ī, N., lead: album plumbum, tin (c. v, 12).

plūrēs : see multus.

plūrimum, adv., superl. of multum; longe plurimum valet, is by far the most powerful (c. v, 3).

plūrimus, -a, -um, adj. superl. of multus.

plūs, adj., comp. of multus.

pōculum, -ī, N., drinking cup.

poena, -ae, F., compensation, punishment, penalty; poenas dare, to pay the penalty, to be punished; poenas sumere, to exact a penalty, to punish.

poēta, -ae, M., poet.

polliceor, -ērī, -itus sum, v. tr. dep., promise.

Polītēs, -ae, N. m., *Polites,* a son of Priam, slain by Pyrrhus before his father's eyes during the sacking of 'Troy.

Pompēius, -ī, M., *Pompey,* Cnēius Pompēius Magnus, a Roman general, born 106 B.C., Consul 70 B.C., 55 and 52, defeated by Caesar at Pharsalia, 48 B.C., and afterwards assassinated in Egypt.

pōmum, -ī, N., an apple.

pondus, -eris, N., weight.

pōne, adv., behind.

pōnō, pōnere, posuī, positum, v. tr., place, put, lay down; ponere arma, to lay down arms (c. iv., 37); castra ponere, to pitch a camp: put aside

pontus, -ī, M., sea.

populātiō, -ōnis, F., devastation, ravaging.

populus, -ī, M., people; populi, nations.

porta, -ae, F., gate, door.

porticus, -ūs, F., arcade, colonnade.

portus, -ūs, M., port, harbor.

poscō. poscere, poposcī, no sup., v. tr., beg, demand, ask.

possideō, -ēre, possēdī, possessum, v. tr., hold, own.

possīdō, -ere, possēdī, possessum, v. tr., win, get possession of.

possum, posse, potuī, no sup.; v. irreg., be able, can; multum posse, to have great power; plurimum posse, to have very great power.

post, adv. after, later; (often with the abl. of measure) anno post, a year

afterwards; paucis diebus post, a few days afterwards.

post, prep. (with acc.), after; post tergum, in the rear; post paucos annos, after a few years; post hominum memoriam, within the memory of man.

posteā, adv., afterwards.

posteāquam, conj., after that, after.

posterus, -a, -um, adj., the following, next; (comp., posterior; sup., postrēmus); pl., posteri, -orum, descendants.

postis, -is, M., post.

postpōnō, -ere, -posuī,-positum, v. tr., put off : (c. v, 7).

postquam, adv., after that, after, when.

postrīdiē, adv., the next day; postridie ejus diei mane, early next day (c. v, 10).

postulō, -āre, -āvī, -ātum, v. tr., ask, demand, request

potens, -tis, adj., powerful.

potestās, -ātis, F., power.

potissimum, adv., sup., chiefly, principally, especially.

potius, adv., rather, preferably; sup. potissimum, no positive.

praeacūtus, -a, -um, adj., sharpened at the end, pointed.

praebeō, -ēre, -uī, -itum, v. tr., offer, show, furnish.

praeceps, -cipitis, adj., headlong, teed, precipitious; praecipites hostes agere, to drive the enemy headlong (c. v, 17).

praeceptum, -ī, N., teaching, advice, order, command.

praecipiō, -cipere, -cēpī, -ceptum, v. intr. (with dative), order, direct.

praecipitō, -āre, -āvī, -ātum, v. tr. and intr., rush headlong, throw headlong; mentem praecipitare, to hasten one's resolve

praecipuē, adv., especially, particularly.

praeclārus, -a, -um, adj., distinguished.

praeclūdō, -ere, -clūsī, -clūsum, v. tr., close up (c. v, 9).

praecordia, -ōrum, N. pl., heart, breast

praeda, -ae, F., booty, plunder.

praedicō, -āre, -dicāvī, dicātum, v. tr., proclaim, boast.

praedīcō, -ere, -dixī, -dictum, v. tr., foretell.

praeditus, -a, -um, adj. (with abl.), endowed with.

praedor, -ārī, -ātus sum, v. dep. tr., plunder, pillage, obtain booty.

praeficiō, -ficere, -fēcī, -fectum, v. tr., put over, put in command of.

praefigō, -ere, fixī, -fixum, v. tr., fix or place in front of.

praefixus, perf. part. pass. of praefigō.

praemetuō, -ere, -uī, no sup., v. intr., fear for, be anxious for.

praemittō, -ere, -mīsī, -missum, v. tr., send before, send forward.

praemium, -ī, N., reward.

praeparō, -āre, -āvī, -ātum, v. tr., prepare.

praepōnō, -ere, -posuī, -positum, v. tr., set over, place in command of.

praesens, -tis, adj., at hand, present.

praesertim, adv., especially.

praesidium, -ī, N., guard, defence, garrison; praesidio navibus esse, to guard the ships (c. v, 9).

praestō, -stāre, -stitī, -stitum, stand before, show, perform; officium praestare, to fulfil a duty (c. iv, 25).

praesum, -esse, -fuī, v. intr. (with dative), be over, have command of; negotio praeesse, to have charge of the matter (c. v, 2).

praeter, prep. (with acc.), beyond, except, contrary to.

praetereā, adv., besides.

praetermittō, -mittere, -mīsī, -missum, v. tr., let pass, let slip.

praetervehor, -vehī, -vectus sum, v. tr., be carried beyond, sail past, coast along.

precī, precem, prece (no nom. or gen. sing.); pl. preces, precum, etc.; F., prayer, request.

premō, -ere, pressī, pressum, v. tr., press, harass, crush.

prehendō (or prendō), -ere, -dī, -sum, v. tr., seize, lay hold of.

prensō, -āre, -āvī, -ātum, v. tr., grasp.

(prex, precis), F., supposed form; see precī.

prīdiē, adv., the day before.

prīmō, adv., at first.

prīmum, adv., firstly, in the first place; ubi prīmum, as soon as; cum prīmum, as soon as possible; cum (quum) prīmum, as soon as.

Priamēius, -a, -um, adj., of or belonging to Priam.

Priamus, -ī, M., Priam, the last king of Troy.

prīmus, -a, -um, adj., sup. of the comp., prior, no positive: prima luce, at daybreak; prima nocte, at night fall; primum agmen, the vanguard; in primis, especially.

princeps, -cipis, M., chief man, chief, prince.

principātus, -ūs, chief authority, leadership.

principium, -ī, N., beginning.

prior, prius, adj., comp.(no positive; sup. prīmus); former, previous.

pristinus, -a, -um, adj., old, former.

prius, adv., before, sooner, earlier; followed by quam, and often written with it as one word, priusquam before, before that.

priusquam, conj., before.

prīvātim, adv., privately, individually.

prīvātus, -a, -um, adj., private.

prō, prep. (with abl.), in front of, before; for, in proportion to; pro merito ejus, as he deserved (c. v, 4); pro tempore et pro re, suited to the time and the conditions (c. v, 8); pro sano, as a sane man (c. v, 7); pro nummo, as money (c. v, 12); pro sua virtute, in consideration of his excellence.

prōcēdō, -ere, -cessī, -cessum, v. intr., advance, succeed.

procul, adv., afar, at a distance.

prōcumbō, -ere, -cubuī, cubitum, v. intr., fall, sink down.

prōditiō, -ōnis, F., treachery, betraying.

prōditor, -ōris, M., traitor, betrayer.

prōdō, -ere, -didī, ditum, v. tr., betray, surrender; memoria proditum, handed down by tradition (c. v, 12).

prōdūcō, -ere, -duxī, -ductum, v. tr., prolong.

proelior, -ārī, -ātus sum, v. intr., fight.

proelium, -ī, N., battle; proelium facere, to fight a battle.

profectiō, -ōnis, F., a departure; setting out.

profectō, adv., for a fact, indeed.

proficiscor, -cī, -fectus sum, v. intr. dep., set out, depart.

prōgredior, -gredī, -gressus sum, v. tr. dep., advance, go forward.

212   VOCABULARY

prohibeō, -hibēre, -hibuī, hibitum, v. tr., hold, defend, protect (c. v, ⁹¹).

prōjiciō, -jicere, -jēcī, jectum, v. tr., throw, throw forward.

prōinde, adv., henceforth, therefore.

prōlābor, -ī, -lapsus sum, v. dep., glide forward, sink down.

prōmissum, -ī, N., promise.

prōmissus, -a, -um, adj., long, flowing; capillo sunt promisso, they have long hair (c. v, 14).

prōmittō, -ere, -mīsī, -missum, v. tr., promise.

prōmō, -ere, prompsī, promptum, v. tr., put forth ; se prōmunt, issue from

prōmoveō, -ēre, -mōvī, -mōtum, v. tr., move forward.

prōnē, adv., headlong, leaning forward.

prōnuntiō, -āre, -āvī, -ātum, v.tr., tell, announce, declare.

prōnus, -a, -um, adj., steep.

prope, adv , near, nearly, almost ; comp., propius ; sup., proximē.

prōpellō, -ere, -pulī, -pulsum, v. tr., drive away, put to flight.

properō, -āre, -āvī, -ātum, v. tr. and intr., hurry, hasten.

propinquō, -āre, -āvī, -ātum, v. intr. (with dat.), approach.

propinquus, -a, -um, adj., near, with dative ; as a noun, propinquus, -ī, M., relation.

propior, -us, adj., comparative of obsolete propis ; sup. proximus ; nocte proxima, last night.

propius : see prope and propior.

proprius, -a, -um, adj., one's own, particular, peculiar.

propter, prep. (with acc.), on account of, in consequence of.

proptereā, adv., for this reason, therefore ; proptereā quod, because.

prōpugnō, -āre, -āvī, -ātum, v. tr., fight.

prōsequor, -sequī, -secūtus sum, v. tr., dep., follow after, follow, attend.

prōspiciō, -ere, -spexī, -spectum, v. tr., look forward, take care.

prōsum, -prōd-esse, prō-fuī, v. intr., be of benefit to, benefit (with dative).

prōtegō, -ere, -texī, -tectum, v. tr., protect.

prōtinus, adv., at once, forthwith, immediately ; ex hac fuga protinus, immediately after this defeat (c. v, 17).

prōtrahō, -ere, -traxī, -tractum, v. tr., drag forth.

prōvehō, -ere, -vexī, -vectum, v. tr., carry forward ; in pass., sail along, coast.

prōvideō, -ēre, -vīdī, -vīsum, v. tr., foresee, take care.

prōvidus, -a, -um, adj., foreseeing.

proximē : see prope.

proximus : see propior.

pūbēs, -is, F., youth.

publicus, -a, -um, adj., public, common ; res publica, the commonwealth ; publico consilio, by a public plan.

Publius, -ī, M., Publius, a Roman praenomen.

puella, -ae, F., girl.

puer, puerī, M., boy, youth.

pugna, -ae, F., fight, combat.

pugnō, -āre, -āvī, -ātum, v. intr., fight ; acriter pugnatum est, a fierce battle was fought (c. iv, 26).

pulcher, -chra, -chrum, adj., beautiful.

pulvis, -eris, M., dust.

puppis, -is, F., stern of a vessel ; a ship.

pūrus, -a, -um, adj., pure, bright.

putō, -āre, -āvī, -ātum, v. tr., think, fancy, consider.

Pyrrhus, -ī, M., Pyrrhus, also called Neoptolemus, son of Achilles.

Q

Q = Quintus (which see).

qua, nom. sing. fem. or neut. pl. nom. or acc. of quis or qui.

quā (abl. fem. of qui, supply viā or parte) adv., where.

quadrāgintā, nom. card. adj., forty.

quaerō, ere, quaesivī, quaesītum, v. tr., seek, look for, ask, enquire.

quaestiō, -ōnis, F., enquiry, investigation.

quaestor, -ōris, M., quaestor ; the quaestors were officers who acted as government treasurers, received tribute and paid the soldiers.

quālis, -e, adj., of what sort or kind ; talis . . qualis, such…as ; talis omitted ; quālis erat ! what a sight was he !

quam, conj., than (after comparatives); with superlatives (with or without **possum**)=as possible : **quam primum**, as soon as possible; **quam plurimi**, as many as possible; **quam maximi**, as large as possible.

quamquam, conj., though, although, however, and yet.

quandō, interrog. adv., when? rel. adv., when, whenever; **si quando**, if at any time.

quantō (abl. of difference from **quantus**), adv., by how much; **quanto...tanto, as...so; the...the.**

quantum (acc. of **quantus**), adv., how much, how far, as far as.

quantus, **a**, **-um**, adj., interrog. or rel., how great, how much, how large, as large as.

quārē, interrog. and rel. adv., wherefore, why.

quartus, **-a**, **-um**, ord. num. adj., fourth.

quasi, conj., as if.

quater, adv., four times.

quatiō, **-ere**, no perf., **quassum**, v. tr., shake.

quattuor, card. num. adj., four.

-que, conj., and ; always appended to the word, which in construction belongs to it ; generally to the first word of the clause or to the word it couples.

queror, **queri**, **questus sum**, v. tr. dep., complain, lament.

qui, **quae**, **quod**, rel. pro., who, which, what.

quicquam : see **quisquam**.

quicumque, **quaecumque**, **quodcumque**, indef. pro., whoever, whatever.

quidam, **quaedam**, **quoddam** or **quiddam**, indef. pro., a certain one ; pl., some, certain.

quidem, adv., indeed, at least; **ne...quidem**, not...even : the emphatic word is always placed between **ne** and **quidem**.

quiēs, **-ētis**, F., rest, repose.

quin (old abl. **qui**, how and **ne**, not), conj., that not, but that, without ; after words expressing doubt or suspicion, that ; after words of preventing, etc., translated by *from* with verbals in -ing.

quingenti, **-ae**, **-a**, card. num. adj., five hundred.

quini, **-ae**, **-a**, distrib. num. adj., five

quinquāgintā, card. adj., fifty.

quinque, card. num. adj., five.

quintus, **-a**, **-um**, ord. num. adj., fifth.

Quintus, **-ī**, **M.**, *Quintus*, a Roman praenomen (see **cognomen**); see **Atrius, Titurius, Laberius**).

quis, **quae** or **qua**, **quid** or **quod**, indef. pro., anyone, any ; **ne quid**, nothing (c. v, 7); interrog., who?

quisquam, **quaequam**, **quicquam** or **quidquam**, indef. pro., any one ; **neque quisquam**, no one (c. iv, 20); **neque quicquam**, and nothing (c. iv, 20); always in connection with negatives or implied negatives.

quisque, **quaeque**, **quidque** or **quodque**, indef. pro., each, every, every one; with superlatives in sing., all ; **optimus quisque**, all the best.

quisquis, **quidquid** or **quicquid**, indefinite relative pronoun, whoever, whatever.

quivis, **quaevis**, **quidvis** or **quodvis**, indef. pro., any one you please, any.

quō, adv., (1) rel. and interrog., whither, where (c. v, 21) ; (2), interrog., why ; rel., when.

quō (abl. of **qui**), final conj., used with comparatives and followed by subjunctive ; in order that (c. v. 3).

quoad, adv. (with indic. in Caesar), as long as, until, till.

quod, conj., because, inasmuch as (with indicative or subjunctive) ; the fact that; **propterea quod**, because ; **quod si**, but if, if.

quōmínus, conj., that not; often best translated by *from* after verbs of hindering, preventing, etc., with an English verbal noun in -*ing*.

quōnam, interr. adv., whither pray?

quondam, adv., once, formerly, at times

quoniam, conj., since, seeing that, because.

quoque, adv. (following the emphatic word of a clause), also, too.

quot, indecl. adj., how many? often correlative of **tot**; **tot...quot**, as many as.

quotannis, adv., yearly, every year.

quotidiānus, **-a**, **-um**, adj., daily, every day.

quotidie, adv., every day, daily.

R

rabiēs, no gen. or dat., rabiem, rabiē, F., rage.

rādō, -ere, rāsī, rasum, v. tr., shave.

rapidus, -a, -um, adj., swift, quick.

rapiō, rapere, rapuī, raptum, v. tr., snatch, seize, hurry off.

raptō, -āre, -āvī, -ātum, v. tr., drag.

raptor, -ōris, M., plunderer, lupi raptores, prowling wolves

rārus, -a, -um, adj., few, scattered, in small parties.

ratiō, -ōnis, F., reckoning, calculation, account; rationem inire, to form a plan; ratio atque usus belli, the theory and practice of war = the systematic practice of war; equestris proelii ratio, the style of the cavalry battle (c. v, 16); ratio pontis, the plan of the bridge; rei militaris ratio, military science (c. iv, 23); omnibus rationibus, in every way (c. v, 1); reason, nec sat rationis in armis; nor was there sufficient reason in (taking) arms

raucus, -a, -um, adj., hoarse.

rebelliō, -ōnis, F., renewal of war, uprising; rebellione facta, by a renewal of the war (c. iv, 30, 38).

recēdō, -ere, -cessī, -cessum, v. intr., go back, withdraw.

recens, -tis, adj., fresh, late, recent.

receptus, -ūs, M., retreat; expeditūs receptus, a convenient retreat (c. iv, 33).

recipiō, -cipere, -cēpī, -ceptum, v. tr., take back, recover, win; in fidem recipere, to take under one's protection or to receive as a pledge of faith (c. iv, 22); se recipere, to retreat (c. iv, 2); se a fuga recipere, to recover from the flight (c. iv, 27); in deditionem recipere, to admit to a surrender.

recondō, -ere, -didī, -ditum, v. tr., hide (far back).

recūsō, -āre, -āvī, -ātum, v. tr., refuse, decline, deny; often followed by quin or quominus.

recutiō, -ere, -cussī, -cussum, v. tr., strike.

reddō, -ere, -didī, -ditum, v. tr., give back, restore.

redeō, -īre, -iī (īvī), -itum, v. intr., go back, return.

reditus, -ūs, M., return.

redūcō, -ere, -duxī, ductum, v. tr., lead back.

referō, -ferre, -tulī, -lātum, v. tr., bring, carry back; gratias referre, to return thanks; gratiam referre, to requite, to repay; ad suos referre, to report to their people; pedem referre, to retreat (c. iv, 25).

reficiō, ficere, -fēci, -fectum, v. tr., repair, refit.

reflectō, -ere, -flexī, -flexum, v. tr., bend back.

refugiō, -fugere, -fūgi, -fugitum, v. tr. and intr., flee back or away, retreat, escape : shrink back

refulgeō, -ēre, -fulsi, no sup., v. intr., shine out.

rēgīna, -ae, F., queen.

regiō, -ōnis, F., district, country.

rēgius, -a, -um, adj., kingly, royal.

regnātor, -ōris, M., ruler.

regnum, -ī, N., kingdom (c. v. 20); regnum civitatis, sovereignty of the state (c. v, 6).

rējiciō, -jicere, -jeci, -jectum, v. tr., hurl back, drive back, repulse; tempestate rejici, to be driven back by the storm (c. v, 5).

rēligiō, -ōnis, F., religion; religionibus, impediri, to be hampered by religious scruples (c. v, 6); quae religio? what object of religious awe?

rēligiōsus, -a, -um, adj., holy, venerable.

relinquō, -ere, -liqui, -lictum, v. tr., leave, abandon, leave behind; relinquebatur ut, the only course left was that (c. v, 19).

reliquus, -a, -um, adj., remaining; nihil reliqui est, there is nothing left; in reliquum tempus, for all time to come; reliquus exercitus, the remainder of the army (c. iv, 22).

reluceō, -ēre, -luxī, no sup., v. intr., flash, gleam.

remaneō, -ēre, -mansi, mansum, v. intr., remain, await.

remeō, -āre, -āvī, -ātum, v. intr., return.

remetior, -īrī, -mensus sum, v. dep., retrace.

rēmex, -igis, M., a rower.

rēmigō, -āre, -āvī, -ātum, v. intr., row.

remigrō, -āre, no perf., no sup., v. intr., depart, return.

remissus, -a, -um, adj., relaxed; remissioribus frigoribus, since the cold is less intense (c. v, 12).

remittō, -ere, -misi, -missum, v. tr., send back.

removeō, -ēre, -mōvī, -mōtum, v. tr., renove, dismiss, get rid of.

rēmus, -ī, M., oar.

Rōmi, -ōrum, pl. M., the *Remi*, a powerful people of Gaul, whose capital was Durocortorum (now *Rheims*)

renovō, āre, -āvī, -ātum, v. tr., renew.

renuntiō, -āre, -āvī, -ātum, v. tr., bring back word, report.

reor, rēri, ratus sum, v. dep., think.

repellō, -ere, -pulī, -pulsum, v. tr., drive back, repulse.

rependō, -ere, -dī, -sum, v. tr., pay back.

repente, adv., suddenly.

repentinō, adv., suddenly, unexpectedly.

repentinus, -a, -um, adj., sudden, unexpected, hasty.

reperiō, -īre, repperī, repertum, v. tr., discover, find, ascertain.

repetō, -ere, -ivi or ii, -itum, v. tr., reseek, seek anew.

repleō, -ēre, -plēvī, -plētum, v. tr., fill.

reportō, -āre, -āvī, -ātum, v. tr., carry back.

reposcō, -ere, no perf., no sup., v. tr., claim in return, exact.

reprimō, -ere, -pressi, -pressum. v. tr., check.

requiescō, -ere, -quiēvī, -quiētum, v. intr., rest.

requirō, -ere, -quīsīvī, -quīsītum, v. tr., seek to know, ask.

rēs,-reī, F., natter, affair, (the neaning will depend on the context); res militaris, nilitary science; res novae, a change in governnent, a revolution; res publica, the state, con nonwealth, politics; res divina, a sacred rite; res frumentaria, supply of corn; his rebus, on these terns (c. iv, 28).

resideō, -ēre, -sēdi, no sup., v. intr., sit down, stay behind.

resistō, -ere, -stitī, no sup., v. intr., resist, oppose, withstand (with dative).

resolvō, -ere, -vī, solūtum, v. tr., unloose.

respiciō, -spicere, -spexī, -spectum, v. tr., look back for or at.

respondeō, -ēre, -spondī, -sponsum, v. tr., reply, answer.

responsum, -ī, N., answer, rely.

respublica, reīpublicae. (for declension), state, con nonwealth.

restat, restāre, no perf., no sup., in pers., it renains.

restinguō, -ere, -nxī, -nctum, v. tr., put out.

restō, -āre, -stitī, no sup., v. intr., renain, am left.

retineō, -ēre, -tinui, -tentum, v tr, restrain, detain, keep back.

retrahō, -ere, -traxī, -tractum v. tr., draw back, save, preserve.

revertō, -ere, -verti, -versum, v. tr., turn back, return.

revertor, reverti, reverti, reversum, v. intr., return.

revinciō, -īre, -vinxī, -vinctum, v. tr., bind back.

revīsō, -ere, -visi, vīsum, v. tr., revisit.

revocō, -āre, -āvī, -ātum, v. tr., call back, recall.

revolvō, -ere, -volvī, -volūtum, v. tr., roll back.

rex, rōgis, M., king.

Rhēnus, -ī, M., the Rhine.

Rhīpeūs, -ī, M., Rhipeus, a con rade of Aeneas.

ripa, -ae, F., a bank.

rivus, -ī, M., brook.

rōbur, -oris, N., oak.

rogō, -āre, -āvī, -ātum, v. tr., ask.

Rōmānus, -a, -um, adj., Ronan.

Rōmāni, -ōrum, M., pl., Ronans.

roseus, -a, -um, adj., rosy.

rota, -ae, F., wheel.

Rūfus, -ī, M., Publius Sulpicius Rufus, one of Caesar's lieutenants (c. iv, 22).

ruina, -ae, F., downfall.

rumpō, -ere, rūpi, ruptum, v. tr., break.

ruō, ruere, ruī, rutum, v. intr., rush, fall.

rūpēs, -is, F., rock, cliff.

rursum, adv., back again, anew.

rursus : see rursum.

S

Sabīnus, -ī, M., Sabinus; Quintus Titurius Sabinus, one of Caesar's lieutenants in Gaul. He was slain by the treachery of Ambiorix, 54 B.C.

sacer, -cra, -crum, adj., holy, sacred; as a noun, sacra, -ōrum, sacred rites sacerdōs, -ōtis, M. or F., priest or priestess.

sacrāmentum, -ī, N., the military oath taken by a Roman soldier. The chief obligations were obedience to the commander, loyalty to the country, etc.

sācrātus, -a, -um, perf. part. pass., used as an adj., hallowed.

sācrō, -āre, -āvī, -ātum, v. tr., make holy, hallow.

saepe, adv., often ; minimē saepe, very seldom ; comp., saepius ; sup., saepissimē.

saeviō, -ire, -īvī, -itum, v. intr., be cruel, rage, be furious.

saevus, -a, -um, adj., cruel, fierce.

sagitta, -ae, F., arrow.

salsus, -a, -um, adj., salt.

saltus, -ūs, M., leap (salio).

sālum, -ī, N., surf (of the sea).

salūs, -ūtis, F., safety, health.

sanctus, -a, -um, adj., sacred, solemn.

sanguineus, -a, -um, adj., bloody.

sanguis, -inis, M., blood.

saniēs, ēī, F., gore.

sānus, -a, -um, adj., sound, healthy ; pro sano facere, to act as a sane man (c. v, 7).

sarmentum, -ī, N., twig.

sat = satis

sata, -ōrum, N. pl., perf. part. pass. of sero ; crops.

satelles, -itis, M. or F., attendant, guard.

satiō, -āre, -āvī, ātum, satisfy.

satis, adv., enough ; used as an indecl. neut. noun. ; satis militum, enough of soldiers (c. v, 2) ; or as adv. limiting an adj.: satis magnus, very large (c. v, 21).

satisfaciō, -facere, -fēci, -factum, v. intr. with dative, satisfy ; in pass., satisfio.

saucius, -a, -um, adj., wounded.

saxum, -ī, N., a rock, stone.

Scaeus, -a, -um, adj., Scaean ; used in the phrase Scaeae portae, the famous Scaean or Western Gates of Troy.

scāla, -ae, F., ladder.

scandō, ere, scandi, scansum, v. tr., climb, mount

scapha, -ae, F., boat, skiff.

scelerātus, -a, -um, adj., wicked.

scelus, -eris, N., wickedness, sin.

scīlicet, adv., doubtless, forsooth (scire licet).

scindō, ere, scidi, scissum, v. tr., cut, tear, destroy.

sciō, scire, scīvī, scītum, v. tr., know.

scitor, -āri, -ātus sum, v. dep., seek to know, ask.

scrībo, ere, scripsī, scriptum, v. tr., write.

Scȳrius, -a, -um, adj., of or belonging to Scyros, an island east of Euboea.

scūtum, -ī, N., a shield (of oblong shape, while the clipeus was round).

se : see sui,

sēcernō, -ere, -crēvī, crētum, v. tr., separate.

secō, -āre, -uī, -tum, v. tr., cut.

sēcrētus, -a, -um, adj., separate, secret, private.

sēcum, with him, with themselves.

secundus, -a, -um, adj., following, second, favorable.

secūris, -is, F., axe (acc. securim).

sēcius, adj. (comp. of secus) ; nihilo secius, less by nothing, nevertheless ; haud secus ac = just as.

secus, adv., otherwise, differently.

sed, conj., but, yet ; sed enim, but indeed.

sedeō, -ēre, sēdī, sessum, v. intr., sit.

sēdēs, -is, F., seat, abode.

seges, -etis, F , crop, harvest.

segnitiēs, -ēī, F., slowness.

Segontiacī, -ōrum, M., pl., the Segontiaci, a British tribe belonging to Hampshire.

Segovax, -ācis, M., Segovax, one of the petty princes of Kent (c. v, 22).

sēmita, -ae, F., a path.

semper, adv., always.

senātus, -ūs, M., senate.

senectūs, -ūtis, F., old age.

senex, senis, M., an old man.

senior, -ōris (comp. of senex, older.

sententia, -ae, F., opinion, decision.

sentiō, sentire, sensī, sensum, v. tr.; think, know, observe.

sentis, -is, M., thorn, briar.

sepeliō, -ire, -īvī, sepultum, bury.

sēpēs, -is, F., hedge.

septem, card. num. adj., seven

septentriōnēs, -um, the Seven Stars, the constellation of the Great Bear (Ursa Major); hence, the North.

septimus, -a, -um, ord. num. adj., seventh.

septingentī, -ae, -a, card. num. adj., seven hundred.

sepulchrum, -ī, N., tomb(sepelio).

sequor, sequī, secūtus sum, v. tr. dep. follow, pursue; aestus commutationem secutus, following the turn of the tide (c. v, 8); Caesaris fidem sequi, to be loyal to Caesar (c. v, 20).

serēnus, -a, -um, adj., clear, bright.

sermō, -ōnis, M., talk, language, speech, discourse; sermo Latinus, the Latin language.

sērō, -ere, sēvi, satum, v. tr., sow, plant.

sēro, adv., late, too late.

serpens, -ntis, F., snake, serpent.

serpō, -ere, serpsī, serptum, v. intr., creep.

sērus, -a, -um, adj., late.

serviō, -īre, -īvī, -ītum (with dat.), be a servant, serve.

servans, -tis, adj. (with gen.), observant of; servantissimus aequi, most observant of right

servō, -āre, -āvī, -ātum, v. tr., keep, save, preserve; servare ordines to keep the ranks (c. iv, 26).

servus, -ī, M., slave

sese, reduplicated form of se (see sui).

sēvocō, -āre, -āvī, -ātum, v. tr., call aside.

seu: see sive.

sexāgintā, card. num. adj., sixty.

sexcentī, -ae, -a, card. num. adj., six hundred.

sī, conj., if, whether.

sibilus, -a, -um, adj., hissing.

sic, adv., thus, in this manner.

siccitās, -ātis, F., dryness, drought.

siccus, -a, -um, adj., dry, thirsty.

sidus, -eris, N., star, constellation.

Sigēus, -a, -um, adj., of or belonging to Sigeum, a promontory of the Troad.

significō, -āre, -āvi, -ātum, v. tr., show, mean.

signō, -āre, -āvī, -ātum, v.tr., mark.

signum, -ī, N., sign, signal.

silentium, -ī, N., silence.

sileō, -ēre, -uī, no sup., v. intr., be silent.

silva, -ae, F., wood, forest.

silvestris, -e, adj., wooded.

similis, -e, adj., like, similar (with dat.); comp. similior; sup., simillimus.

simul, adv., at the same time; simul atque (ac), as soon as.

simulācrum, -ī, N., image.

simulō, -āre, -āvī, -ātum, v. tr., pretend (pretend that a thing is what it is not; dissimulo, pretend that a thing is not what it is).

sin, conj., but if.

sine, prep. (with abl.), without

singillātim, adv., one by one, singly.

singulāris, -e, adj., extraordinary, single; aliquos singulares, some scattered soldiers (c. iv, 26); singulari studio, with especial zeal (c. v, 2).

singulī, -ae, -a, num. distrib. adj., one by one, one each, one apiece; in singulos annos, from year to year, i.e., yearly (c. v, 22).

sinister, -tra, -trum, adj., left; sub sinistra relictus, behind him on the left (c. v, 8).

sinistra, -ae, F. (sc. manus), left hand.

sinō, -ere, sīvi, situm, v. tr., let be, permit, allow.

Sinōn, -ōnis, M., Sinon, a Greek who induced the Trojans to admit the wooden horse into their city.

sinuō, -āre, -āvī, -ātum, v. tr., bend, writhe

sinus, -ūs, M., bay, gulf.

sistō, sistere, stitī, statum, v. intr., place.

sive (seu), conj., or if; sive...sive or seu, whether...or.

socer, -eri, M., father-in-law.

socius, -ī, M., companion, ally, associate.

socius, -a, -um, adj., confederate; socia agmina, confederate hands.

sōl, sōlis, M., sun; sole oriente, solis ortu, at sunrise; sole occidente, solis occasu, at sunset; ad solis occasum, to the West (c. v, 8).

soleō, solēre, solitus sum, v. intr., semi-dep., to be accustomed, be wont.

solidus, -a, -um, adj., solid, whole.

sollemnis, -e, adj., annual; arae sollemnes, customary altars.

sollicitō, -āre, -āvī, -ātum, v. tr., stir up, incite.

solum, -ī, N., ground.

sōlum, adv., alone, only, merely.

sōlus, -a, -um, adj., alone, only, single.

solvō, -ere, solvi, solūtum, v. tr., loose, unbind; solvere navem, or naves, to set sail; naves solverunt, sc. funes, the ships set sail (c. iv, 28); solvit se Teucria luctu, the Trojan land releases itself from sorrow

somnus, -ī, M., sleep; in somnis = in somniis, in my dreams

sonitus, -ūs, M., a sound.

sonō, -āre -ui, -itum, v. intr., sound.

soror, -ōris, F., a sister.

sors, sortis, F., lot, fate.

sopor, -ōris, M., sleep.

sortior, -īrī, sortītus sum, v. dep., draw lots, draw by lot.

spargō, -ere, -sī -sum, v. tr., scatter.

Sparta, -ae; N. f. : the chief city of Laconia in the Peloponnesus, and home of Menelaus and Helen; Sparta, sometimes called Lacedaemon.

spatium, -ī, N., space, time.

speciēs, -ēī. F. (gen. and dat. pl. not found), appearance, form ; sight.

spectō, -āre, -āvi, -ātum, v. tr., look, observe; ad orientem solem spectat, it faces the East (c. v, 13).

speculātor, -ōris, M., scout, spy.

speculātōrius, -a, -um, adj., scouting, spying; navigia speculatoria, despatch boats, rowed with a single bank of oars, generally ten in number on each side, and employed for reconnoitring purposes.

speculor, -ārī, -ātus sum, v. tr., watch.

spērō, -āre, -āvi, -ātum, v. tr. and intr., hope, expect.

spēs, -spel (gen. and dat. pl., rare), F., hope; in spem venire, to have hopes, to entertain hopes.

spira, -ae, F., coil.

spissus, -a, -um, adj., thick.

spoliō, -āre, -āvi, -ātum, v. tr., rob, plunder.

spolium, -ī, N., spoil, booty.

sponsa, -ae, F., betrothed.

spūmeus, -a, -um, adj., forming.

spūmō, -āre, -āvi, -ātum, v. intr., foam.

squālens, -ntis, adj., rough.

squāleō, -ēre, -ui, no sup., v. intr., be rough.

squāmeus, -a, -um, adj., scaly.

stabilitās, -ātis, F., firmness, steadiness (c. iv, 33).

stabulum, -ī, N., stall, stable.

statim, adv., instantly, at once, immediately.

statiō, -ōnis, F., outpost, picket, guard; in statione esse, to be on guard (c. iv, 32) = in stationibus esse (c. v, 15); in stationem succedere, to take their place on guard (c. iv, 32); anchorage.

statuō, -ere, -uī, -ūtum, v. tr., decide, resolve (c. v. 7, 11); build.

statūra, -ae, F., height, size.

stella, -ae, F., star.

sternō, -ere, strāvī, strātum, v. tr., lay low.

Sthenelus, -ī, M., Sthenelus, a leader of the Greeks.

stipendium, -ī, N., pay, tax, tribute.

stō, stāre, stetī, stātum, v. intr. stand stand firm; Palladis auxiliis, semper stetit, ever rested on the aid of Pallas.

strepitus, -ūs, M., noise, din.

strictus, -a, -um, perf. part. pass. from stringo, drawn.

strīdō, -ere, strīdi, no sup., creak.

stringō, -ere, strinxī, strictum, v. tr., draw, unsheath.

struō, struere, struxī, structum, v. tr., build.

studeō, -ēre, -ui, no sup., v. intr. (with dat.), be eager about, aim at; novis rebus studere, to aim at a change in the government.

studiōsē, adv., eagerly, zealously.

studium, -ī, N., zeal, devotion; summo studio, with the greatest zeal (c. v, 8).

stultē, adv., foolishly.

stultitia, -ae, F., foolishness.

stultus, -a, -um, adj., foolish.

stupeō, -ēre, stupui, no sup., be amazed.

stuppeus, -a, -um, adj., hempen.

suādeō, suādēre, suāsī, suā-
____, v. intr., reconmend, advise (with dat m

sub, prep. (with acc. and abl.), beneath, under, near, just before, at the
foot of; sub sinistra, on the left (c. v,
8); sub bruma, at the time of the
winter solstice (c. v, 13).

subducō, -ducere, -duxī, -duc-
tum, v. tr., draw up on shore; navem
subducere, to beach a ship (c. v, 11).

subductiō, -ōnis, F., drawing up
on shore, beaching a vessel.

subeō, -īre, -iī (īvī), -itum, v. tr.,
come up, approach; auxilio subeun-
tem, coming up to aid; illa subit, it
approaches; ast alii subeunt, but
others come up.

subiciō, -jicere, -jēcī, -jectum,
v. tr., place near, expose; hiemi navigationem subjicere, to expose his
voyage to the winter, i.e., to run the risk
of sailing in winter (c. iv, 36).

subjectus, -a, -um (perf. part. pass.
of subjicio), adj., adjacent, near; insulae subjectae, islands lying near
(c. v, 13); subjectis flammis, with
flames placed beneath

subitō, adv., suddenly, quickly.

subitus, -a, -um, adj., sudden,
unexpected.

sublābor, -lābī, lapsus sum, v.
dep., slip down, sink.

sub-ministrō, -āre, -āvī, -ātum,
v. tr., supply (c. iv, 50).

submittō, -ere, -mīsi, -missum,
v. tr., send secretly.

submoveō, -ēre, -mōvī, -mōtum,
tr. v., dislodge, draw off.

suboles, -is, F., posterity; race.

subsequor, -sequī, -secūtus
sum, v. tr., dep., follow closely, follow.

subsidium, -ī, N., auxiliary troops
reserve, aid; ad omnes casus subsidia componere, to make provision
for all emergencies (c. iv, 31).

subsistō, -ere, -stitī, no sup., v.
intr., halt, make a stand; neque
ancorae funesque subsistunt,
neither the anchors nor the cables
hold out (c. v, 10); substitit, it
halted.

subsum, -esse, -fuī, v. intr., be
near; aequinoctium subest, the
equinox is at hand (c. v, 23).

succēdō, -ere, -cessī, -cessum,
v. intr., approach, take the place of; ad
stationem succedere, to take their
place on guard (c. iv, 32).

successus, -ūs, M., success.

succīdō, -ere, -cīdī, -cīsum, v. tr.,
cut down.

succīsus, -a, -um, perf. part. pass.
of succido, cut down.

succurrō, -ere, -currī, -cursum,
v. intr. (with dat.), help, aid; succur-
ritis urbi incensae, you are aiding a
city in flames; succurrit=succurrit
menti=occurrit menti, the thought
comes to my mind.

sūdes, -is, F., stake; acutis sudibus praefixis, with sharp stakes fixed
in front (of the bank) (c. v, 18).

sūdō, -āre, -āvī, -ātum, v. intr.,
sweat.

sūdor, -ōris, M., sweat.

suffectus, -a, um, perf. part. pass.
of sufficio, suffused

sufferō, -ferre, sustulī, sublātum, v. tr., bear, endure.

sufficiō, -ficere, -fēcī, -fectum,
v. tr., to tinge.

suī, reflex. pro., of himself, herself,
itself.

sulcus, -ī, M., furrow.

sulfur, -uris, N., brimstone, sulphur.

Sulpicius, -ī, M., Sulpicius: a Roman
nomen (see cognomen); Publius Sulpicius Rufus, a lieutenant of Caesar in
Gaul (c. iv, 22).

sum, esse, fuī, v. intr., be.

summa, -ae, F., total, whole; general administration, control; summa
imperii bellique administrandi
permissa, the supreme command in con-
ducting the war being entrusted (c. v, 11).

summoveō: see submoveō.

summus, -a, -um, adj., highest,
greatest, very great, chief (superl. of
superus); summus mons, the top
of the mountain; summa res, a most
important matter; summis copiis,
with their entire forces (c. v, 17); summa
ab arce, from the top of the citadel;
summa dies, the last day; summa
=suprema.

sūmō, sūmere, sumpsī, sumptum, v. tr., take, assume; poenas
sumere, to exact a penalty.

super, prep. (with acc. and abl.)
above; et super, and further; super
his (dictis), moreover, with these
(words).

superbus, -ā, -um, adj., proud,
haughty.

superior, -us, (comp. of superus),
higher, previous; nocte superiore,

on the previous night (c. v, 10);
superiore aestate, in the preceding
summer (c. iv, 21; v. 8), superius
tempus, former time (c. iv, 22; v. 11);
superiore anno, in the previous year
(c. iv, 38); in loca superiora, up the
country, c. v, 8); locus superior, a
height (c. v, 9).

superō, -āre, -āvī, -ātum, v. tr.,
conquer, defeat; superare undas,
rise above the waves; mount.

supersum, -esse, -fuī, v. intr.,
remain, survive; neque multum
aestatis superest, and not much of
the summer is left (c. v, 22).

superus, -a, -um, adj., high (comp.,
superior; sup., suprēmus, or summus); superi, -orum, those above,
the gods

supplex, -icis, adj., suppliant.

supplicātiō, ōnis, F., thanksgiving.

suprā, prep. (with acc.) and adv.,
above, over.

surgō, -ere, surrexī, surrectum,
v. intr., rise.

suscitō, -āre, -āvī, -ātum, v. tr.,
stir up.

suspectus, -a, -um, perf. part. pass.
of suspicio, suspected.

suspensus, -a, -um, adj., in doubt.

suspīciō, -ōnis, F., suspicion; in
suspicionem venire, to be suspected;
neque ulla belli suspicione interposita, and no suspicion of war having
arisen (c. iv, 32).

suspiciō, -ere, suspexī, suspec-
tum, v. tr., suspect.

suspicor, -ārī, -ātus sum, v. tr.
dep., suspect, distrust.

sustineō, -ēre, -tinuī, -tentum,
v. tr., withstand (c. iv, 37); check, rein
in (c. iv, 33); hold one's ground (c. iv,
32).

suus, -a, -um, reflexive, adj. pro.,
his, her, its, their.

T

T. = Titus, a Roman praenomen:
see cognomen

tabulātum, -ī, N., storey, floor.

taceō, -ēre -uī, -ītum, v. tr. and
intr., be silent; pass over in silence.

tacitus, -a, -um, adj., silent.

tactus, -ūs, M., touching, touch.

tālea, -ae, F., bar; taleae ferreae,
iron bars (c. v, 12).

tālis, -e, adj., such.

tam, adv., so (before adverbs and adjectives); tam...quam..., as much...as.

tamdiū, adv., so long.

tamen, adv., yet, still, for all that,
however, nevertheless.

Tamesis, -is (acc. Tamesim), M.,
the Thames.

tandem, adv., at length, finally; in
questions, pray? now? as quis tandem? who, pray?

tangō, tangere, tetigī, tactum,
v. tr., touch, border on.

tantō, adv. of comparison, by so much;
with comparatives, tanto brevior, so
much the shorter.

tantulus, -a, -um, adj., so very
small, so slight, so trifling; has tantularum rerum occupationes,
this business consisting of such trifles
(c. iv, 22).

tantum, adv., only, so much, so far,
merely.

tantus, -a, -um, adj., so great, so
large, such; tanto spatio, so far (c. iv,
35).

tardō, adv., slowly.

tardus, -a, -um, adj., slow.

taurus, -ī, M., bull.

Taximagulus, -ī, M., Taximagulus,
one of the petty kings of Kent (c. v, 22).

tectum, -ī, N., house.

tectus, -a, -um, perf. part. pass. of
tego, shut up; tectus, shutting himself up in his tent

tegō, tegere, texī, tectum, v. tr.,
cover; si qua tegunt, if anything
they conceal (Verg. 159); protect, nec
Apollinis infula texit, nor did the
fillet of Apollo protect thee

tellūs, -ūris, F., land.

tēlum, -ī, N., weapon, dart.

temerō, adv., at random, without a
purpose (c. iv, 20).

tēmō, -ōnis, M., pole (of a chariot).

temperantia, -ae, F., self-control,
moderation.

temperātus, -a, -um, adj., temper
ate, mild; loca sunt temperatiora,
the climate is milder (c. v, 12).

temperō, -āre, -āvī, ātum, v. tr.
and intr., with acc., rule, manage; with
dat., restrain.

tempestās, -ātis, F., weather;
idonea ad navigandum tempes-
tas, weather suitable for sailing (c. iv,
23;) so, iv, 36; v, 7; storm (c. iv, 28, 29,
34;) rejici tempestate, to be driven
back by a storm (c. v, 5).

templum -ī, N., temple.

temptō (or tentō), -āre, -āvī, -ātum, v. tr., try, attempt.

tempus, -oris, N., time, season, occasion; in reliquum tempus, for the future; omnī tempore, always; tempus ducere, to protract the time; tempore dato, at an appointed time; ad tempus, at a moment's notice (c. iv, 23); pro tempore et pro re, suited to the time and conditions (c. vi, 8); temples (of the head); circum tempora, around my temples

tenebrae, -ārum, F. pl., darkness.

tendō, -ere, tetendī, tentum (or tensum), v. tr., stretch; tendens lumina, raising her eyes; tendit divellere, he strives to undo; ad litora tendunt, make for the shore.

Tenedos, -ī, F., Tenedos, an island near Troy.

teneō, -ēre, -uī, -tum, v. tr., hold, possess; navem tenere in ancoris, to keep a ship at anchor; cursum tenere, to hold on its course (c. iv, 26; iv, 28); vento teneri, to be kept back by the wind (c. iv, 22); teneor patriae nec legibus ullis, nor am I bound by any laws of my native land

tener, -era, -erum, adj., tender.

tenuis, -e, adj., thin, weak.

tenus, prep., with abl. (placed after the noun), as far as.

ter, num. adv., thrice.

terebrō, -āre, -āvī, -ātum, v. tr., bore through.

tergum, -ī, N., back; a tergo, in the rear; post tergum, behind the back; terga vertere, to flee (c. iv, 35; 37).

ternī, -ae, -a, distrib. num. adj., three each, three apiece.

terra, -ae, F., land, earth, country.

terreō, -ēre, -uī, -itum, v. tr., frighten, terrify, alarm.

terrestris, -e, adj., of or belonging to land; exercitus terrestris, land army, opposed to exercitus navalis, sea forces.

territō, -āre, -āvī, -ātum, v. tr., terrify, frighten.

terror, -ōris, M., fear, dread : ipso terrore, by the sheer terror (c. iv, 38).

testor, -ārī, -ātus sum, v. tr. dep., call to witness.

testūdō, inis, F., a tortoise, a covering formed by the shields of the soldiers held above their heads so as to ward off the weapons hurled by the enemy; so called from the fancied resemblance to a tortoise shell. The term was also applied to the different kinds of sheds under which the soldiers worked when attacking a town.

Teucer, -crī, M., Teucer, king of Troy, ancestor of Priam.

Teucrī, -ōrum, M. pl., Trojans.

Teucria, -ae, F., land of Teucer, i.e., Troy.

texō, -ere, -uī, textum, v. tr., weave.

thalamus, -ī, M., bedchamber.

Thessandrus, -ī, M., Thessandrus, one of the Greek heroes in the wooden horse.

Thoās, -antis, M., Thoas, one of the Greeks in the wooden horse.

Thȳbris (Tybris), -is or idis; M., old name for the Tiber, a river in Italy on which Rome is situated.

Thymoetēs, -ae, M., Thymoetes, a Trojan who was the first to counsel that the wooden horse be brought within the city.

timeō, -ēre, -uī, no sup., v. tr. and intr., fear, be afraid.

timor, -ōris, M., fear, dread.

Titūrius, -ī, M., Titurius; see Sabinus.

Titus, -ī, M., Titus; see Labienus.

tōlerō, -āre, -āvī, -ātum, v. tr., bear, support.

tollō, -ere, sustulī, sublātum, v. tr., lift, raise, carry away, destroy; ancoram tollere, to weigh anchor (c. iv, 23).

tormentum, -ī, N., military engine for throwing missiles against the enemy.

torrens, -ntis, M., torrent.

torus, -ī, M., couch.

tot, indecl. adj., so many; tot...quot, as many as.

totiens, adv., so many times.

tōtus, -a, -um, adj., whole, all.

trabs, trabis, F., beam, timber.

trādō, -ere, -didī, -ditum, v. tr., hand over, give over, deliver, surrender; hand down to posterity; traditur, it is said; traditum est, the tradition is.

trādūcō, -ere, -duxī, -ductum, v. tr., lead across, or over.

trahō, -ere, traxī, tractum, v. tr., draw, drag; vitam trahere, to drag out one's life

trājiciō, -jicere, -jēcī, -jectum, v. tr., throw across, lead across, pierce.

222 VOCABULARY

trājectus, -ūs, M., passage, distance, across.

tranquilitās, -ātis, F., calm weather; summa tranquillitas, a dead calm (c. V, 23).

tranquillus, -a, -um, adj., calm.

trans, prep. (with acc.), across, over, on the other side, beyond.

transeō, -īre, iī (īvī), -itum, v. tr., cross over, cross.

transferō, -ferre, -tulī, -lātum, v. tr., bear or carry across; summam imperii transferre, to transfer the supreme power.

transgredior, -gredī, -gressus sum, v. tr., pass over, cross.

transigō, -ere, -ēgī, -actum, v. tr., pass through; tempus transigere, to pass the time.

transitus, -ūs, M., a going or crossing over, passing, crossing.

transjectus, -ūs, M., passage, distance across (c. V, 2).

transmissus, -ūs, M., passage (c. V, 13).

transportō, -āre, -āvī, -ātum, v. tr., carry over, transport.

Transrhēnānī, -ōrum, pl. M., those living across the Rhine (c. V, 2).

Trebōnius, -ī, M., Trebonius; Caius Trebonius, one of Caesar's lieutenants in Gaul.

trecentī, -ae, -a, card. num. adj., three hundred.

tremefactus, -a, -um, adj., dismayed.

tremens, -tis, adj., trembling.

tremendus, -a, -um, adj., terrible.

tremō, -ere, -uī, no sup., v. intr., tremble, quiver.

tremor, -ōris, M., trembling, fear.

trepidō, -āre, -āvī, -ātum, v. intr., tremble much; hasten.

trepidus, -a, -um, adj., alarmed.

trēs, tria, card. num. adj., three.

Trevirī, -ōrum, pl., M., the Treviri, a people of Gallica Belgica, who dwelt between the Meuse and the Rhine; their capital was Augusta Trevirorum, now Trèves.

tribūnus, -ī, M., a commander of a tribe; hence, one of military officers, six in number, attached to each legion.

tribuō, -ere, -ī, tribūtum, v. tr., give, show.

tribūtum, ī, N., tribute, tax.

tridens, -tis, M., trident.

triduum, -ī, N., space of three days; tridui via, a three days' march.

trigintā, card. num. adj., thirty.

Trinobantēs, -um, pl., M., the Trinobantes, a people of Britain who occupied Essex and part of Suffolk.

tripertītō, adv., in three divisions.

triplex, -plicis, adj., threefold, triple.

triquetrus, -a, -um, adj., three-cornered, triangular.

tris, num. adv., thrice.

tristis, -e, adj., sad, sorrowful, dejected.

trisulcus, -a, -um, adj., three-forked.

tristitia, -ae, F., sadness.

Trītōnia, -ae, F., Tritonia or Minerva.

Trītōnis, -idis, adj., Tritonian, an epithet of Minerva, who was also called Tritonia.

triumphus, -ī, M., triumph.

Trōēs, -um, pl., The Trojans.

Trōja, -ae, F., Troy.

Trōjānus, -a, -um, adj., Trojan.

tropaeum, -ī, N., trophy, i.e., a memorial or monument of victory; hence victory.

Trōs, Trōis, M., Tros, a king of Troy.

trucīdō, -āre, -āvī, -ātum, v. tr., butcher, slaughter.

truncus, -ī, M., trunk, body without limbs.

tū, tuī, pl. vos, thou, you.

tuba, -ae, F., trumpet (with a straight tube).

tueor, tuērī, tuitus sum, v. dep., preserve, defend, protect.

tum, adv., then.

tumens, -tis, adj., swelling.

tumeō, -ēre, -uī, no sup., swell.

tumidus, -a, -um, adj., swelling.

tumultus, -ūs, M., disturbance, disorder.

tumulus, -ī, M. mound.

tunc, adv., then, at that time.

turba, -ae, F., crowd, throng.

turbātus, -a, -um, adj., alarmed.

turbō, -āre, -āvī, -ātum, v. tr., disturb.

turbō, -inis, M., whirlwind.

turma, -ae, F., a troop of 30 cavalry; the cavalry (ala) of the legion was divided into 10 turmae.

turpis, -e, adj., base, disgraceful.

turris, -is, F., tower.

tūtē, adv., in safety, safely.

tutor, -ārī, -ātus sum, v. dep., protect.

tūtus, -a, -um, adj., safe, secure.

tuus, -a, -um, pro. adj., thy, yonr.

Tȳdidēs, -ae, M., *son of Tydeus*, an epithet of Dionede, one of the Greek warriors at the siege of Troy.

Tyndaris, -idis, F., *daughter of Tyndarus*, an epithet of Helen, wife of Menelaus: (see Helena).

U

ubi, adv., where, when; ubi primum, as soon as.

ubique, adv., everywhere.

Ūcalegōn, -ontis, M., *Ucalegon*, a Trojan

ulciscor, ulciscī, ultus sum, v. tr. dep., avenge, punish.

Ulixēs, -is or -ī, M., *Ulysses*, king of Ithaca, noted anong the Greeks for his cleverness in strategy. His wanderings on his return hone after the fall of Troy form the subject of Honer's Odyssey, upon which nuch of the Aeneid is nodelled. He is always referred to by Vergil as a type of Greek cunning.

ullus, -a, -um, adj., any.

ulterior, -ius, conp. adj., further, beyond, nore renote; sup., ultimus.

ultimus, -a, -um, adj., farthest, most distant.

ultor, -ōris, M., an avenger.

ultrā, adv., and prep. (with acc.), beyond, on the other side; ultra fidem, beyond belief.

ultrō, adv., of one's own accord; without provocation; bellum ultro inferre, to nake war without provocation (c. iv, 13); voluntarily

ultus,-a,-um, perf. part. of ulciscor, having avenged.

ululō, -āre, -āvī, -ātum, v. intr., howl.

umbō, ōnis, M., boss (of a shield).

umbra, -ae, F., shade.

umerus, -ī, M., shoulder, arm.

umidus, -a, -um, adj., noist, dewy.

ūnā, adv., along with; usually with cum; una cum his legatis, along with these envoys (c. iv, 26); una cum ceteris, along with the others (c. v, 6).

unda, -ae, F., wave.

unde, adv., fron which place, whence.

undique, adv., fron all sides, on all sides, everywhere.

undō, -āre, -āvī, -ātum, v. intr., rise in waves, swell.

ūniversus, -a, -um, adj., whole, all (in a body).

unquam, adv., ever, at any tine; non unquam = nunquam.

ūnus, -a, -um, card, num. adj., one, alone; uno tempore, at one and the sane tine; omnes ad unum, all to a man; hoc unum, only this (c. iv, 26); justissimus unus, above all others the nost just

urbis, F., city.

urgeō, -ēre, ursi, no. sup., v. tr., press hard.

ūrō, -ere, ussī, ustum, v. tr., burn.

usquam, adv., anywhere.

usque, adv., right on, ever.

ūsus, -ūs, M., use, experience, practice, advantage; ratio atque usus belli, theory and practice of war, *i.e*, the systenatic practice of war; magno usui sibi esse, to be of great advantage to him (c. iv, 20); usus belli, skill in war (c. iv, 20); ex usu, of advantage (c. v, 6); pervius usus, a connecting passage

ut (or utī), conj., that, in order that (Final); that, so that (Consecutive); that (in Substantive clauses); that not (with verbs of fearing).

uter, utra, utrum, interrog. pro., which of two?

uterque, utraque, utrumque, adj. pro., each (of two), both: ex utraque part, on both sides; in utrunique paratus, ready for either result.

uturus, -ī, M., belly, wonb.

utinam, adv., O that.

ūtor, ūtī, ūsus sum, v. intr. dep. (with abl.), use, enploy, enjoy; alacritate uti, to show dash (c. iv, 24).

utrimque, adv., fron or on both sides.

utrique, pl. of uterque.

utrum, conj., whether; utrum... an, whether...or; often not translated in direct questions.

uxor, -ōris, F., wife.

V

vacuus, -a, -um, adj., enpty.

vādō, -ere, no pf., no sup., v. intr., go, advance.

vadum, -ī, N., ford.

vagor, -ārī, -ātus sum, v. intr., dep., wander; ea fāma vagatur; that report spreads

valens, -tis (pres. part. of valeo used as an) adj., powerful.

valeō, -ēre, -uī, -itum, v. intr., be powerful, strong; have power or influence; longe plurimum valet, is by far the nost powerful (c. v, 3); quam plurimum valere, to be as powerful as possible (c. v, 4); avail.

validus, -a, -um, adj., strong.

vallis, -is, F., valley.

vallum, -ī, N., ranpart, breastwork of a canp.

vānus, -a, -um, adj., enpty, vain.

varius, -a, -um, adj., different, changing.

vastō, -āre, -āvī, -ātum, v. tr., lay waste, devastate.

vastus, -a, -um, adj., vast.

vātēs, -is, M. or F., a soothsayer, prophet.

-ve, enclitic conjunction, or; giving a choice between two or nore things.

vectigal, -ālis, N., tax, toll, revenue.

vectōrius, -a, -um, adj., adapted for carrying; navigium vectorium, a transport ship.

yehiculum, -ī, N., a carriage.

vehō, vehere, vexī, vectum, v. tr., bear, carry, convey.

vel, conj., or; vel . vel, either... or; with sup., even, indeed; vel optimus, the very best.

vellō, -ere, velli, vulsum, v. tr., pluck.

vēlō, -āre, -āvī, -ātum, v. tr., cover, veil.

vōlum, -ī, N., sail; dare vela ventis, to set sail.

velut, adv., just as; velut sī, just as if.

vendō, -ere, -didī, -ditum, v. tr., sell, offer for sale; pass., veneo (which see).

venenum, -ī, N., poison.

vēneō, -īre, ii (īvī), -itum, v. pass. (see vendo), be sold.

veneror, -ārī, -ātus sum, v. tr., adore, worship.

Veneticns, -a, -um, adj., of or belonging to the Veneti, a tribe on the west coast of France, north of the Loire, in the vicinity of the bay of Quiberon: Caesar subdued then 54 B.C.

venia, -ae, F., favor, forgiveness.

veniō, -venire, vēni, ventum, v. intr., cone; est ventum (=venerunt), they cane (c. iv, 28).

venter, -tris, M., belly; hunger (Verg. 356).

ventūra, -ōrum, neut. pl. fut. part. act., coning events.

ventus, i, M., wind; dare vela ventis, to set sail.

vēr, vēris, N., spring; primo vere, at the beginning of spring; extremo vere, at the end of spring.

verbum, -ī, N., word; in pl., conversation.

vērō, adv., truly, in truth (conp., verius; sup., verissime).

vereor, -ērī, -itus sum, v. tr., dep., fear, dread; navibus veritus, fearing for the safety of the ships (c. v, 9).

vergō, -ere, no perf., no sup., v. intr., incline, slope; ad septentriones vergit, it has a northerly slope (c. iv, 20).

vērō, adv., in truth, in fact, truly, certainly; but, indeed.

versātus, perf. part. dep., versor, skilled in

versō, -āre, -āvī, -ātum, v. tr., turn often, change.

versor. -ārī, -ātus sum, v. intr., dwell in, be occupied with, engaged in.

vertex, -icis, M., top, head.

vertō, vertere, verti, versum, v. tr., turn, change; terga vertere, to turn their backs, flee (c. iv, 35).

vertor, verti, verti, versum, v. seni-dep., turn, change

vērum, adv., see vero.

vērus, -a, -um, adj., true.

vescor, vescī, no perf. or sup., intr. dep. (with abl.), feed, live upon.

vesper, -eris (or -erī), M., evening; vespere, or vesperi, in the evening.

Vesta, -ae, F., Vesta, the Ronan goddess of the hearth and hone.

vester, -tra, -trum, adj. pro., your, yours.

vestibulum, -ī, N., porch, entrance.

vestigium, -ī, N., footstep, track.

vestiō, -īre, -īvī, -ītum, v. tr., clothe, dress; pellibus vestīrī, to clothe oneself in skins (c. v, 14).

vestis, -is, F., dress.

veterānus, -a, -um, adj., old; as a noun, veterānī, -ōrum, pl. M., veteran troops (scil. milites).

vetō, -āre, -uī, -itum, v. tr., forbid.

vetus, -eris, adj., old, ancient; no conp.; sup., veterrimus.

vetustus, -a, -um, adj., ancient, old.

vexō, -āre, -āvī, -ātum, v. tr., harass, plunder, waste.

via, -ae, F., way, road, journey; tridui via, a journey of three days.

vībrans, -tis, adj., quivering.

vibrō, -āre, -āvī, -ātum, v. tr., shake.

vīciēs, num. adv., twenty tines.

vīcīnus, -ī, M., neighbor.

vicis (genitive), vicim, vice, F. (no nom. sing.), change; vices vitavisse Danaum, to have avoided the onsets of the Greeks

victor, -ōris, M., victor, conqueror; as an adj., victorious.

victōria, -ae, F., victory.

victus, -a, -um, perf. part. pass. of vinco, conquered.

videō, vidēre, vīdi, visum, v. tr., see; videor, vidērī, visus sum, intr. dep., seen, appear.

vigeō, vigēre, no perf., no sup., be vigorous, thrive, flourish.

vigil, -is, M., watchnan, guard.

vigilia, -ae, F., watch, guard. The Ronans had four night watches: prima vigilia, from 6 p.m. to 9 p.m.; secunda vigilia, fron 9 p.m. to 12 p.m.; tertia vigilia, fron 12 p.m. to 3 a.m.; quarta vigilia, fron 3 a.m. to 6 a.m.; secundā initā vigiliā, at the beginning of the second watch (c. v, 23).

vigintī, card. num. adj., twenty.

vimen, -inis, N., twig, osier:

vinciō, -īre, vinxī, vinctum, v. tr., bind.

vincō, vincere, vici, victum, v. tr., conquer.

vinculum, -ī, N., chain; in vincula conjicere, throw into prison.

vīnum, -ī, N., wine.

violābilis, -e, adj., that may be profaned; non violabile, inviolable.

vir, virī, M., man, husband.

virga, -ae, F., twig.

virgineus, -a, -um, adj., of a naiden, virgin (Verg. 168).

virgō, -inis, F., naiden; Priameia virgo, virgin daughter of Prian = Cassandra

virtūs, -ūtis, F., nanliness, virtue, courage, bravery (c. iv, 21).

vis, vīs, F., strength, power, vim facere, to offer violence; vi or per vim expugnare, to take by storn; vim sustinere, to withstand an attack; vim facere, to offer resistance (c. v, 7); endurance (c. v, 8); plural, strength

visō, vīsere, visi, visum, v. tr., go to see, visit.

visus, -ūs, M., sight.

vita, -ae, F., life.

vitō, -āre, -āvi, -ātum, v. tr., avoid, shun.

vitrum, -ī, N., woad; a plant known to botanists as Isatis tinctoria, which produced a blue dye. Till the introduction of indigo in the 17th century it was largely cultivated.

vitta, -ae, F., fillet.

vituperō, -āre, -āvī, -ātum, v. tr., abuse, revile.

vivō, vivere, vixi, victum, v. intr., live; lacte et carne vivunt, they live on nilk and flesh (c. v, 14).

vīvus, -a -um, adj., alive, living.

vix, adv., hardly, scarcely.

yōciferor, ārī, ātus sum, v. dep., cry aloud, (vox, fero).

vocō, -āre, -āvī, ātum, v. tr., call, sunnon.

volō, -āre, -āvī, -ātum, v. tr., fly, hasten.

volō, velle, volui, no sup., irregular verb, intr., be willing, wish, desire.

volitō, -āre, -āvī, -ātum, v. intr., flit about.

volucer, -cris, -cre, ad., swift.

volūmen, -inis, N., fold.

voluntās, ātis, F., good will; in se voluntas, his good will towards hinself (Caesar), (c. v, 4).

voluptās, -ātis, F., pleasure; animi voluptatisque causā, for sentinent and pleasure (c. v, 12).

Volusēnus, -ī, M., Volusenus; Caius Volusenus Quadratus, a nilitary tribune in Caesar's arny.

vōtum, -ī, N., vow; or = votum esse, that it had been vowed

voveō, vovēre, vōvī, vōtum, v. tr., vow.

VOCABULARY.

volvō, -ere, volvi, volūtum, v. tr., roll.

vōs: see tu.

vox, vōcis, F., voice; magnā voce, in a loud voice (c. iv, 25); voces ambiguae, dark sayings; rumpit vocem, he breaks silence.

Vulcānus, -ī, M., *Vulcan*, the Fire-god of the Romans, hence, fire.

vulgō, (abl. of vulgus used as an) adv., generally, commonly.

vulgus, -ī, N. (rarely M.), con non people, multitude.

vulnerō, -āre, -āvī, -ātum, v. tr., wound, hurt.

vulnus, -eris, N., wound; paucis vulneribus acceptis, with slight loss (c. v, 10).

vultus, -ūs, M., expression, countenance.

Z

Zephyrus, -ī, M., *Zephyrus, the west wind.*

Made in the USA
Middletown, DE
25 April 2017